THE KENNEDY LEGACY

Previous books by Theodore C. Sorensen

DECISION-MAKING IN THE WHITE HOUSE

KENNEDY

Theodore C. Sorensen

THE KENNEDY LEGACY

MACMILLAN PUBLISHING COMPANY
New York

MAXWELL MACMILLAN CANADA
Toronto

MAXWELL MACMILLAN INTERNATIONAL
New York Oxford Singapore Sydney

Macmillan Publishing Company   Maxwell Macmillan Canada, Inc.
866 Third Avenue   1200 Eglinton Avenue East
New York, NY 10022   Suite 200
                                      Don Mills, Ontario M3C 3N1

Macmillan Publishing Company is part of the Maxwell Communication Group of Companies.

Library of Congress Cataloging-in-Publication Data
Sorensen, Theodore C.
The Kennedy legacy / Theodore C. Sorensen. — Special 25th
anniversary ed.
    p.   cm.
Includes index.
ISBN 0-02-612405-X
1. Kennedy, John F. (John Fitzgerald), 1917–1963. 2. Kennedy,
Robert F., 1925–1968. 3. Presidents—United States—Biography.
4. Legislators—United States—Biography. 5. United States. Congress.
Senate—Biography. I. Title.
E842.S57   1993   92-43703   CIP
973.922'092'2—dc20
[B]

Macmillan books are available at special discounts for bulk purchases
for sales promotions, premiums, fund-raising, or educational use.
For details, contact:

Special Sales Director
Macmillan Publishing Company
866 Third Avenue
New York, NY 10022

SPECIAL TWENTY-FIFTH ANNIVERSARY EDITION 1993

10   9   8   7   6   5   4   3   2

Printed in the United States of America

FOR

Eric, Steve, and Phil

AND ALL THE OTHER YOUNG PEOPLE IN THE COUNTRY

FOR WHOM THE LEGACY WAS INTENDED, AND FROM

WHOM MUST COME ITS FULFILLMENT

Acknowledgments

AMONG all those I have already thanked for their help in making this book possible, I want to convey special gratitude to the many friends (including my brothers Tom and Phil) who offered suggestions and encouragement regarding the contents and concept of this book, especially Senator Edward Kennedy, Steve Smith, Peter Edelman, and Victor Temkin; to my patient but persistent editor at Macmillan, Peter Ritner, and his research assistant, Susan Hall; to my secretary, Mrs. Marge Hornblower, who devoted every night and weekend to this project for months; to the College of the Virgin Islands and its president, Lawrence Wanlass, with whom I had the good fortune to stay as writer-in-residence during the drafting of the original manuscript; and to my wife, Gillian, who made life during this writing not only happier but more meaningful.

Contents

Foreword

In 1968, as in 1963, an assassin's bullets changed history. Had Robert Kennedy not been suddenly, senselessly taken from us, the world would be a better place today.

He would have won the Democratic Party nomination for President in 1968. The momentum of his victory in the California Democratic Primary would have enabled him to pick up speed and delegates on the road to the National Convention in Chicago. Many if not most of those delegates supporting each of the remaining candidates on the Convention floor—largely because they could not bring themselves to vote for any of the other candidates—would have gladly thrown their support to him. Many if not most of the Democratic Party leaders of the sixties, followers of JFK who had long worked with RFK, would have recognized that his series of primary victories entitled him to the nomination.

He then would have won that year's Presidential election. The Democratic nominee in 1968, Vice President Hubert Humphrey, after making a valiant effort to heal the divisive party wounds inflicted in bitterness and anger both inside and outside that tumultuous Convention Hall, came within an eyelash of winning. Robert Kennedy would have waged a more effective campaign—Kennedys always have. Unlike Humphrey, he would not have been burdened with the "baggage" of the incumbent administration, the war that it was unsuccessfully waging, and the antagonisms among the young, black, and liberal voters that it had generated.

He then would have been an extraordinary President—fearless, controversial, in some quarters unpopular, but more passionate, more committed, and more effective than any of the six U.S. Presidents who served between the time of his death and the time this is written. Under an RFK Presidency, the war in Vietnam would not have been widened and prolonged. Countless lives and limbs would have been saved from battlefield destruction. Far more time and money would have been available to save our cities and their least advantaged citizens from poverty, drugs, crime, and despair. Far less time and money would have been devoted to the stockpiling of strategic weapons and the arming of undeserving, undemocratic, and unreliable client states.

But, sadly, Robert Kennedy did not live and he was not elected President. Of those six who served in that office in the twenty-four years following his death, only one served the two full four-year terms permitted under the Constitution, and all six left that office defeated, discredited or disgraced in the eyes of millions of Americans. Not one of them had RFK's unique combination of strong leadership, deep compassion, and the ability to inspire confidence and hope among Americans in every walk of life.

Too often in those twenty-four years, 1968–1992, the American people were disillusioned by the actions or inactions of their President. Not surprisingly, cynicism, disdain, indifference, even anger characterized the attitude of an increasing number of voters toward politics in general and the Presidency in particular until Bill Clinton, consciously invoking the Kennedy standard, gave them reason to hope once again.

Perhaps it is too long a leap (and certainly too long a sentence) to speculate that, had Robert Kennedy lived and been elected, Richard Nixon never would have occupied the Presidency, or resigned from it in 1974, turning it over to the

unelected Gerald Ford, whose pardon of Nixon was among
the factors that fueled the anti-Washington sentiment
among the voters that Vietnam and Watergate had already
built to an all-time high, high enough to elect a one-term
Governor of Georgia with no experience in Washington,
Jimmy Carter, whose inability to persuade an unhappy
Congress and country to halt skyrocketing inflation, deficits, and interest rates helped turn the electorate rightward
for ex-screen star Ronald Reagan, who was succeeded by
his Vice President, George Bush. But that long sentence
leads to a short question: Had Robert Kennedy lived to be
elected in 1968, would any one of these five gentlemen (three
of whom had failed in their previous bids for the Presidency)
ever have held that position?

Perhaps not. No one can be certain in which direction a
stream, diverted by a mighty fallen oak, will twist and turn.
We will never know. But we do know that a Robert Kennedy
Presidency would surely have been free from the corruption,
deception, and deadlock that characterized so many of the
years that followed; that the special pleaders and PACs
would have wielded considerably less power in Washington;
and that the poor, the African-Americans, the Latinos, the
Native Americans, and all the others left behind by our
society would have had in the Oval Office someone who
listened and cared. We do know that the sense of despair
that bred demonstrations and riots in our inner cities and on
our college campuses in the late sixties and early seventies
would have given way much sooner to a sense of hope,
including the hope that a speedy end to the war in Vietnam
meant more resources for the war on poverty that had
partly originated in the office of Attorney General Robert
F. Kennedy. That much we know.

We know as well that no Presidential campaign since the
RFK campaign of 1968 has been characterized by more

idealism and energy. Throughout those few extraordinary months, his crowds grew, their enthusiasm grew, the excitement grew. He did not try to please everyone—and succeeded in displeasing many—but he was uniquely determined, unlike any previous Presidential candidate in history, to bridge the gap between black and white, between the comfortable and the afflicted, between blue collar and professional, to challenge all Americans to meet their responsibilities as citizens of this country and as members of the human race.

Many a subsequent candidate in both major political parties has invoked his words or manner, not always with attribution, perhaps not always consciously. But none of those candidates had his special qualities of candor and courage. Like a biblical hero, he was strong and he was not afraid. He was not afraid to tackle any major controversy, from black-white relations to reproductive rights. He was not afraid to disagree with his own party leaders, or to discomfort his own financial backers. He was not afraid to stand up against the war, or to speak up for the underdog and the overlooked, for those who had no money for his campaign and even for those who had no votes. And, unlike so many other politicians throughout history, he was not afraid to lose, to go down to defeat if sticking fast to his principles so required, secure in the knowledge that he had done his best and kept the faith and would return, head high, to the family and friends who loved him.

I was one of those who loved him. Months after his death, I wrote this little book, in haste and in pain but out of love as well. It is flawed in many ways. It could have been better reasoned, better written, and better organized. Nevertheless, I hope it remains useful as a contemporaneous, firsthand look at the ideas and ideals for which Robert Kennedy fought, on which he worked with his brother John, and to which his shining 1968 campaign was dedicated—the essence of the Kennedy legacy.

Is that legacy gone? Is it at all relevant today, nearly twenty-five years later? The clock has moved on and cannot be turned back. The world has moved on, the issues have changed, the Cold War is over, the Vietnam War is history, the arms race is winding down, and South Africa is on the road to freedom. New challenges of international trade, energy dependence, and terrorism have come to the fore. A new President is determined, like the Kennedys, "to get this country moving again," to make the Presidency a "vital center of action," to get things done, to do better.

But the real Kennedy legacy—the standards that Jack and Bob Kennedy set, the goals they articulated, the measures they advanced, the young people they moved—that legacy is with us still, not irrelevant but renewed, not forgotten but, by many, revered.

No one knows better than our new President that the problems of race and poverty so eloquently and fiercely addressed by Robert F. Kennedy are with us still; that the cities of America are in more difficult straits now than they were when Bobby walked their streets in 1968; that too many Americans are still denied access to affordable, quality health care and homes; that these and other issues confronted head-on by Bobby Kennedy in the campaign of 1968 still need to be confronted head-on today; and that his words are as timely and moving and valuable today for their wisdom and inspiration on these issues as they were in 1968.

That campaign ended in tragedy. And yet, like Al Smith's losing campaign of 1928, the RFK campaign of 1968 was in many ways a turning point for the Democratic Party and the country, a redefinition of the Party's future strategy and strengths. For it was a campaign that reached beyond the traditional party leaders and organizations into suburbs and ghettos and campuses and grass-roots operations as never before, a campaign that looked beyond the superpower struggle and the Cold War itself, a campaign that was unashamedly based on high moral principles and dedication. It was that campaign, tracing many of its roots to the campaign and Presidency of John F. Kennedy, but expanding and strengthening those roots and adding to them, that sharpened and confirmed and left behind, for all of us to ponder and remember, the Kennedy legacy.

Ted Sorensen
New York City
December 1992

We need not feel the bitterness of the past to discover its meaning for the present and future.

—William Butler Yeats

Prologue

I WRITE NOT OUT OF SADNESS BUT OUT OF HOPE. John Kennedy is gone. Robert Kennedy is gone. Ted Kennedy remains, his prospects for the Presidency in 1972 diminished if not destroyed by his involvement in a fatal automobile accident. Some wrote that his plea of guilty for leaving the scene of that accident, and his public confession that his rational judgment had been overcome by a jumble of emotions during the grotesque hours that followed, marked "the end of the Kennedy era . . . the last of the Kennedy legacy."

I disagree. What John and Robert Kennedy built with such effort and imagination does not depend upon their brother being elected President in order to endure. What they left behind is too sturdy and too involved in the lives of countless others either to die suddenly and senselessly with them or to be destroyed by an automobile overturning in a pond. No one at this time can foretell with certainty the political future of Ted Kennedy. But I can say with certainty that the legacy of John and Robert Kennedy lives on.

It is more than fading memories, monuments, myths, and a sense of martyrdom. What they started, others are still determined to finish. What they stood for, millions now stand for. More than the laws, the books, and the speeches that bear their imprint, it is a unique and priceless set of concepts that to me represents the Kennedy legacy. It is of this legacy that I feel compelled to write. It is this legacy that endures and gives us hope.

Legacy is not legend. Indeed the gap between posthumous legend and legacy is greater in the case of the two Kennedys than that of any other public figure since Lincoln. This is not merely the result of cultists romanticizing their heroes. Too many supposedly serious scholars have implied that all our nation's problems began when Lyndon Johnson succeeded John Kennedy in 1963. Too many evaluations of Robert Kennedy make him an ethereal myth, a political Roland, omitting his concrete accomplishments and the obstacles he would have faced. At the same time the old hostile exaggerations persist—such as those about JFK's getting nothing through the Congress and RFK's entering the 1968 Presidential race only because Eugene McCarthy had won the New Hampshire primary. No myth or exaggeration, admiring or adverse, can help or hurt the dead; but it can make true perspective more difficult for the living.

Adding to the legend, not the legacy, is the tendency even among Kennedy admirers to pay more attention to their style than to their substance. Style is a part of the Kennedy legacy; a cool, convincing, self-confident style that spoke to and for the young at heart, cut through cant, overrode trivia, and elevated eloquence and gallantry and wit. But the ratio in their legacy as in their lives was roughly one part style to nine parts substance. Personal presence and eloquence helped both men achieve their gains and articulate their goals. But the solid significance of those gains and goals mattered far more to them—and will matter far more to history—than the spirit of their personal styles.

Let me make clear at the outset that I knew Bob Kennedy not only less intimately than I knew his brother John but also considerably less intimately than many of his close friends and staff associates knew him. I have already set forth my knowledge and impressions of John F. Kennedy, the man and the President. I feel no need now either to repeat or to retract any of those observations, nor to make any revelations or identifications deliberately withheld from the previous volume out of a sense of propriety. Thus more of this book will deal with RFK than with JFK. But time and travel have enlarged my perspective of President Kennedy. The questions asked of me in some three dozen capitals of the world, and by students at more than a hundred colleges, have shed additional light on what he bequeathed to us all; and comparisons and contrasts with his late brother—far more than with his successors—illuminate John Kennedy in new ways as well as telling us much about Robert.

Both John and Robert Kennedy (and the same has been true of Senator Edward Kennedy) displayed throughout their careers an unusual capacity for growth. Had their views simply reflected Boston, Harvard, the Court of St. James's, the Navy, and the Kennedy family, this book could have been written twenty years ago, if it were written at all. But they changed as they grew, their views and values changed, and this book seeks the story of that change.

Enough has been written—and will be written—about both Kennedys to provide a full record of their lives and deeds. I write not to repeat a recitation of their history but to trace the evolution of their philosophy—to distill from those lives and deeds a personal and national way of life that can meaningfully guide and inspire their legatees. This is not a detached account, for I remain devoted to them both. Where I am critical, I freely confess to writing with the benefit of hindsight. As Clark Clifford once observed to me, "The average high-school junior in Kansas City, Missouri, equipped with hindsight, is smarter than any President of the United States." Nor is this an official account, for the Kennedy legacy has many executors and each will have his own interpretation. What follows is simply the personal point of view of one who regards the legacy of the two Kennedys as the most important body of ideas in our time. It is not the exclusive province of the Kennedy family, much less those who sat at their feet or supped at their table, as some of my fellow "keepers of the flame" sometimes imply; nor is it only for intellectuals, Democrats, liberals, radicals, or even Americans. It is a legacy for all those who, in the phrase both brothers admired, now "seek a newer world."

The Kennedy legacy can no more be described in this or any other book than a Mozart concerto can be summed up by listing a series of black notes on white score paper. The whole of the Kennedy legacy is more than the sum of its parts. The following chapters will attempt to examine whence it came, what it included, and where it is headed. But there was in the lives of John and Robert Kennedy an indescribable essence that those not close to them may never fully understand. I do not wish to sound mystical or presumptuous, but there was a spirit emanating from these brothers, a sense of purpose, a quality of life, that the printed page cannot wholly capture.

However one defines that quality, we urgently need their legacy today. After the world recovered from the shock and grief of John Kennedy's assassination, his closest associates and followers vowed to carry on his work in private life or in public. The majority of us ultimately rallied around the banner of RFK as a means of fulfilling the Kennedy dream. We sought not the restoration of Camelot but a continuation of our effort to build a better society. As I traveled about the country and world, I found countless others keeping alive their hopes for our national destiny by this same reliance on the dead President's brother. But when he, too, was gunned down—and shortly thereafter the McCarthy–McGovern forces and their "peace plank" were routed at the Chicago Convention—it was not so easy to carry on. Bitterness, despair, and disillusionment engulfed many both inside and outside the Kennedy camp.

In particular, the young, the black, and the poor saw less hope of making their voices heard, of rising above the system. PRAY FOR US, BOBBY, said a hand-lettered sign held up to the passing funeral train. No one else seemed able to fill his role as their bridge to American society. Extremists on both the left and the right made new gains. The prospects for this nation's solving swiftly, peacefully, and effectively the mammoth problems confronting us at home and abroad, the prospects for a future America filled with something more meaningful than greater material wealth and more forms of entertainment, the prospects for politics free from dreary mediocrity and age-old proposals—all seemed dimmer if not hopeless. As bitter divisions deepened in 1968, there was a feeling in this country that somehow we had lost our way. Then in the summer of 1969, when Ted Kennedy's accident removed him from the Presidential picture for 1972, many felt that we had lost our best chance for leadership capable of showing us the way.

Yet I write because hope is not lost. We still have the Kennedy legacy, a legacy of hope.

Both John and Robert Kennedy, as devoted as they were

to this country and as hopeful as they were about its future, recognized the hypocrisy and irrelevance ingrained in so much of American policies and society; and both helped spark the current sense of revolt against the inadequacies and inequities of American life. But both believed that the necessary reforms could be achieved without violence, within the system, by making that system more open, more responsive, more relevant, by closing the gap between aspirations and performance, by going beyond New Deal liberalism and radically revising our institutions to make them serve us all. Death, not defeat, interrupted their success. They were on their way to proving that peaceful political change of revolutionary proportions was possible in the United States. Their leadership, if only they could have lived, might well have prevented the present splits in America's social fabric. Their legacy, if only it can be applied, may yet save it.

PART ONE

Evolution

ONLY AN ARBITRARY LINE DIVIDES THE
substantive meaning of the Kennedy legacy—summarized
later—from the evolution of that legacy in the lives of two
brothers. To what extent was that evolution shaped by
family, church, school, aides, and advisers? How was it
affected by personalities, politics, and public opinion, by
the press and by the Presidency? What happened to it after
John Kennedy's death? It is necessary that we now ask
these questions. But we can only guess at the answers.

One wellspring is unmistakable. The story of the
Kennedy legacy begins with the story of the Kennedy
family. All public men trace their success back to their
upbringing. But few if any were influenced by their families in the way the Kennedy boys were, because there has
never been in American public life a family like the
Kennedys. For three brothers to have become President,
Presidential candidate, and Presidential prospect within
a brief span of years requires more than an accidental
combination of tragedy and talent. It is an indication of the
qualities instilled in all three since childhood—aspiration

for public service and ambition to succeed, courage in the face of adversity and the will to win, a feel for the public pulse and the ability to quicken it.

In the early neighborhood softball and touch-football games, it was "the Kennedys versus the world." Much of the same spirit dominated their outlook on life. Their father, hard-driving, no-nonsense Joseph P. Kennedy—who set high standards for each child and was tough on any one who failed to meet them—was determined to acquire enough money and power to insulate himself and his children against the uncertain, indifferent, and hostile winds he felt as a young Irish Catholic in Brahmin Boston and at Harvard. As he became active in national and international affairs under Franklin Roosevelt, the dinner-table conversation which he dominated—when he was home—focused on public personalities and issues. Rose Kennedy was determined to give her children a combination of family affection and religious, educational, and parental discipline that would bind them together all their lives.

All nine Kennedy children maintained active lifetime memberships in their own exclusive "club," which outsiders—with rare exceptions, such as Lem Billings, who was an associate member—could join only through marriage. No one's presence, advice, or approval was as strongly desired by any Kennedy as that of another club member. The club's influence in their lives was somewhat diminished by the 1961 stroke that felled its founder and leader, Joseph P. Kennedy, Sr., and by the death of John Kennedy in 1963; but it was at all times for each of the Kennedy brothers his primary source of strength, fun, affection, assistance, and money.

Between Jack and Bob, during the time I knew them, there was no jealous competition for the limelight, only an intimate sharing of secrets, plans, and worries and a love that was unusually strong even between brothers. Jack Kennedy would not have considered anyone other than his brother Bob—except his brother Ted—to be his campaign manager; and neither Bob nor Ted would have considered turning him down, whatever else they were doing. All brothers and sisters—and brothers-in-law Stephen Smith and Sargent Shriver—were considered automatic members of every campaign team; Rose Kennedy was an effective stump speaker and television performer; and, until his illness, "the Ambassador" loved the role of *éminence grise*. Every campaign or other effort followed the father's theory: "If you have your family with you, you have a head start on others who must rely on making friends."

Both Jack and Bob Kennedy loved their parents with a devotion all too rare among modern adults, differing only as their circumstances and personalities differed. When Jack Kennedy was seeking major elective office, some observers felt he was keeping himself aloof from his father's conservative views and controversial past; but it was simply Jack's way to reserve his displays of affection and emotion for private occasions. His father's shrewd judgment and unqualified enthusiasm were, in fact, important to him. Bob at this period had not yet developed the strong contrary views that might otherwise have caused him to answer back at the dinner table even more than Jack, and the pride that he and his father took in each other's aggressive ways was known to all.

The sons' love for their father was redoubled by the latter's illness. Bob's campaign schedule for May 9, 1968, for example, was incredibly heavy and hectic. It began in New York City, ended in Lincoln, Nebraska, featured an address to the United Auto Workers' convention in Atlantic City and sandwiched in dinner at home with his children in McLean, Virginia, before a four-week Western trip for the Nebraska, South Dakota, Oregon, and California primaries. Yet he insisted on adding in the middle of that schedule a chartered jet flight to Cape Cod to have lunch with his father. The UAW convention ran late and the jet was unavailable. Still he persisted, hitching a ride on a corporate plane that detoured to drop us at Hyannis. At lunch, Bob told his father, helplessly confined to his wheelchair and unable to respond, how the campaign was coming, how much the old warrior's advice and assistance were needed, where the campaign trail had been and was headed, who was being helpful and who was hanging back. He made his father feel wanted and involved in the effort and excitement. On the plane returning to Washington, he fell asleep in his seat, content that his exhausting effort had made possible this brief and not easy visit that sadly turned out to be his last.

Bob's love for his mother shone through on that same visit. They talked both seriously and humorously about her role in his campaign, and she urged him to get more rest and take better care of himself. I chose not to remind either of them of an evening in 1962 when Mrs. Kennedy remarked to us both that she would campaign for Ted in 1962, then once more for Jack in 1964, and that would be enough at her age. When Bob had said, "What about me, Mother?" she had said she never would, and they teased each other about it. When I later asked him the reason (she had simply said to him, "You know why"), he told me it was because as a teen-ager he had not kept his clothes and room neat. Whatever the reason, in 1968 he was grateful that she had relented.

It is usually assumed that the toughness of fiber in the Kennedy children came from their father. But, like Bob, he was in many ways soft and emotional beneath his fierce exterior, while their mother, like Jack, was made of far

more steel than her gentle disposition conveyed to outsiders. Rose Kennedy has now seen two sons assassinated,
another son killed in war, another son nearly killed in a
plane and then involved in a fatal automobile accident,
a daughter killed in a plane crash, another daughter
mentally retarded, and her husband totally incapacitated.
It should be clear that her continuing faith in man is
upheld by a great faith in God as well as pride in her blood.

Neither John nor Robert was as devoutly Catholic as
their mother, but both had a genuine devotion to the
Church. Each had unquestioningly accepted Catholicism
as a part of his heritage, along with wealth, intelligence,
and the Democratic Party. President Kennedy showed
none of the authoritarian nature of the Catholic Church
in his dealings with his aides, his domestic staff, or his
children, and he did not embrace it in his Church. His
religion, like other aspects of his personal life, was a
private matter. No one who knew him believed the allegation of Jim Bishop that JFK had fallen sobbing on his
knees in prayer the dawn after the Bay of Pigs venture
failed; but if he had, he would not have disclosed it to
anyone.

Bob was more faithful than Jack in observing Catholic
ritual in his home as well as church and found that it
sustained his courage in the face of reality rather than
providing any escape from reality. But both brothers were
only generally—although sometimes adversely—concerned
with the position of the Catholic Church on social and
economic issues, and neither had, except on rare occasions,
any deep interest in the questions of church doctrine and
renewal that were of concern to Catholic scholars. One
revealing exception occurred during RFK's Harvard days.
Attending a meeting of Catholic students, he listened with
growing anger to a priest's assertion that there was no

salvation outside the Catholic faith. To everyone's aston-
ishment Bob rose to contest that point of view (for which
the priest, Boston's famed Father Feeney, was later ex-
communicated), and then stormed out of the meeting—an
action that shocked his mother when she heard about it.

Nor was there any direct ethnic motivation to the
careers of the two men—no deep-seated need to be the
first Catholic President, or to revenge themselves on the
Brahmins who had snubbed their father, or to adhere to
the Irish tradition of primogeniture in their Presidential
efforts. But there is no mistaking the Catholic Church's
influence, primarily via their mother, on the compassion
they possessed for their fellow human beings.

The difference in their public attitudes toward the
Church was brought about by a difference in their political circumstances. RFK ran for the Presidency in 1968
with virtually no opposition for religious reasons. JFK
ran for the Presidency in 1960 with religion his major
handicap. He had started as a parochial Congressman from
Boston, where he at first strongly defended the Catholic
position on aid to education and won the plaudits of the
Boston Archdiocese, to which his family would always have
close connections and make heavy contributions. Upon
entering the national arena in 1956, he was at first startled
to learn that many well-meaning, unbigoted Protestants
and Jews genuinely feared that his Church might tell him
how to act on matters of state and might excommunicate
him if he refused. Some Catholic newspaper editors and
others reacted adversely to his reply that his oath of office
took precedence. Thereafter he generally responded to
questions about church-state issues not with a philosophical
explanation but with a recital of his position: opposing
public aid to parochial schools (once he became a Senator),
opposing creation of the post of Ambassador to the Vatican,

and supporting the First Amendment generally. He dispatched me twice to obtain from his friend Bishop John Wright of Pittsburgh a professional explanation on why his First Amendment stand was not inconsistent with his membership in the Church.

The issue that personally gave him the most difficulty in the late 1950s was birth control. It was a relatively new issue in national elections, and the then Senator was reluctant to dissent from what appeared to be the solid opposition of his Church. Having won the enmity of the Church's detractors, he wanted to hold on to whatever support he had from adherents to the Church position.

The birth-control issue presented itself, moreover, in terms of an amendment to the foreign-aid bill; and JFK sincerely feared that this would be the final straw to break the back of that already foundering program. As President, he remained cautious on this subject, making important but very quiet strides forward in supporting research and other programs through the National Institutes of Health and the United Nations. He was only half joking when he asked economist Barbara Ward (Lady Jackson) how she squared her Catholicism with her public advocacy of birth control; and he valued her answer which compared it to money-lending in the sixteenth century just before the Church declared that charging interest was no longer a sin. She was certain that another such declaration was on its way regarding contraception and that no one should be troubled for having preceded it.

RFK as a Senator, on the other hand, took a bolder stand on this issue and on abortion reform as well. Operating in a more relaxed climate, he moved easily with the growing public support for progress in this area, and felt his Church should move also.

Except for one year Jack spent at a Catholic institution

run by laymen, neither brother attended parochial school. Reportedly Bob refused to attend compulsory chapel at one Protestant prep school, but his reasons are not known. In any event, their education—unlike that of their sisters— was basically secular. Jack graduated from Choate and Harvard, and Bob graduated from Milton, Harvard, and the University of Virginia Law School; but it is difficult to credit any of these institutions with extensive influence on the Kennedy legacy. Neither Kennedy was a star student. Both showed more interest in the athletic activities that would interest them the rest of their lives—football, swimming, sailing, and general physical fitness. JFK as boy and man suffered more than his share of illness and injury but never lost either his physical vigor or his love of the sea. When it was no longer summer at Hyannis Port, he sought out Palm Beach or island vacations. Bob was a sportsman for all seasons. Even more than Jack, he sought and enjoyed as a student the companionship of star athletes more than scholars. (Later in life he would warm to scholars, but he still liked to be with athletes.) He compensated for his shorter stature by a rugged determination to best every physical challenge, whether it was mountain climbing, rapids running, skiing, or swimming in the piranha-filled waters of an Amazon tributary. No doubt, as his wife remarked, he wished he had time to be an astronaut. He loved the out-of-doors, the countryside, and small towns— the latter in contrast with the big cities where JFK was at home.

In the middle of his four years at Harvard, Jack Kennedy's intellectual development began to take hold. He still had no fixed point of view—as one professor said, he approached political-science problems as "the young scientist in the laboratory"—and he was still basically a wealthy, charming, conservative Democrat with no flair for campus politics and no plans for national politics. But his readings and travels were more important than his formal studies, and they continued to expand and shape his mind after graduation. Traveling in Europe, visiting England, where his father was Ambassador, talking with young Europeans and second-level diplomats, observing firsthand the rise and fall of governments, parties, and doctrines, he began to perceive the logic and desirability of diverse systems in a diverse world. Reading biography and history, jotting down favorite passages, questioning his father and various experts on other passages, he began to see how mortal men can sometimes change the flow of history and how some tides cannot be turned back.

Jack Kennedy's reading habits had been developed during the long sieges of illness that confined him to bed as a youngster. Bob Kennedy, always an activist, did not have this early discipline. By his own admission, his mind, like Jack's, also blossomed after his formal education had nearly ended. But he shared that remarkable Kennedy quality of continuing growth; and his reading, observing, traveling, and learning continued after graduation from college, service as a naval seaman, and graduation from law school. He covered the Middle East war for the *Boston Post* in 1948, just as Jack had covered the Potsdam Conference, the British elections, and the founding of the United Nations for the Hearst newspapers in 1945. He was not until his last years as serious a reader or as intellectually inclined generally as Jack. Unlike Jack, he usually preferred to be briefed out loud on a subject facing him in elective office rather than to read a comprehensive analysis, although he wanted the latter for back-up. But neither one of them would have labeled himself a pure "intellectual."

Certainly Jack Kennedy was far from the sober, scholarly

type during his years as Washington's gay young bachelor. His marriage to Jacqueline Bouvier in 1953, when he was thirty-six, was followed by his second brush with death—a dangerous operation on his back. (The first occurred when his PT boat was sliced by a Japanese destroyer during World War II.) The combined effect settled him down. Jacqueline possessed a quality of strong independence and, occasionally, saucy irreverence that made him all the more pleased to impress her in his work. Her love of life enriched his, and she provided a continuity of affection and relaxation that a man who drove himself so hard found particularly welcome. Their marriage was not always smooth in its early years, but it brought them both an increasing amount of happiness, particularly in the White House. His desire to have her present when he announced the Cuban missile quarantine, and her desire to share whatever fate befell him in that crisis, were but illustrations of the bond between them.

Although he started comparatively late in life to raise children, JFK was fascinated by the growth process, curious about the practices of others, and delightfully surprised at how completely and quickly his own offspring altered his outlook on life. More than ever, he saw the world's needs in terms of children, the gap between what they needed or deserved and what they were likely to receive. Even though Caroline and John, Jr., were still very young when he died, their father had discovered a kind of satisfaction in playing and talking with them that neither political nor social life had ever given him.

Bob Kennedy was profoundly influenced by and dependent upon his wife and children over a much longer time. Ethel Skakel is a rugged and exuberant member of the female species, and this befitted RFK. It was a strong and mutual love. He paid thoughtful attention to her reactions and to her judgments on events, policies, and particularly people, feeling that this gave him some sense of how others felt. Sometimes, in mock sternness, he would chastise her for berating his detractors, or hush her for volunteering amateurish views in the presence of supposed experts, or tease her about some new expenditure for their house. But it always seemed to me that he was secretly proud and impressed and that she knew it.

He, too, was increasingly moved by the notion that his children and all children deserved a better world. Although JFK could relax on the campaign trail or abroad and move from one abode to another, RFK felt really at home only at home. He gave his ten children—the eleventh was born after his death—more time and affection than most fathers half as busy. He shared his sorrows as well as his successes with them. He took them to his office (where he hung their drawings), on trips abroad, and on vacation adventures in this country; but he took pains to prevent politics from interfering with their studies, manners, and friendships, and tried to minimize their share of publicity. In the midst of important political meetings at his home, he would excuse himself to be with his children during dinner, even if he and Ethel would be dining with adult guests later. Despite his many absences and the sheer number of his flock, he knew intimately each child's strengths, weaknesses, and needs.

His tenderness to Jacqueline and her children after JFK's death was especially moving, but his warmth was not confined to members of his family. Gripping the hand of a dying woman in a nursing home until she was gone, talking with a little retarded girl in an institution, sharing the indignation of a Mexican-American migrant farm couple while their children huddled outside their filthy hovel, throwing a football around with teen-age boys in a ghetto—not for photographers, not for effect or even self-gratification, but out of human kindness—such acts were characteristic of RFK. Yet he was called ruthless, selfish, overly aggressive, and cold by many who termed his older brother warm and kindhearted.

A close comparison of the two brothers throws the whole "ruthlessness" charge into new perspective. It is true that Jack Kennedy seemed to the outside world more consistently gentle than Bob. He pressed ahead more quietly and patiently. He could be smoother, more soothing, less intense, less explosive, more given to understatement, less quick to reveal his likes and dislikes. Bob was both tougher and more emotional, or at least more often likely to show emotion. Far from being coldly indifferent, as some thought, he was hot-blooded, sensitive, and compassionate. He reached the zenith of *his* public career at a time when, unlike 1960, the national conscience called for a man of passion; and passion he possessed in abundance—for the black child in the ghetto, the maimed grandmother in Vietnam, the bewildered Indian, the undernourished Appalachian, and future victims of a future nuclear war. JFK, although he had received far less exposure to the suffering of such people, could nevertheless rationally empathize with it. RFK could actually feel it in his own bones.

Bob's spirit had always been tougher and his approach more pugnacious, and he had, in that sense, been more aggressive than Jack ever since they were boys. "I was the seventh of nine children," Robert Kennedy once said, "and when you come from that far down you have to struggle to survive." The President once recalled that when Bobby was four he would jump off the family sailboat, determined to swim with his older brothers, who had to rescue him every time. "It showed either a lot of guts or no sense at all," said JFK, "depending on how you looked at it." The same could be said for some of Bob's daredevil feats on mountains and rivers at a time when not only his family but Jack's widow and children depended on him—and it could be said as well of some of the political risks and challenges he would later undertake. But he had also developed, as the third of four sons in a large family, a sensitivity to individual needs among both older and younger siblings that would later keep him unusually attuned to the feelings of other people.

He could never be as patient as JFK, for there always seemed to him to be so much to do after JFK and so little time to do it. I once watched a female politician grab Bob's arm to pose for a picture. He managed a smile. The flashbulb failed to go off, the photographer fumbled for more, and Bob's smile disappeared. JFK would have had the same inner irritation, but the smile would have remained.

In time Bob's softer traits won out, particularly in his last years. He developed very much the same kind of candid spontaneity and wry wit in public and private utterances that had characterized his older brother. But these were post-Dallas years, and Bob could still not be as lighthearted or easygoing as Jack had been in his final years. Indeed, both John and Robert Kennedy changed so much—and always for the better—since I first met them in 1953 that it is difficult now to remember what they were really like then and, for comparison reasons, what John was like at Robert's age. RFK in particular suffered in his last years from press and public descriptions that never caught up with the changes.

In public appearances and interviews from 1964 to 1968, I often sought to communicate to suspicious liberals the message of Robert Kennedy's growth by first stressing my sympathy with their disapproval of his 1953 qualities and then leading them through all the liberalizing changes that had subsequently occurred. Unfortunately, one TV producer edited the tape of my 1967 interview to retain the full catalogue of horrors regarding 1953 ("militant, aggressive, intolerant, opinionated, somewhat shallow in his convictions . . . more like his father than his brother . . .") but omitting nearly all of the changes and new qualities of compassion and humanitarianism that I had then listed. Bob saw the show and sent me the transcript with a brief handwritten note:

Teddy old pal—Perhaps we could keep down the number of adjectives and adverbs describing me in 1955 [sic] and use a few more in 1967. O.K.—Bob

He would have been entitled to a far angrier reaction, and his critics would have expected it. But the death of his brother had transformed Bob into a more thoughtful, less temperamental human being. More than ever before, his disposition resembled that of Jack, who never lost his temper in the sense of losing control. In Bob's earlier, moodier days his temperamental fuse had been much shorter. JFK could on occasion chew out without mercy anyone whose performance inexcusably failed to meet the high standards he had set for himself and expected of others. He could do his share of grumbling about human and mechanical obstacles. But he never flew into a rage and hated no one.

Bob was not a "hater" either. I know of no one—even among his many harsh critics and opponents—whom he hated. On the contrary, he was capable of deep love, not only for his family but for his country and countrymen, including the very least of them and especially children. His tenderness and romantic idealism were unusual for one so preoccupied and tough-minded. The extraordinary number of fatal tragedies that befell both his family and Ethel's did not harden him to pain. "You had better pretend you don't know me," he told me once in a bitter jest following the death of a friend and relative in a small plane crash, "everyone connected with me seems jinxed."

RFK was less consistently calm and composed than JFK, and more rigid and impulsive, but more often considerate of the other obligations of his associates, and more apt to be sensitive to their needs and feelings. He could also be more demanding, rougher, tougher, more belligerent with those who crossed or double-crossed the Kennedys. He had a louder bark than his brother Jack, more intense feelings for and against individuals. Both brothers, in complete contrast with their deceased older brother Joe, Jr., and younger brother Edward, had qualities of shyness, terseness, and sometimes tenseness that caused people to feel they were arrogant and aloof. But both tempered their zeal in pursuit of good by frequently laughing at themselves and their own seriousness.

Bob drove himself even harder than his brother, if that is possible, and the fatigue of campaigning showed more clearly on his face and frame. But he was no more ambitious, no more reluctant to take advantage of his family name and money, no more determined to succeed, no more pragmatic about the realities of opportunity than his brother Jack and no less tender a soul. He did have more political enemies than Jack, a tougher exterior to bear the "ruthless" accusation, and a reputation as a hardheaded campaign manager, a carpetbagger in the New York Senate race and, most important, a "prosecutor" in his Senate Rackets Committee and Justice Department roles. In a country where all too few love a cop, Robert Kennedy had "cop" written all over his public image. Moreover, he was fearless about the truth, and, as Averell Harriman said in his eulogy, "At times the truth is ruthless."

Certainly both brothers were possessed with strong but nevertheless well-governed ambitions. Both, reflecting the competitive instincts of their upbringing, wanted to reach the top of their chosen profession of politics and public service—and the top is the Presidency. Each objectively considered himself more capable of handling the burdens of that post at the time he was running than any other candidate. Both felt frustrated as Senators that they were not making their maximum contribution to the shaping of a better world—and that the place to make it was the Presidency, which had far more influence on the course of history. "It seems to make so little difference sometimes what we do down here," Jack Kennedy remarked to me one day in the Senate. "Only the Executive Branch can really move things." RFK made similar remarks to his aides. (After JFK was President, however, he ruefully remarked that he had not realized, when a Senator, how much power the Congress had.)

Jack Kennedy was suddenly propelled into the Presidential picture by his unexpected showing in the Vice Presidential contest at the 1956 Democratic Convention, after which he was wholly uninterested in second place. He was not motivated by any special tasks he wanted to accomplish in the White House, only a conviction that he had developed the qualities needed to lead the country forward. "I run for the Presidency of the United States," he said on election eve in November 1960, "because it is the center of action." That summed it up, and that was clearly "ambition."

Bob Kennedy, who had sought for years not only to serve and assist his brother but also to stride not too far behind him, was suddenly propelled into the Presidential picture by his brother's death and by a determination to carry forward the policies and principles his brother had started. He, too, felt that he was the one man who could best do that—and that, too, was clearly "ambition."

Yet it is the country's good fortune that the Kennedys possessed these ambitions in the world of politics and public service, and that their talents and energies had not been confined to the world of private business in which their father largely moved. Neither brother ever wanted for money, thanks to Joseph P. Kennedy's financial success and his establishment of trusts enabling each child—he liked to say—to look him in the eye and tell him to go to hell. None ever did. But it was not because they feared being cut off financially, and it was more than gratitude. It was simply because they loved him.

Nor did Ambassador Kennedy ever make any attempt to interest any of his sons in the family business, in the deals he made, or in the income he made. Even as adults, the Kennedy children left the handling of their personal financial affairs to their father's office in New York. They had comparatively little interest in how their own funds were being invested and what their own annual incomes totaled, much less their father's.

Clearly, the brothers in public office would not have been influenced by their father's holdings even if they had known more about them. On one occasion President Kennedy asked me to meet with Tom Walsh of "the New York office," as it was called, to make certain that legitimate foundations such as the Joseph P. Kennedy Jr. Foundation—which channeled the bulk of the family's charitable donations into the fight against mental retardation—would not be adversely affected by proposed language in a Presidential message relating to the tax-exempt status of charitable trusts. But on every other occasion the actions of

John Kennedy as Senator and President, and of Robert Kennedy as Attorney General and Senator, were taken without regard to and frequently in opposition to the business interests of the far-flung family enterprises in oil, gas, theaters, real estate, and other fields. Both joked about the extent to which the tax reforms they favored would hurt them financially. They were neither ashamed of their good fortune and what it enabled them to do nor condescending to those less fortunate. That they could spend far less time courting rich contributors was a blessing for them and for the nation.

The Kennedys, to be sure, are not the Rockefellers, or even close. There was some limit on the amounts available, and a pooling or borrowing of funds was sometimes required to meet major expenditures approved by all. Presidential campaigns were too exorbitantly expensive to be financed within the family. But family money was a help —to purchase the campaign plane *Caroline* in 1959, for example, to start RFK's sudden Presidential race in 1968 until a fund-raising campaign could begin, or to help those friends of JFK in the 1958 election whom he undoubtedly hoped might help him in his 1960 quest for the Presidency. (There was no understanding of *quid pro quo,* and some of those 1958 recipients, such as Eugene McCarthy, did not support him, which was wholly within their right.)

Both Bob and Jack expressed occasional concern in typical husbandly fashion over their spouses' rate of expenditure; and both would occasionally forgo desired purchases, trips, or campaign efforts on the grounds that they were not worth the money. But neither carried much if any money, neither cared much about money, and neither wanted a career making money. "The political world," said JFK in 1960, "beats following the dollar. It's . . . so much more stimulating . . . and you can do something about what you think."

The earnest and thoughtful conviction accurately reflected in that statement had not characterized either brother in the eyes of many during their first few years in Washington. Jack was a lackluster Congressman from January 1947 to January 1953; and Bob, after a short stint in the Justice Department, joined the staff of Senator Joseph McCarthy's notorious Senate Committee on Government Operations, also in January 1953, for six short months that would haunt him in liberal circles thereafter.

There is no purpose in attempting to excuse or explain Bob Kennedy's relationship with Joe McCarthy. The simplistic views of militant patriotism, anti-Communism, and internal security which were a part of his upbringing had, in 1953, not yet been balanced by the deep devotion to Constitutional rights and civil liberties that he would ultimately hold. His father, sisters, and brother-in-law Sargent Shriver were personal friends of McCarthy's; his brother Jack, as a member of the House Labor Committee, had made headlines in the conservative Boston Irish press by stiffly cross-examining suspected Communists in the union movement; and no one in that family had the background to understand the motivations of anyone who was blinded by either the despair of the Depression or the hopes of the postwar period into collaborating with the Communists. Nor were they as sensitive then to the hurt inflicted by the McCarthy committee's shabby treatment of persons who had committed no real crime, however foolish or even unpatriotic they might have been. John Kennedy told me that he hoped Bob would not take the McCarthy post, but his reasons were political, not ideological.

JFK's liberalism grew in the Senate, and he opposed McCarthy on a surprising number of votes without ever directly tangling with him on the Communist issue. His back operation in 1954 forced him to miss the McCarthy censure vote, but the two men had broken long before on JFK's refusal to support a hunt for Red witches at Harvard. "Perhaps we were not as sensitive as some and should have acted earlier," he later admitted.

Bob Kennedy's duties with one of McCarthy's subcommittees had nothing to do with domestic subversives and had been originally requested by a staff member not connected with McCarthy. Six months later he came to the conclusion that subcommittee counsel Roy Cohn was consistently conducting investigations with McCarthy's consent on the basis of preconceived prejudices instead of developing hard evidence. He informed McCarthy that he felt this to be wrong and resigned, obviously influenced by the fact that all the Democratic members of the subcommittee had walked out a month earlier. Other twenty-eight-year-old lawyers might have recognized the McCarthy–Cohn pattern before joining the staff and wanted no part of such investigations even if hard evidence were developed. But Bob liked Joe McCarthy, found him a much more complex and sensitive man than the public believed, pitied his appetite for headlines, and continued—long after McCarthy had been censured and broken and Bob had become a national personality through his role as Chief Counsel to the Special Senate Rackets Committee—to befriend the man who had befriended him when he was a fledgling lawyer. Moreover, even as Rackets Committee Counsel, he dealt with recalcitrant witnesses with such wrath and zeal that the American Civil Liberties Union was moved to remind him of witnesses' rights.

He would hear all the rest of his life about those first six months with McCarthy. Clearly, they did not represent an auspicious start on Capitol Hill—but neither did JFK's first six years. His service in the House of Representatives, to which he was elected in 1946, was marked by an inconsistent voting record that was basically conservative on international and fiscal issues, basically liberal on domestic, social, and economic issues, and plagued by a high rate of absenteeism on all issues. The first reflected the fact that he was only beginning to develop convictions independent of his father's; the second reflected the fact that he represented a "bread-and-butter" district in East Boston where housing, social security, rent and price controls, and similar issues were all-important; and the third reflected his frequent illnesses, world travels, and crisscrossing of Massachusetts in preparation for a state-wide campaign.

Some positions he took as a Congressman showed courage—such as his favoring a large increase in taxes to pay for the Korean War and his opposing a popular veterans' pension boost. (He was also the only Massachusetts Democrat to oppose clemency for James Michael Curley, then serving in Federal prison; but, as Ted Kennedy pointed out later, "Grampa [Fitzgerald, an old Curley rival] had something to do with that one!") Some showed the first beginnings of those notions that would later bloom as full-fledged principles—such as a condemnation of imperialism and colonialism all over the world, including French Indochina, and a recognition that the United States cannot solve all the world's problems. But far more often his positions, when consistent at all, were contrary to those which with greater experience and responsibility he would later take. He opposed, for example, some foreign-aid and most foreign-trade liberalization; he favored cuts in domestic programs not beneficial to Massachusetts; and he supported limitations on Presidential power.

His travels to Europe, the Middle East, and Asia during this period had a broadening effect, however; and his travels across Massachusetts culminated in the 1952 Senate campaign that tested his political mettle far more than his easy Congressional victories. That campaign tested as well the political techniques that would become famous in the 1960 Presidential race. It was a pragmatic, personal campaign led by the candidate's family and friends that carried him directly to the voters (and even their children) at tea parties, high schools, and an endless, exhausting round of stump speeches and handshaking in the traditionally Republican towns as well as the city of Boston. Instead of holding meetings and hearing complaints day after day, Kennedy campaign leaders were out working in the grass roots. The candidate's brothers and sisters were as willing to hand out bumper stickers or ask store managers to put signs in their windows as they were to make speeches or plan high strategy. "You know something is wrong with the campaign," Bob Kennedy said to me later, "if the campaign manager has time to ride in the motorcades with the candidate."

There was not one headquarters but one hundred, each one manned by volunteers receiving constant instructions on what must be done and others checking constantly on whether it had been done. Talented but nonpolitical aides worked on speeches and issues. Money fueled the machine. The Ambassador was never present, but his presence was never absent. Polls, card files, clipping services, and constant communication kept the campaign team in close touch with the thinking of the electorate.

Above all, the campaign relied on an enormous number of volunteers instead of professionals, a broadening of the effort far beyond the regular party machinery to enlist students, housewives, college faculty members, young business and professional men, and many, many others. As many signatures as could be gathered were placed on nominating petitions, for example, in order to involve as many voters as possible; then each signer received a letter of thanks from the candidate in order to make use of as many volunteers as possible in that process. As later codified in Lawrence O'Brien's sixty-four-page manual on organization, the campaign's basic premise, as the astute Theodore White has described it, was

that every citizen likes to feel he is somehow wired into the structure of power; that making a man or woman seem useful and important to himself (or herself) in the power system of American life takes advantage of one of the simplest and noblest urges of politics in the most effective way.

That was participatory politics long before the phrase became popular.

Many of the old-school Massachusetts politicians did not like the new methods, the new people brought in, RFK as campaign manager, or JFK's independence—but in time, as their national counterparts would in 1960, they reluctantly "led" their followers who were already in the Kennedy camp. JFK's upset victory over Henry Cabot Lodge, although narrow, stood out in the 1952 Eisenhower sweep of Massachusetts and the nation.

Twelve years later RFK was elected to the Senate with the same campaign techniques, by then further perfected, but in very different circumstances. Jack Kennedy's apartment in his home district may have been rarely used as his "residence," but at least he had represented Massachusetts for six years in the House before he ran for the Senate. Bob Kennedy entered the Senate race in New York —where he had grown up but moved away from—without an established residence and ineligible to vote in his own election. He did not have to fight the party machine; most of it pleaded with him to come into the race. He did not need several years to make himself known; he was a former Attorney General of the United States and the eldest surviving brother of one of the nation's most famous families. He did not win in the face of a Republican landslide but with the help of a Democratic landslide, including the personal campaign help of Lyndon Johnson, who stumped the state with him one day as their two campaigns fused.

During the summer of 1964, still uncertain about his future, Bob had talked with me more than once about the New York Senate possibility. The post interested him. He had rejected appointment to his brother's seat in 1960 but not the notion of someday seeking it. Now his brother Ted had that position. It seemed incredible to him that a state Democratic Party as large and diverse as New York's would not already have a candidate who could oust the incumbent Republican Senator Kenneth Keating. But Averell Harriman would not run, Robert Wagner would not commit himself to running, and other would-be contenders, such as Congressmen Samuel Stratton and Otis Pike, fared poorly in polls showing RFK a potential victor. Lyndon Johnson once told me that Adlai Stevenson had privately wanted that New York Senatorial nomination and had asked President Johnson during an automobile ride to the airport to obtain the support of party leaders for him. "When I told him I was for Bobby, he never said another kind word about me."

Nomination at that time was by state convention. With the reluctant endorsement of Wagner, the divided backing of reform Democrats, and the continued opposition of Stratton and Pike, but with the enthusiastic support of the city leaders and party workers—some of whom Bob, as campaign manager for his brother, had treated roughly when they refused to work with the reformers, but all of whom now recognized a winner—the nomination was easily his.

The election was not so easy. Initially he refused to attack Keating's record, and many voters saw no reason to oust a popular moderate. Handicapped by insufficient time to familiarize himself with the state, he was berated as a ruthless carpetbagger. Many liberals felt a lingering suspicion of him for his McCarthy past and "cop" image. A controversy arose over distortions in Keating's record once it was attacked. All of this added to RFK's concern and spurred him to direct pleas for campaign help to his scattered colleagues from the days of the New Frontier. Then a second-half surge gave him a large margin of victory, though not as large as L.B.J.'s edge in the state. Observing that his victory was no reflection of the strength of the organized party structure in New York, Bob set out to do something about it.

Jack Kennedy had involved himself in Massachusetts party politics only once—in 1956, when he committed himself to wresting control of the state committee away from some John McCormack allies whose reputations, ambitions, and anti-Stevenson attitudes would, he felt, adversely affect him and his position at that year's Democratic National Convention. It was a hard, close struggle, requiring him to woo assiduously small-town Democratic barons who cared little for his fame and not at all for his independence. But he won and promptly abandoned interest once again, save for occasional inquiries through Ken O'Donnell and Larry O'Brien. His massive Senate re-election victory in 1958 was conducted as usual outside the state-party apparatus, even though the latter was then in friendly hands.

Bob Kennedy was far more ambitious in this regard and far less successful. He, too, was able in time to install a state chairman of his own choosing and to obtain the grudging respect of most party leaders. He scored a single-handed victory in a local New York City judicial race as well when his candidate upset the choice of patronage-minded leaders of both parties. But his efforts to prevent a party-splitting battle for the state legislative leadership posts, to obtain a strong, openly chosen gubernatorial nominee in 1966, to promote a state-wide atmosphere of Constitutional reform in 1967, and to build a united, enthusiastic, and fully democratic state Democratic Party were all doomed to failure.

Despite general agreement on progressive policies, the divisions among New York Democrats were so many, deep-seated, and long-standing, and the various factions were so intent on pursuing their own goals, that such concepts as party unity, loyalty, and even success were matters considered by some local leaders to be more of convenience than consistent principle. Preoccupied with national and international affairs in Washington, finding himself constantly in opposition to the party's national leader (President Johnson, who had strength of his own in New York) and allocated very little Federal patronage or other influence to dispense, Senator Kennedy could make only partial headway in turning back the traditional tide of disunity among the members of his party in New York.

His relations with the state's senior Senator, Republican Jacob Javits, were not as consistently close as Jack Kennedy's relations had been with his Republican colleague and senior, Leverett Saltonstall; but after a shaky start they were basically friendly and cooperative. His relations with the state's Republican Governor Nelson Rockefeller, were not as close. Kennedy contradicted the Governor's position that eligible New York counties needed no aid under the Appalachia bill, refuted the Governor's assertions regarding mental-retardation requirements in the state, and even opposed some state legislative proposals of Rockefeller's on public power and other issues.

He had least respect of all for New York City's Republican Mayor, John Lindsay, whose 1965 mayoralty campaign, he felt, had carefully imitated the JFK style and mannerisms without providing as much substance. He was grateful for Lindsay's help in Bedford-Stuyvesant but generally felt that the Mayor's public-relations image was maintained by a press that was far less generous to the Kennedys. He was, in 1968, in the process of organizing a group of civic leaders who would speak out on Lindsay's mismanagement of city problems. In 1967 he predicted to me that Lindsay would challenge him for his Senate seat in 1970, seeking a victory that would not only guarantee the Mayor the Republican Presidential nomination in 1972 but at the same time eliminate his toughest opponent. For the same reason, RFK hoped Lindsay would be his 1970 opponent, remarking, "I couldn't beat him nationally anyway if I can't beat him state-wide in New York . . . but I think I can."

Robert Kennedy's role as United States Senator was largely overshadowed by the attention he earned during that period on statements and efforts that went beyond the legislative process. As a result, it is widely assumed that he accomplished nothing legislatively and disliked his Senate years. In truth, he did dislike much of the verbosity and pomposity he encountered in the Senate and had little patience for petty arguments, routine subcommittee meetings, and time-consuming hearings. But he was conscientious—as JFK had been—about not missing roll-call votes, whatever the effect on his speaking schedule. He attended working sessions of his committees and subcommittees in which pending bills were considered and amended, and, attended—or as subcommittee chairman convened—hearings shedding new light on major problems. The Ribicoff hearings on urban problems, which led to Kennedy's tax-incentive bills discussed in the next chapter, were a prime example. Frequently he himself testified before Congressional committees, administrative hearings, the New York City Council, and other panels. His colleagues respected him for having done his homework, for possessing a good staff, and for offering concrete suggestions and carefully drafted bills regarding major problem areas.

Inasmuch as the Executive Branch effectively initiates most legislation, few Senators can point to major bills bearing their names. RFK achieved passage of a score of measures of importance to New York and to his wider constituencies and was a leader from beginning to end in the Senate fights over poverty, welfare, and airline-strike legislation. Nevertheless, he was not a "Senate man" like his brother Ted or even to the extent that his brother John had been. From 1965 to 1968 the Senate and his fellow Senators sometimes stimulated and shaped the then-developing Kennedy legacy but they had little direct effect on it.

Bob was a leader in that body only in the sense that he had power—not Senate power as a committee chairman or floor leader but national power as a man who had a popular following in the home states of his colleagues, a man whose help they might need in their own campaigns and whose path would surely someday lead him to greater power in the White House. For these reasons, and because he became an articulate advocate for points of view that many of his colleagues shared, they generally respected him and listened to him, but many did not warm to him.

Jack Kennedy, on the other hand, had no such power or prominence in the Senate until his last several months as a member of that body, and by then he was rarely there. But he liked the Senate, despite its frustrations, for, unlike Bob, his Senate service preceded his taste of Executive power. The Senate also liked him better and liked his acceptance of Senate customs and his effort to befriend the older, more conservative, and Southern members who comprised the Senate establishment. He would never be a member of that establishment in view of his youth, his independent liberal record, and his ambitions beyond the Senate. But more mutual respect prevailed between JFK and the "club" than would later be true of RFK, and that respect was of some assistance to him when he entered the White House. Unlike his brother Ted, however, John Kennedy had no desire to rise to a Senate leadership position. One day, observing Majority Leader Lyndon Johnson and his Senate Whip employing their arm-twisting, finger-wagging, favor-dispensing techniques for building Democratic unity, he remarked to me what a miserable job he would find either of those posts.

Part of JFK's success with his colleagues and his Massachusetts constituency stemmed from his quiet manner, his tendency toward objectivity and understatement, and his well-prepared, temperate and rational remarks on all subjects to which he addressed himself. Robert Kennedy, as an instant national figure in the Senate, frequently took part even in his first two years as Senator in debates on major national and international issues. John Kennedy, a little-known freshman Senator who was acutely conscious of the narrow margin by which he had carried his state, spent more time on Massachusetts and New England matters.

Some of John Kennedy's work, however, reflected the growth of his perspective. His speeches on Indochina and Algeria were remarkably accurate analyses of the West's inability to halt the power and appeal of nationalism. His speech on Poland recognized the need for diversity and discretion in America's approach to Eastern Europe. His efforts on labor reform—undertaken despite warnings that it would alienate union support in 1960—sought to assure "participatory democracy" to that segment of society. That fight also gave him more valuable experience in piloting a bill through the shoals of the Senate than all his other efforts combined. His support of the St. Lawrence Seaway and reciprocal trade indicated a courageous adherence to broader national interests instead of the narrow sectionalism of his House days. His sponsorship of the Development Loan Program for poorer countries, his proposal of a multilateral aid consortium for India and her neighbors, his preference of economic aid over military aid, his backing of injunctive powers against racial discrimination, and his consistent efforts on behalf of the underprivileged and unemployed, all contained overtones of the philosophy and program he would later offer as President.

But, in general, his posture in the 1950s was too moderate by today's standards and his contribution as a freshman Senator too modest for the work of JFK's Senate years (as distinguished from RFK's Senate years) to be included in what I have termed the Kennedy legacy. His philosophy was still developing, his ties to provincial Massachusetts matters were still too close, his politically motivated caution was too inhibiting, and his exposure to the problems, power, viewpoints, and values which would later shape his program was still too limited. But his record from 1953 onward did demonstrate that the conservative and indifferent Congressman was fast becoming a courageous and liberal Senator.

Because I first joined John Kennedy in 1953 as an aide in his new Senate office, I am frequently asked to what extent I am responsible for the philosophical and political evolution in his thinking that began that year. Even after all these years, I cannot give an objective answer to that question.

My recommendations on bills, suggestions for speech themes, initial phrasing of statements, encouragement, analyses, ideas, and ideals all had some influence on a young Senator building his philosophy, just as his political realism, experience, and responsibilities influenced me. I came from a more liberal background than he did. My parents were outspoken progressives and pacifists, my sister was a civil-rights activist, my brothers were internationalists by occupation. My legislative and legal efforts against segregation, my Selective Service preference for noncombat duty, my membership in Americans for Democratic Action and civil-rights organizations, my published writings against loyalty oaths and Joe McCarthy's type of inquisitions—all these were a part of my record when he employed me at age twenty-four.

The fact that, in the second and final interview that preceded his hiring me, I raised some question about his reported views on Communist investigations must have alerted him to the possibility that I could be a troublemaker. But because there was no trouble, no argument ever, not even important disagreements, because our minds meshed despite our different backgrounds, because he was open to reason and evidence and grew increasingly thoughtful and compassionate, I cannot say with any certainty that his evolution in the Senate would have been any different had he employed someone else in my spot.

Other associates, Senate colleagues and hearings, informal meetings with experts, his wife, his brothers, his writing of *Profiles in Courage*, his travel, and—always of immense importance—his reading all helped map out the path he chose to take. In part, his own impatient energies were simply reacting to the tedious mediocrity of ideas produced during the sugar-coated Eisenhower years, when nothing went wrong enough for revolution or right enough for celebration. While his intimates were fewer than RFK's, he had a remarkable circle of friends—in fact a remarkable number of circles of friends, a PT-boat circle, a social circle, a Boston-politics circle, a Washington circle, and others. No one fully knew, much less dominated, all sides of his life and mind.

What I can assert unequivocally is that I had less than a marginal role in the intellectual development of Robert Kennedy. When he was still a Senate committee counsel, his close association with union leader Walter Reuther inspired new liberal insights that would mature through intimacy with JFK's own growing idealism. His Justice Department associates—Nick Katzenbach, Burke Marshall, John Seigenthaler, Ed Guthman, Byron White, Lou Oberdorfer, John Douglas, Dave Hackett, John Nolan, John Doar, Jack Miller, Bill Orrick, Ramsey Clark, Bill vanden Heuvel, Barrett Prettyman, and other members of a brilliant team—were his close friends as well as associates, and sources of ideas as well as support.

His Senate aides were particularly influential in providing him with solid substance to fill in the outline of his deepening convictions. Ideas and initiatives poured from the pens of Adam Walinsky and Peter Edelman, with deft touches from press aide Frank Mankiewicz and political leavening from administrative assistants Joe Dolan in Washington and Tom Johnston in New York. Still others, including Earl Graves, Dal Forsythe, and Carter Burden, provided important help in his New York office, as did Milton Gwirtzman, Wendell Pigman, Jeff Greenfield, and others in the Washington office. Dick Goodwin, Adam Yarmolinsky, and Arthur Schlesinger were major sources of opinion and advice; and there was again so varied an assortment of political colleagues, social friends, family influences, and visitors from the worlds of business, sports,

journalism, education, society, entertainment, and government (and a few revolutionaries as well) that no single
individual's influence could be measured with precise proportions and compared with RFK's own reading, travel,
experience, and other sources. He did not make friends
quickly. But once tested and accepted, any new friend was
bound to him for life by a bond of mutual loyalty, whether
it was Bronx boss Charles Buckley or New Left commenta-
tor Jack Newfield.

Bob Kennedy made his Senate office such a center of
intellectual ferment that it is hard to understand his frustration in that post unless one recalls that he had previously
exercised high-level Executive authority. What is much
harder to understand was his desire, before running for
the Senate, to be selected by Lyndon Johnson as his 1964
Vice Presidential running mate. For a man of his energies,
independence, and candor to be confined to presiding over
the Senate and kowtowing to a President he did not respect
should have been instantly seen by us all as an absurdity.
But urged on by many political associates, he somehow
thought that in this way he could continue to influence
policy at the top, as a Johnson-Kennedy team succeeded
the Kennedy-Johnson team; or that the Kennedy wing of
the party deserved one of the top spots and he was its
leader; or that any other choice by Johnson might lock
RFK out of a Presidential race for years to come. It was
all mixed up—his sense of obligation and ambition—and
the summer of 1964 was still too close to November 22,
1963, for any of us to think very clearly.

In 1956, eight years earlier, Jack Kennedy had also
sought the Vice Presidential nomination, but not too de-
terminedly until it turned into a horse race with Estes
Kefauver when Adlai Stevenson as Presidential nominee
threw the nomination open to the convention. Winning

that nomination made little sense for JFK either, not because he would have been elected Vice President but because he would not have been. Nothing could have enabled
Stevenson to oust Eisenhower that year, but all the professionals would undoubtedly have attributed his defeat to
the presence of a Catholic on the ticket. The competitive
instincts and ambitions honed on the playing fields of
Hyannis Port nevertheless caused JFK to desire that nomination that year—because that was where the action was.
Clearly, Robert Kennedy was driven to some extent by
the same instinct in 1964. A year later we laughed together
over Lyndon Johnson's good judgment and Robert Kennedy's good luck in avoiding this particular mixed marriage.

Bob overcame his disappointment over the Vice Presidency in 1964 by immediately starting his campaign for
the Senate. Jack overcame his disappointment over the
Vice Presidency in 1956 by immediately starting his campaign for the Presidency.

It was not an announced decision on his part or even
an inner commitment. He simply recognized that his
sudden new national status had opened a door that until
then had seemed unlikely to open for some years. Without
knowing how far he would be able to go beyond that door,
where it would lead him, or who else would be there when
a final commitment had to be made, he started through it.
Had his subsequent travels and organizational efforts across
the country proved unrewarding, he would have stayed out
of the 1960 race and waited for another year. Had his religion and age proved to be insuperable obstacles, he might
have reluctantly accepted the Vice Presidential nomination. But his goal from 1956 on was the Presidential
nomination in 1960; and unlike Bob in March 1968, there
was no final moment or crucial turning point that definitely

committed him. He simply started running in 1956 and never stopped until he was President.

During those four years virtually my entire time was given over to the Presidential campaign, with Mike Feld-man, Ralph Dungan, and Ted Reardon handling most Senate chores. Beginning with his speeches on behalf of Stevenson in the fall of 1956, JFK and I traveled to every state, some more than once, meeting party leaders whose dinners he addressed, acquiring supporters whose names and addresses I took, learning about each state's concerns and factions and power structure, ascertaining who talked and who worked, who had press clippings and who had delegates. There was no need for him to define our goal; it was an unspoken assumption between us. In his name and sometimes in my own, I kept in touch with our new friends and acquaintances by mail and telephone, relaying his progress in the public-opinion polls and in various states, sending Christmas cards and autographed copies of his book, inviting visits to his Senate office, and preparing schedules, press releases, and speech texts for his next trip.

We concentrated almost entirely on the nomination, as distinct from the election. The two efforts are hardly separable, inasmuch as any evidence of popular support would be weighed by delegates who wanted a winner. But to the extent that time and resources had to be allocated according to priority, our number-one priority was winning the 761 majority of the 1520 delegate votes in the 1960 convention. We assumed that obtaining the nomination from a basically unfriendly convention would be an even more difficult hurdle than defeating Richard Nixon among rank-and-file voters and that, in any event, the first job would occupy our full time and energy until it was completed. Thus our efforts were focused more on Democrats than on the general public, more on party leaders than on party members, and more on delegate-vote projections than on electoral-vote projections.

Nevertheless, the grass roots—the precinct workers, the county chairmen, the party members, and public opinion —had to be won over in order to bring around or go around those national Democratic Party leaders who were either skeptical or hostile. (That included virtually all of the better-known ones at the start.)

A delegate search can teach a student of the English language a lot about the parlance of political commitment. Most politicians are to a surprising degree men of their word; but one has to learn when he has been given the word. We learned not to be too impressed with "I'll do all I can, Senator" or "I'll be all right when the time comes." We quickly saw through "You have what it takes to be President, and you can put me down as supporting your entry into the race one thousand per cent." Even "Let me know if I can help in any way" was not a commitment. A simple "I'm for you" was.

Our own approach was equally careful. "An Eastern Catholic Senator's need to balance his ticket" perked up the ears of a Midwestern Protestant Governor without anyone's crassly discussing the Vice Presidency. "JFK after election will need to rely on those whose ability he has come to know and trust during the campaign" eliminated any need for unseemly talk about patronage. An indication to politicians anxious to be with the winner that the next primary would "lock up" the nomination for Kennedy suggested not only that the bandwagon was rolling but that they had better jump aboard while there was still room.

In 1959 Steve Smith brought his experienced operational judgment to our new Washington office on a full-time basis, and gradually Larry O'Brien, Kenny O'Donnell,

Bob Kennedy, Pierre Salinger, John Bailey, Dave Powers, and others left their other duties to join the effort. Because I had been so close to JFK, because he and I alone had built the beginnings of a nation-wide campaign and network of contacts, and because I had moved outside my intellectual area of competence into their operational area of competence, there was at first some disdain and resentment regarding my role on the part of those more experienced in politics, including RFK. Because his joining the campaign on a full-time basis as a member of the family "club" immediately reduced me from number-one to number-two man in the throne room, there was at first some resentment on my part as well. But there was more than enough for everyone to do. Bob and I each recognized very quickly that the other had not only a unique devotion but also a contribution to make to JFK's success that no one else could make. And the common affection we all had for our candidate and our common determination to put him across soon swallowed up all outward signs of dissension.

A Kennedy campaign was fun. It was excruciatingly hard work and exhaustingly long hours, and we were lucky that the candidate's history of bed-confining fevers did not recur. But it was all carried out with a certain gusto, gaiety, and, despite all the prevailing predictions to the contrary, full confidence that we had not only the best man but the winner.

JFK in 1960 staked everything on winning all the Presidential primaries he could reasonably enter, not because their cumulative votes amounted to much but because those victories would prove to the delegates and others that he was a winner and disprove the allegation that a young Catholic had little appeal in those states containing few members of that faith. If he won the primaries and continued to lead all the polls, we reasoned, the big-state professionals would expose themselves to the charge of anti-Catholic prejudice (although most of them were Catholic) if they still turned thumbs down on his nomination.

Each primary state, therefore, was subjected to the same kind of massive assault on the electorate first practiced on Massachusetts. Volunteers were recruited by the hundreds, sometimes thousands. Kennedy ladies gave tea parties in every corner of the state. Prominent speakers, a plethora of pamphlets, and old friends from Choate, Harvard, PT-109, Washington, Boston, and New York fanned out into all parts of the state. Each county had its local chairman, beneath him the district chairman, beneath him chairmen for primary day and candidate's day and press relations, transportation, and whatever else seemed worthwhile. The point was to involve people and get them working, not to give them titles. The object was not to have someone whom RFK and O'Brien could blame if things went wrong. The object was to make certain that things went right.

In such a hasty surge of activity there was waste, duplication, and failure of communication and coordination. Mistakes were made. Stop-gap decisions or substitutes had to make do. Often, as we fumbled our way through, we laughed about the press reports of the smooth, efficient, well-oiled Kennedy machine. But we were able to keep laughing because we were able to keep winning. Together, JFK and RFK forged a political approach that revolutionized campaign techniques and shattered religious barriers, setting a standard of excellence against which subsequent candidates for many offices and in many countries would attempt to measure themselves.

Bob Kennedy's reputation as a tough and sometimes abrasive campaign manager was fully deserved. Other men in the Kennedy camp performed well, but the hard decisions and skillful judgments that produced victory were all made by the two older brothers. RFK had neither the time nor the temperament to spend much effort slapping politicians' backs or buttering up their pride. He had no interest in the long talk fests, endless griping, and selfish demands that occupied so much of professional politics. He considered his task not winning friends for himself but winning delegates for his brother. "It doesn't matter if they like me or not," he once said. "Jack can be nice to them." He would, it turned out, need friends for himself in 1968 among some of the political leaders he overrode or ordered about in 1960, but that year he fashioned a successful campaign organization.

Had Bob been more easygoing, it is questionable whether he would have been successful, particularly in the fall campaign. He had to obtain an all-out effort for JFK from local chairmen who saw a Catholic candidate ruining their local ticket, from feuding factions whose future success depended upon keeping each other out of the campaign, and from powerful leaders whose control would be reduced by a Democratic President. He had to say no to those who wanted commitments on patronage before they would help. He had to say no to those in states clearly for Nixon who nevertheless needed help for their local candidates. He had to tell those with more experience or prestige than he that they were not doing enough or not doing it right.

No doubt he could have been softer, more patient, more complimentary at times. But he had the offsetting advantage of being a campaign manager who could be accepted as speaking with absolute authority for the candidate and who, in the difficult and sometimes devious world of politics, had the absolute trust and confidence of the candidate. He had proven himself to JFK in the 1952

Senatorial campaign, which had brought them much closer together than they had been either as children or as young men pursuing separate paths. Even in 1952, JFK recalled, "every politician was mad at Bobby—but what friend who was really worthwhile has he lost?"

Moreover, most of the successful political moves in any Presidential campaign by any candidate or campaign manager can be equally well described as ruthless or fair. I say, for example, that JFK was willing, if Ohio party leaders denied him their delegates, to prove in a primary that he was the choice of the Democratic voters in that state. Others might say that he coerced Governor Mike DiSalle into pledging an entire favorite-son delegation to him by threatening DiSalle with division and humiliating defeat in his own state.

I say that JFK victories in the primaries and public opinion polls convinced reluctant powerhouses—such as Pennsylvania's Governor David Lawrence—that Kennedy, having proven he could win despite his Catholicism, deserved the support of anyone who was not holding back on grounds of personal religious prejudice. Others might say that Kennedy's victories in the primaries and polls enabled him to frighten the party leaders with the prospects of political retribution from Catholic voters if the Democrats did not nominate the first member of their faith since 1928 to have a chance for the Presidency.

I say we won New York because such political leaders as Charles Buckley, Peter Crotty, and Eugene Keogh rounded up delegates until bosses Carmine DeSapio and Mike Prendergast had no other choice. Others might say that bosses friendly to Kennedy took the other bosses along with them.

This is not to say that the Kennedys operated on the principle that "all is fair in love, war, and politics—or at least in politics." They refused to make deals with any leader who hinted that he could attend the Los Angeles convention as a delegate to vote for JFK if only he could somehow afford the travel, lodging, and other expenses involved. They refused assorted offers of "sale" of various kinds of endorsement. They avoided personal attacks on their adversaries, false allegations about their past records, commitments for future jobs, and exaggerated promises of future solutions. But they campaigned hard and relentlessly within the limits of decency because they sincerely believed that the country needed John F. Kennedy, his talents, and his principles in the White House.

Political pressure in that context is rough but not necessarily "ruthless." It was assumed, for example, in April 1960 that those financing Hubert Humphrey's campaign against JFK in the West Virginia primary knew that their candidate, having lost in Wisconsin, had no chance for the nomination; that they were merely using him to eliminate JFK in an anti-Catholic tide; and that they therefore deserved whatever political pressure could be brought to dissuade them. Needless to say, Humphrey was not required to drop out of the West Virginia primary for lack of money. By staying in, he gave Kennedy an astonishing victory that more than anything else proved we were right in saying a Catholic could win—and wrong in seeking pressure on Humphrey's backers.

West Virginia gave Kennedy something more—a firsthand feel for the conditions of poverty and squalor that had previously held only intellectual and political, not emotional, meaning for him. He saw idle, wasting, but able-bodied men trained only to mine coal waiting hopelessly for the coal mines to reopen. He traveled through beautiful green mountains isolated from major highways and scarred by dying towns and deserted buildings. He talked with mothers already old in their twenties whose children ate only one real meal a day—surplus rice, lard, and cornmeal. He recognized as never before the inadequacy of welfare, the necessity for Medicare, the importance of enough good schools and enough good housing and, most of all, enough good jobs. The Kennedy legacy was taking shape. Part of it was what he said in West Virginia; part of it was what West Virginia said to him.

That 1960 campaign also extended Robert Kennedy's horizons. He was exposed to more different kinds of people, problems, and parts of the country than ever before. The fall campaign meant winning voters in all states, not merely Democrats in the primary states and delegates in the rest. It meant an examination of his own values on race, religion, Soviet-American relations, and other issues of the campaign so as not to misspeak his position or mislead his brother. Although pamphlets and position papers poured out of the Washington headquarters he headed, most of the substance of the campaign was worked out by the candidate and me, assisted by Dick Goodwin, on the campaign trail. But problems of organization, distribution, manpower, and supervision engulfed Bob every waking hour. On one occasion I handed the candidate a press report that his brother, in the midst of a talk defending the family against the charge that their religion made suspect their allegiance, had referred emotionally to their older brother's death in the war and then sat down too overcome to continue. JFK shook his head. "Bobby must be getting tired," he said.

Religious bias was the principal obstacle to election victory. Before obtaining the Democratic nomination, we had to convince delegates, including many Catholics, that Kennedy, although a Catholic, *could* be elected.

After obtaining the nomination, we had to convince voters, including many Democrats, that Kennedy, although a Catholic, *should* be elected. Opposition on religious grounds came from respectable pulpits, such as that of Dr. Norman Vincent Peale, and from disreputable publications that ranged from the obscene to the absurd. It came from liberal religionists and fundamentalists, Protestants and Jews, believers and nonbelievers. Much of it was open, some of it was intelligent, but the bulk of it and the worst of it was an unreasoning, unanswerable bigotry just below the surface.

It did not have to be raised by Kennedy; it was always there, in every state. The polls showed it, the telephone campaign heard it, the canvassers felt it. The most difficult question was how to combat it without appearing to exploit it and without focusing the campaign upon it—for if the electorate ever split along religious lines, Kennedy was through.

To be sure we had raised the issue in 1956 in the "Bailey Memorandum" I wrote, which pointed out the strength of the Catholic vote in key states to those weighing a running mate for Adlai Stevenson. But that was to offset fears of an anti-Catholic vote hurting the ticket if JFK were chosen and was in keeping with the traditional notion that a Vice Presidential candidate should bring some special regional, factional, or ethnic strength to the ticket. Neither that memorandum nor any other estimates of Catholic voting strength figured in our 1960 election calculations.

When, in the 1960 West Virginia primary, the religious issue threatened to obscure all others without ever being faced publicly, John Kennedy himself decided to bring the subject up, preferring to combat it out in the open then and there instead of permitting it to fester until fall or prevent his candidacy from surviving until fall. Then, in September, following a "respectable" attack by the Peale group attempting to disqualify all Catholics from the Presidency, JFK also accepted the request of the Houston Ministerial Association to discuss the subject in full.

In short, if appealing for fair play in West Virginia, accepting the invitation and questions of the Houston ministers, enlisting impartial Protestant clergymen to fight bigotry, and similar steps constitute "exploiting" the issue, then exploit it we did. But not one of us in the Kennedy circle ever suggested that Nixon in the election or Humphrey in the primaries was stirring up the issue. Not one of us ever asked people to vote for Kennedy to prove they were not bigots, or termed it a contest between religious liberty and bigotry, or publicized anti-Catholic attacks on Kennedy in order to woo Catholics and other minority voters.

Postelection surveys made clear that Catholic Republicans in Ohio, California, Wisconsin, and across the country did not budge toward Kennedy, while Protestant Democrats in those states and others— including Kentucky, Tennessee, Oklahoma, Virginia, and Florida—deserted him in droves. That is the key statistic. To be sure, Catholics who were already Democrats (and a majority had been for many years) did vote Democratic, some of them no doubt with more enthusiasm than before and some of whom had strayed from Stevenson to Eisenhower in 1952 and 1956. And no doubt some other voters did rally to Kennedy's side because they felt he was being unfairly attacked. But postelection studies by the University of Michigan survey and Professor V. O. Key, Jr., among others, made clear that religion alone prevented JFK from winning by a more comfortable majority. Only a practitioner of religious prejudice could ignore the unmistakable evidence that Kennedy was its chief victim in the 1960 campaign.

Today that issue seems surprisingly remote because of JFK. What he *said* at Houston, and earlier to the nation's editors, on the complete and rational separation of church and state—as applied to all religious groups—is an important part of the Kennedy legacy. But equally important is what he *did* in winning the understanding of previously prejudiced Protestants, in winning the election and thereby shattering religious barriers to the White House, and in conducting the Presidency in such a manner as to disprove all lingering doubts about a Catholic President's independence from the Vatican's position on legislative issues.

His religion had played at least a subconscious role in the initial opposition to his candidacy from many liberals and intellectuals. But there were other reasons for their opposition. Their affection for Stevenson, their suspicions of father Joe and brother Bob, their recollection of JFK's equivocation on Joe McCarthy, their feeling that he was a young, pushy opportunist whose money and machine would run down anyone in his way—all these and other criticisms which today seem more reminiscent of the attacks on RFK in 1968 were leveled at John Kennedy in 1960 by some of those who have since professed their devotion to his memory.

It was in part to offset those suspicions that JFK enlarged and publicized during the campaign his group of "academic advisers." Principally professors in the Cambridge area who specialized in economics, science, government, military affairs, housing, and specific areas of foreign policy, these men provided in time more than an impressive show of Kennedy's links to the academic community. They also provided ideas, statistics, reports, concepts, and memoranda of use in the campaign speeches and position papers which became the bases for the Task Force reports of the transition period and the legislative proposals of the first year. Although many of those most helpful—including Professors Paul Samuelson, Earl Latham, Max Millikan, and others—remained in academia, others in the group later occupied important posts in the Kennedy Administration.

The political atmosphere was right in one sense for this kind of infusion of new intellectual currents but wrong in another. The drabness and complacency of the Eisenhower years had created among many a sense of tedium and indifference that seems hard to believe in today's turbulent times. Some observers with a more long-range perspective wondered aloud whether our nation had lost its spiritual vitality, its willingness to dare and to change, and whether it had a national purpose any longer without the benefit of President Eisenhower's committee to find one. The sterility and timidity of most government proposals, the prevalence of clichés in political speeches, the passivity of the young, and the pessimism of the poor seemed almost to be waiting for a clarion call to "get this country moving again."

JFK provided it. But, in fact, not that many voters wanted to be moved. Not that many liked the thought of facing up to their responsibilities to our own poor, or to the developing nations, or to our blighted cities, or to world peace. Not that many welcomed so sudden a change from the quiet complacency and comfort to which the preceding eight years had accustomed them. John Kennedy's call to action, mild by the standards of 1968, when war and revolution threatened everywhere, was disturbingly loud to much of the electorate he sought to stir in 1960.

Not all of the issues to which he addressed himself were meaningful. The "missile gap" alarm, for example, turned out to be unjustified in the light of evidence subsequently available. The "gap" charge was based on the statements of those Senators, columnists, military figures, and others who were concerned in the late 1950s by the potential difference between Soviet missile capabilities and our own. The innovation of U-2 and particularly space-satellite photography indicated some time during 1960 that these fears were unfounded. Richard Nixon—if he knew of these findings before the election—deserves credit for not compromising security in order to answer the "gap" charge. Kennedy, whose briefings as a candidate contained no information to refute the "gap," made use of the issue. At times, when not speaking from a prepared text, he was guilty of oversimplifying and overstating the supporting evidence. But he used it largely as a part of his over-all charge that the United States had been drifting, slipping, and dawdling in the world. And that charge was true.

JFK did not take this or other stands on the basis of public-opinion polls, nor did he later in the White House. He did use private polls in the preconvention battle more than they had previously been used by any candidate—to ascertain his relative standing in various states, to determine his prospects in primary states, to ascertain his progress and areas of weakness in the course of those primaries, and to obtain evidence of strength with which to persuade leaders and delegates. Poll figures were not falsified, but at times we could be "ruthlessly" selective in deciding which polls or parts of polls we would show "in strict confidence" to reporters and politicians, depending on whether we sought to convey the impression that JFK was an underdog deserving their sympathy for his uphill battle or an unbeatable winner whose team they should promptly join.

In the course of that campaign we learned a lot about polls, their uses and limitations. We learned, too, to be suspicious of those polls that reflected the bias of the pollster, his desire to deliver good news or warnings, or his attempt to adjust his poll results to conform to his sense of the electorate. Polls were of little value, we discovered, in ascertaining the voters' views on most issues or in ascertaining why they favored or opposed a candidate of their own party. Robert Kennedy, in his Senate and Presidential races in later years, held much the same view of both the uses and the limitations of public-opinion polls, which he, too, used extensively.

Yet public opinion itself was important in the Kennedy White House. No President can get very far ahead of it. No President can succeed very long with Congress without it. Every President needs to know the state of American public opinion, not because his role is to reflect it like a barometer but because his task is to lead it, educate it, and mobilize it behind what he believes to be the national interest. For this John Kennedy did not depend on polls, although he received and read many as President and followed as well the United States Information Agency polls on foreign opinion. He relied on his own sense of the public mind that had helped him gain the Presidency, on a feel for the public pulse that resulted from talks with politicians, trips around the country, a sampling of his mail, and a reading of the press.

The press—including television, radio, and magazines as well as newspapers—was important to the Kennedys as a source of what the public was saying and even more important as a source of what the public was hearing. Both John and Robert Kennedy gained new ideas and insights from their constant attention to the press. Many newsmen and news stories had a role in shaping the Kennedy legacy. Both brothers relied on the press as unofficial channels of information, particularly as a means of obtaining the bad news, the independent criticisms, and the overlooked details that might not filter through the well-meaning subordinates around them. Newsmen, untroubled by bureaucratic illusions, often reported more accurate, reliable, and relevant information—on Vietnam, for example, although JFK discovered this too late, if at all—than could be obtained by the White House from within the government.

But the primary reason President Kennedy devoted so much time to monitoring the press—and this was true to a lesser degree of Senator Robert Kennedy because of the differences in their offices—was not that the press told him very much he had not already learned from official sources but that the press told him what the general public was learning about official actions. Both brothers resented distortions of their views in the press, not merely because they were sensitive to criticism—JFK even more than RFK—but because the public upon which their acts as public servants depended was being misinformed and misled.

If editors, leaders, teachers, preachers, and plain citizens back home and Congressmen in Washington were receiving inaccurate or unfair accounts of what a President or other public official was doing, that could have serious repercussions in a government based on the consent of the governed. Experience even indicated that it was harmful for other reporters to read it; for the Washington press corps often ran in a pack, and a myth or misconception appearing once was likely to appear twenty times.

The New York Times was in a sense the Kennedy's second bible, devoured each day from start to finish and credited with great influence for its news and editorial judgments; and yet both brothers were troubled by what they felt to be a basic hostility on the part of some *Times* personnel. Any criticisms of a Kennedy's personal qualities, it should be added—any challenge to his integrity or compassion or truthfulness—always hurt far more than assaults on his policies and programs. Both brothers became more philosophical and thick-skinned about press attacks as the years went on. JFK, his wife once told me, "learned how to roll with the punches in his last two years and they bemused rather than upset him. Whenever I was upset by something in the papers, he always told me to be more tolerant, like a horse flicking away flies in the summer."

The Kennedys were not hostile to the press, particularly the working press in Washington, which had some very bright and energetic members of special appeal to them. They trusted newsmen more than most politicians and were trusted by them. Having both served brief stints as foreign correspondents and having the kind of minds and interests that matched those of most reporters, Jack and Bob Kennedy maintained extremely close friendships with many members of the Washington press corps and provided unusually easy access for almost any interested reporter. They were not wholly unmindful of the value of such friendships but were basically attracted to these men and women as human beings.

Their friends did not always write favorable material. Columnist Joseph Alsop, for example, was immensely fond of both Kennedys but held increasingly divergent views from them on Southeast Asia policy. JFK was usually able to persuade his friend in personal or telephone conversations that their differences were not so great as to deserve a public attack. But Joe often delivered avuncular lectures to Bob Kennedy through his column when those same lectures failed in private. Even those columns, however, were restrained by the mutual affection and respect that continued between them to the end.

A special problem for any President is posed by foreign governments who gravely weigh and interpret, and sometimes angrily answer, all kinds of speculative items in the American press (including the *Times*) in much the same manner as our Kremlinologists analyze items in *Pravda*. The difference is that any discrepancy between *Pravda*'s position and the Kremlin's position is sheer accident, while any similarity between an American newspaper's position (including the *Times*) and the White House's position is sheer coincidence.

When a foreign leader is pilloried by the American press, he may for that reason alone become hostile to the American government. When he is idolized by the American press, our government may have difficulty disengaging from him if that becomes necessary. President Kennedy tried to make clear to other nations that he had no control whatsoever over the contents of our newspapers and magazines; and he tried to make clear to the American press (including those who praised Adenauer and pilloried De Gaulle) that there were no angels or devils in foreign governments, only imperfect politicians who might shift from an allied to an adversary position and back again at different times on different issues.

President Kennedy discovered early in his Administration, however, that even the mildest suggestion to the press of voluntary self-imposed restraint in the national interest fell on deaf ears and raised angry voices. He realized, moreover, that less restraint by the press preceding the Bay of Pigs invasion might have demonstrated that the CIA's promise of a quiet, unpublicized landing was not only unfulfillable but contrary to that agency's own actions. In that event, he reasoned, he might well have re-examined all CIA promises and premises regarding that effort, found them all wanting, and called the whole plan off. Yet on other occasions he felt that information appearing in the press was saving Soviet espionage agents considerable effort and expense and that too many government officials who relayed confidential information to favorite reporters were doing so not only to promote their own importance but also to grind their own special-interest axes.

There were and are no precise or consistent guidelines, however, even for newspaper executives who seek them. Each publisher must necessarily use his own judgment about any story that appears to have potentially adverse effects on national security. If the President or his press secretary personally requests him (as JFK did at the time of the Cuban missile crisis) to withhold an item for a few days until the whole story can come out, a publisher will no doubt accord that more weight than a request for indefinite suppression by a lesser official. If a clear and present danger to the lives or movements of American servicemen or civilians is involved, he will put that in a different category from obvious attempts to conceal government mistakes.

Television offered the Kennedys many of the same problems, but additional ones as well. Increasingly the American people obtain their public-affairs information and judgments from television. RFK was convinced that the impact, for better or worse, his campaign for the Presidency made in two and one half minutes each evening on the Cronkite or Huntley-Brinkley news shows was far more important than anything he could accomplish in a thirty-minute paid political telecast. The Kennedys' candidacies were tremendously aided by TV. Their natural spontaneity and candor, their engaging good looks, their articulate and vital way of speaking, all gave them advantages they used to the fullest.

JFK was better on television than RFK. It is the "cool tube" and he was a cool candidate. His low-key understatement and detachment came across well in the living room. Bob's words carried equal conviction and sincerity —important on TV—but he was more ill at ease in a studio than JFK and more conscious of the camera's eye. Too many of the television news shots during his brief Presidential campaign featured clawing, screaming mobs of admirers and a hoarsely shouting candidate—a picture with mixed appeal, to say the least, for the living-room viewers.

We were concerned in 1968 about the "crowd" problem, as I will explain later, principally because 1960 had taught us the importance of television. Without this medium— without the many panel and news shows, national and local, that helped spur JFK's rise to fame; without his shrewd use of TV commercials and telecast speeches in that campaign, without television tapes to spread wherever needed his confrontation with the Houston ministers; without the four Great Debates with Richard Nixon which united and activated his party and disproved any difference in experience—John Kennedy would never have been elected President.

But by a very narrow margin he was, as all of us— including JFK, RFK, and especially JPK, Sr.—had expected all along. The discussion of polls and press interrupted my tracing of the development of the Kennedy legacy. It was at this very point, the election of 1960, that it made a quantum jump forward. The responsibility John Kennedy had sought was his. He was not awed or cowed, nor were any of us he took with him into the White House. But there was less assuredness about the national clashes and crises that confronted us then. It was not a lack of confidence in our collective judgment (though a little less confidence would have been both accurate and healthy, as the Bay of Pigs showed). It was, instead, a solemn recognition that the kind of favorable outcome we had always predicted for the election was considerably less certain in these new tests and that an enormous addition of new and different kinds of talent would be required to tackle them.

The President-elect directed the creation of a series of transition task forces to prepare papers on the major problems he would face, at the same time asking me to distill the recommendations contained in his campaign speeches and position papers and the 1960 convention platform. All this formed the basis of his first hundred days of legislative messages, setting the tone as well as the goals of his years in the White House. Meanwhile, aided particularly by his brother Robert, he concentrated on choosing his Cabinet and White House advisers.

It was a difficult chore, this process of selection and rejection, for he knew full well as he undertook it that the capabilities and conduct of his appointees were unlikely to earn for him the commendation of history—that he had to earn for himself—but could earn him its condemnation, should they prove incompetent or corrupt. With RFK at his side, he chose both wisely and well, less concerned than many of his predecessors with political, geographic, and ethnic balance and more trusting of both politicians and scholars.

Bob talked enthusiastically of bringing "new faces . . . to government . . . men who believe their jobs go on forever, not just from nine to five." Yet it is more a part of the legend than the legacy to assert that the Kennedys' brilliant ability to judge and attract top men of talent to the Cabinet set a mark no previous or subsequent President in this century could reach. The new assemblage of brain power in Washington in 1961 was indeed impressive at all levels; and the personal integrity and dedication to the national interest displayed by the new Cabinet set a high standard that is indeed part of the legacy. But at the time of his selection no one could be sure that Robert Mc-Namara would not turn out to be another motorcar-company president like Charles Wilson. At that time the nominations of Arthur Goldberg, Abraham Ribicoff, Stewart Udall, Orville Freeman, and Luther Hodges, all unproven in any Federal Executive capacity, could have been criticized as simply selections from the Presidential campaign circle in much the same way as Richard Nixon's Cabinet choices were criticized eight years later. Nor could anyone have predicted that Robert Kennedy, the wealthy labor-racket-busting pride of Joseph P. Kennedy, would turn out in time to be the most liberal member of that Cabinet.

In 1960 the appointment of RFK as Attorney General was regarded as a daring experiment in nepotism; Douglas Dillon was regarded as a conservative Republican hold-over; Dean Rusk was regarded as an unknown quantity (his critics still feel that way); and surely no one had thought of J. Edward Day for Postmaster General. It turned out to be an excellent Cabinet, with some obviously performing better than others; but JFK deserves credit for leading, molding, and inspiring his Cabinet to excellence and not for any prescience of its excellence.

It would also be well to put into perspective JFK's desire for dissent and diversity among his advisers. The alternative to a bunch of yes men is not a bunch of no men. Kennedy had no wish to place in his Cabinet anyone who might publicly or even privately denounce his policies, lead a palace revolt, or run against him or his party. Nor was he willing to listen endlessly to the minor objections of subordinates to a policy already decided. What he did want was honest, independent judgment from more than one source or point of view *before* a policy was decided. He did not foster division but recognized its advantages, and he encouraged his staff to be skeptical and critical of Cabinet proposals.

He was willing as always to listen to those who had something substantial and significant to say and could say it concisely. He did not want to hear an adviser's conclusion when he asked him for both sides of the question; and he did not want to hear both sides of the question when he asked an adviser for his conclusion. He did not gavel people down in meetings or cut them off in mid-sentence; but the little signs of indifference, then impatience, and finally irritation became recognizable in time to those who were initially inclined to take too long to say too little.

Placing Robert Kennedy as Attorney General made more sense to both brothers than having him breathe down the necks of Rusk or McNamara by becoming an Under Secretary, or lose his administrative talents by becoming a White House aide, or take on an undefined and ill-informed role by becoming a private adviser. But sentimentality should not lead us to exaggerate his role. RFK would have been the first to acknowledge that the President each day made important decisions on which the Attorney General was not his most influential adviser and may not have been consulted at all. He had little interest at that time in fiscal, monetary, and economic questions, no interest in agriculture or conservation, and only marginal interest in business, labor, and government-employee relations. His subsequent concerns with urban affairs, housing, health, welfare, and the whole range of domestic policy had not yet had an opportunity to develop.

There is, however, no mistaking the fact pointed out during the 1968 campaign by Robert McNamara that RFK "functioned as a prime Presidential agent on policy matters across the board." His Justice Department duties took him into many of the major domestic questions—not only race relations but also poverty, the steel-price crisis, the constitutionality of education legislation, and others; and his daily contacts with the President assured him of a strong voice in whatever else was of concern to him. Many of the crucial decisions which helped form the Kennedy legacy—including the President's responses to the Cuban missile crisis and the civil-rights revolution—were made by JFK with both advice and assistance from his brother.

Bob and I had not taken part in the series of small meetings that preceded the Bay of Pigs, and the President asked both of us to involve ourselves more in foreign affairs thereafter. Bob was a prodder and a prober who could offset those hoping to impress the President with their prestige. My preference for peaceful responses helped offset the increased pressure on JFK from other quarters to counter this setback in Cuba with a tough military posture elsewhere. Basically he wanted us in those meetings to observe the judgments of foreign-policy specialists he did not know well with the skeptical eyes of two generalists he did know well.

RFK was far more impatient with the Department of State than JFK was and far more critical of what he regarded to be its unimaginative proposals. His relations with Dean Rusk, like the President's, were amicable but reserved—as distinct from the warm relationship of mutual regard and respect both Kennedys had with Robert McNamara. For all his emerging liberalism, still largely instinctive except in the civil-rights area, Bob Kennedy got along well with conservative Republicans Douglas Dillon and John McCone. His special friend and hero among the military chiefs was Maxwell Taylor. He had favorites

within the Departments of State and Defense such as
Averell Harriman, Roswell Gilpatric, and Llewellyn
Thompson, and worked directly with these men in the
course of his free-ranging activities.

In the White House, where my primary responsibility
was domestic policy, McGeorge Bundy kept a daily watch
on foreign affairs and began without my previously established rapport with RFK. But the dedicated brilliance
of his articulation, the President's increasing reliance on
him, and the zest with which he conducted his arduous
and critical assignments, all fitted so well into the Kennedy
scheme of things that RFK also worked well with Bundy,
despite reservations expressed by both Kennedys at the
time of the two Cuban crises. Press Secretary Salinger and
Appointments Secretary O'Donnell were old sidekicks of
Bob's at the Rackets Committee, and his working relationship with Congressional liaison chief Larry O'Brien dated
back to the 1952 Massachusetts campaign. The principal
White House staff members, in short, were all attuned to
RFK while serving JFK.

The legend about our being a happy band of brothers
is, however, exaggerated. All White House staffs to my
knowledge have had their share of inner rivalries, if not
hostilities, and ours was no exception, as small as it was.
We lived in nearly total harmony because we shared a total
devotion to the President and his success and because he
was careful not to play favorites or deny equal access. But
our interests, tactics, personalities, and private lives were
largely different and separate. Even during "office hours"—
which were eleven or twelve hours on a normal day, and
there were almost no normal days—Salinger and O'Brien
spent far more time and effort in being genial and sociable
with their colleagues than did O'Donnell, Bundy, or I.
But we all worked together well, for we were all young,

liberal, pragmatic, energetic, willing to discipline occasional prima donna tendencies, and familiar with one another's and the President's views, roles, and capabilities.

We were all new to the pinnacle of power and all
exercising it—not because we arrogated to ourselves final
authority properly resting with the President and Cabinet
but because, in the words of Patrick Anderson's *The President's Men,* "not since Roosevelt had there been a President so distrustful of the bureaucracy and so willing to let
his personal aides prod, double-check and bypass it."

Perhaps we were not all as brilliant as the press clippings
we immodestly believed at the time. But I doubt whether
there had ever previously been a Congressional-relations
chief as skillful on the Hill as Larry O'Brien, or a press
secretary as imaginative in new initiatives as Pierre Salinger, or economics and science advisers as influential as
Walter Heller and Jerome Wiesner, to mention only a few
examples. The degree to which we were able to get the
bureaucracy moving, to stimulate, screen, and shape Cabinet recommendations, to refine problems and define conflicts, to inform, advise, and assist the President and free
him for his biggest decisions all comprised our contribution to John F. Kennedy's part of the legacy.

My relationship with the President, earlier described
with respect to the Senate days, remained virtually unchanged. I believed that the nation's success depended on
his success in the White House, and I had no difficulty
opposing any moves that might hamper his success. As
his confidence in the job grew, he became increasingly
compatible to the kind of progressive and peaceful reform
that represented my own natural bent. The drafting of
speeches and messages for the President of the United
States, which remained one of my functions to the end,
provided an outlet for my own idealism. My whole role

seemed to me, at moments of reflection, almost too good to be true and too good to last.

Our brilliant in-house intellectual and historian, Arthur Schlesinger, Jr., was helpful on many speeches, as, during the first year, was Dick Goodwin, whose talents as a speechwriter would later be valued by LBJ, RFK, and Gene McCarthy. Goodwin also deserves credit for helping devise the Alliance for Progress for Latin America. Bundy, his deputy Carl Kaysen, the State Department, and occasionally USIA Director Edward R. Murrow all made contributions on foreign-policy speeches. Walter Heller, Dave Bell, Douglas Dillon, and Kermit Gordon—who as JFK's masterful economic tutors were the fathers of the New Economics —helped formulate economic-policy speeches.

But the final shape of every text was always the President's decision alone. If my ideas had merit, if my arguments had weight, and if my phrases conveyed the message he decided he wanted, there was neither time nor necessity for him to rewrite every page—particularly after years of working together had merged not only our styles of writing but also our thinking about the world. On occasion he rejected my suggestions, just as in policy meetings he might decide contrary to my recommendations. But there were no divisions on principle and no dissent from any of us once his final decision was made.

My watching brief on the domestic departments was never as detailed or frequent as McGeorge Bundy's relationship with the Department of State. Mac Bundy was clearly qualified to be Secretary of State, although he asserted no claim to the job. In a second John Kennedy term he might well have become Secretary of State. Inasmuch as he soon came to believe that the then-Secretary of State's advice on foreign affairs did not wholly fulfill the President's needs for imagination and innovation, Bundy played a major role in the formulation of John Kennedy's foreign policy. Because he was meticulously careful to maintain close communications as well as friendly relations with the Secretary, there was no complaint to the President from the generally unflappable Dean Rusk. Unfortunately, the inevitable growth and strength of Bundy's "little State Department"—inevitable because the Secretary's vast bureaucracy was slow to exercise the over-all authority in national security Kennedy had originally desired—enabled JFK to delay undertaking a long-range and long-needed overhaul of the "big" State Department.

It will be hard to measure objectively Dean Rusk's contribution to the Kennedy legacy until the harsh judgments of his critics can be weighed in historical perspective. Whatever his role may have been under President Johnson, Rusk served President Kennedy, with complete self-effacing loyalty, more as a channel to and from the State Department than as a creative leader or bold originator of ideas. This was not altogether bad. Among the items *not* originated were any more mutual-defense commitments reminiscent of the John Foster Dulles era, or any nuclear wars, or the loss of any free nation. We survived, as the Secretary liked to boast, and there are worse boasts. Nor did he seek either power or publicity for himself.

The assertive and imaginative Kennedy and his active personal aides, moreover, might well have been less comfortable with a stronger and more aggressive Secretary. The President was sometimes disappointed in Rusk, uncertain where he stood, and unsure he was pushing his department to more efficient implementation of Kennedy policy. Except on Vietnam, the Secretary rarely took hard, specific positions on issues presented to him, even when his aides formulated their own. But JFK never voiced regret that he had selected the reticent, soft-spoken Georgian

whose intelligence, integrity, dogged durability, and un-
failing courtesy he genuinely admired. Bob Kennedy, it
should be added, privately felt strongly in 1968 that Rusk's
resignation would be helpful to signal a change in Johnson's Vietnam policy. But when asked in his debate with
Eugene McCarthy about Rusk, whose resignation Mc-
Carthy had publicly demanded, RFK would say only that
Dean Rusk was a dedicated public servant. Both Rusk and
he knew that an RFK Administration would bring in a
new Secretary of State; but Bob wanted his campaign to
deal with issues, not personalities.

Underlying JFK's selection of a Secretary of State in
1960 had been the conviction that no one the President
knew personally could be sufficiently superhuman to
master the burdens of that office. The impossibility of any
one man's staying on top of America's interests and activities in well over one hundred countries excludes as
unrealistic the concept that a modern President can be
his own Secretary of State—or, in that sense, that even the
Secretary of State can be his own Secretary of State. Kennedy knew personally most of those prominently mentioned for the post in 1960. Each had a strike of one kind
or another against him, and JFK knew none was superhuman. He did not know Rusk but had heard only praise
about him, liked his writings, met him, and picked him.
(He did not know McNamara either, which indicates that
unfamiliarity does not always breed discontent.)

Adlai Stevenson had the most support for the Secretary
of State post outside the Kennedy camp in 1960 and the
least support inside. JFK had been an enthusiastic Stevenson supporter in the 1952 and 1956 Presidential elections
(although he regarded Stevenson's 1952 acceptance-speech
statement that he had prayed for that "cup" to pass from
him to be tasteless hypocrisy in view of the Illinois Gover-

nor's telephone and other contacts to delegates asking that they draft him). Their relationship had deteriorated in 1960, however, partly because they were political rivals and partly because JFK regarded Stevenson as weak and indecisive in the convention and preconvention maneuvering. Ironically, had Stevenson been tougher and more determined in battling it out with him for the nomination, JFK would have respected him more. He also thought Stevenson, like Chester Bowles, was too likely to become a prima donna as Secretary of State. He made Bowles Under Secretary, in which post he lasted less than a year, and he made Stevenson UN Ambassador, in which post he outlasted JFK.

He admired Stevenson's eloquence and reputation at the UN and took pains to make clear that he was not undercutting him, as was often rumored. Stevenson's isolation and subsequent embarrassment at the time of the Bay of Pigs occurred contrary to JFK's orders. But he recognized —as other Presidents have recognized regarding their Ambassadors to the UN, with its rarefied atmosphere and separate concerns—that the distance between America's UN Mission offices and the White House is considerably greater than the distance between New York and Washington. At no time did JFK regret appointing Stevenson UN Ambassador or not appointing him Secretary of State. This was a judgment in which RFK fully joined and which Stevenson's own performance during the Cuban missile crisis—as a wavering adviser in the National Security Council but as an articulate advocate in the UN Security Council—fully confirmed.

Dean Rusk had never expressed much interest in administration. Otherwise Lyndon Johnson, who initially lacked Kennedy's background and feel for foreign-affairs leadership, might have done well, upon becoming President, to switch Rusk with McNamara. The latter's managerial reforms as well as strong policy leadership were badly needed in the State Department. It had never fully recovered from the paralyzing purges of the McCarthy-McCarran heyday or efficiently absorbed the rapid growth in this nation's global interests and problems. McNamara's Defense Department was deeply involved anyway in foreign-policy decision-making. Indeed, one of the most persistent problems handicapping Dean Rusk and his predecessors and successors was the proliferation of foreign-policy activities throughout the government—not only to the Pentagon and CIA but to Treasury, Commerce, Agriculture, several other departments and agencies, and especially to the White House staff. The latter is the chief potential cause of tension in most State Departments. But no modern President who has the strength of leadership and depth of conviction to reach the White House can leave all foreign-policy decisions to the State Department or to a vote of the National Security Council.

Rusk and McNamara worked throughout the Kennedy Administration with the utmost harmony. Partly because Rusk seemed intent on demonstrating that the State Department was not a collection of cookie-pushers too cowardly to recommend combat, partly because he was not as assertive or powerful an advocate as Bob McNamara, and partly because he did not have the kind of highly organized and inspired support within his department that McNamara built at the Pentagon, the military resources available to the President often seemed out of balance with the diplomatic. The scales were righted by Kennedy's own dislike for military solutions and by the diplomatic initiatives and considerations put forward by Bundy and other staff members. Nor did McNamara himself believe that national security depended on military hardware alone.

Although he was reluctant to make suggestions that properly were the province of the State Department, his judgment on the whole range of foreign-policy problems was always welcomed by the President.

McNamara has been accurately termed the nation's first real Secretary of Defense; for a truly unified department under Secretarial leadership emerged only after he had abolished the separate supply and intelligence operations, imposed an integrated budget approach, applied a single cost-effectiveness standard to all activities, greatly expanded his civilian staff, and generally dominated the department as no previous Secretary ever had. This firm establishment of civilian control, and the more rational evaluation of weapons needs that resulted, are important parts of the Kennedy legacy that must be allowed to remain; and they were equally important parts of John Kennedy's goals upon his election as President.

Thus he was tremendously pleased with his selection of McNamara and grew increasingly fond of and reliant on him. He did not regard him as infallible—the Bay of Pigs had taught him that no one, including himself, was infallible—and he used the Bundy staff, the science and budget advisers, and other aides as a check on McNamara's authoritative powers of persuasion. He never forgot that his own responsibilities to the nation, the Congress, and the Allies were broader than those of his Secretary of Defense. But he shared RFK's view that McNamara was the star of his Cabinet.

One of McNamara's most useful roles was to keep the Joint Chiefs of Staff both reasonably happy and under control. He would indicate to the President how far he might have to go on a policy or budget question to keep them in line and interpret to the Chiefs the President's other commitments that might prevent him from accepting their recommendations. JFK made certain, however, that the Chiefs had direct access to his office at all times they desired; and he wanted one or more of the Chiefs present at all principal decision-making meetings affecting them. "If we get into real trouble," he remarked, "they will have to operate the military means required to get us out, so I can hardly ignore their views now." He soon learned that the single-mold stereotype of military brass was wholly unfounded. The difference in viewpoint between a Maxwell Taylor and a Curtis LeMay, for example, or between an Arleigh Burke and a David Shoup, was far greater than any differences dividing his civilian appointees.

Marine Commandant Shoup had all the charisma of a Treasury clerk. Seemingly colorless, shy, and reticent, and not as outspoken in private as he has since become in public, he was nevertheless both candid and concise in his blunt advice to the President against military adventures and expenditures generally favored by his colleagues. Taylor, in his service first with the White House staff and then with the Joint Chiefs of Staff, was a handsome, articulate intellectual with a broad-gauged understanding of diplomatic, economic, and domestic political considerations that his colleagues usually lacked. Also quiet-spoken and cool, he won the immense respect of the Kennedys as well as McNamara with his logic and calm. Thus his mistaken if well-motivated advice on Vietnam carried special weight.

As will be noted in the next part in more detail, both Kennedys learned after the Bay of Pigs to be more skeptical of military solutions offered by military men. This reflected not only their doubts about the use of force but their doubts about most narrow-gauged specialists. I have found my fellow lawyers in government, for example, generally convinced that legal tools can resolve almost any problem; they are generally skeptical when challenged by laymen. Scientists, diplomats, and economists are much the same. Thus it should not have been surprising to any of us that men who had spent their entire careers in the armed services of the United States, and talked principally to one another, were genuinely convinced of the efficacy of military solutions alone and were indifferent to the competing considerations offered by civilian aides to Kennedy and McNamara. "Perhaps," as Robert Kennedy wrote, "we would feel even more concerned if they were always opposed to using arms or military means; for if they would not be willing, who would be?"

The Joint Chiefs under Kennedy, moreover, understandably considered themselves to be representatives of the military establishment, not independent advisers or experts in nonmilitary matters. They generally presented a traditional, narrow military point of view, despite Taylor and Shoup; and Kennedy found himself forced to move carefully on the settlement in Laos, the Nuclear Test Ban Treaty, disarmament, and other matters in order to avoid an open break with his military commanders that could alienate much of the Congress and nation. His techniques of clothing a decision in terms most appealing to its opponents, and of never formalizing certain decisions so that they still seemed open to re-examination even as he implemented them, had many drawbacks; but both techniques worked well in soothing the Joint Chiefs.

All the programs and policies devised during those three brief years by John Kennedy, Robert Kennedy, Dean Rusk, Robert McNamara, Douglas Dillon, and others—including Stewart Udall, whose vision of comprehensive conservation fitted perfectly with JFK's concern for future generations, and Arthur Goldberg, whose creative energies before his appointment to the Supreme Court were influential beyond the labor-management field—are a part of the Kennedy legacy. For thirty-four months that legacy grew, expanded, improved, raced ahead—and was suddenly, unbelievably, tragically stopped on November 22, 1963.

The assassination of John F. Kennedy shattered Washington, the world, and particularly the world of Robert Kennedy. He never really got over it. He had not been unaware of the ever-present danger. He and the President had discussed the possibility, often jokingly. An assassination attempt had been made in Palm Beach before JFK had even been sworn in, and the file of threats was a thick one. Nevertheless, for so ghastly a deed actually to have happened, for a man so young and peaceful and loving actually to have been murdered, for Bob's brother, his idol, and his President actually to have been taken was difficult for Robert Kennedy to accept, to believe, and then, once believed, to put aside in order to think of other duties. He had to think of Jacqueline, her children, his parents, and his brother and sisters; he had to think of all the arrangements and ceremonies and eventual memorials; he had to think of the Kennedy team in government and the Kennedy program—and, thinking of all that, he found it once again difficult to believe that it all had actually happened.

For three days nothing but the funeral and family mattered. Only then did he look about him to note how his world had been splintered. Temporarily leaving most of his Justice Department duties to subordinates, he tried his best to console the inconsolable. Even in this family accustomed to sorrow, the grief was shattering. The brutal shock to Jacqueline—whose husband had been

killed before her eyes, his life ebbing out as she held him
in her arms—had plunged her, after a magnificently
brave show of strength to the world for three dramatic
days, into alternating waves of bitterness and despair.
The Kennedy aides, too, were dispirited. Though Bob had
no cheer to share with us, I shall always remember the
day during that first awful week that he came into my
White House office, his puffy eyes still hidden behind dark
glasses, not to mourn the past but to discuss the future.
He looked totally defeated.

I understood how he felt, to the extent an outsider
could understand. His dreams and mine had been wrapped
up in one man for years on end. Our pride in JFK's
success, our love for his life, our joy in his satisfaction—
those had been Bob's life and mine. For thirty-four
months Robert Kennedy had been far more than Attorney
General of the United States. Now he was only Attorney
General. I, too, still had the same title of Special Counsel
to the President; but it was no longer the same job. Bob
and I were proud of our contributions to his brother's
advancement, but we both knew that all that we were we
owed largely to the man who had been cruelly taken from
us. Unlike the Kennedys, I had never really considered the
possibility of a successful assassination. I had never contemplated the loss of the man I served and loved, or any
separation before two full four-year terms had expired.
Too stunned to cry on November 22, too lost to know
what I felt, I had not broken down until that evening
when Lyndon Johnson telephoned to ask my help and I
had called him "Mr. President."

Melancholia hung over the White House. Colleagues
drifted into my office to talk. They had received no instructions, they had no plans. To the enervating effects of
sorrow had been added confusion as a new team arrived in

the White House. Texas Congressmen and Washington lawyers roamed the corridors, and the organization, if any, of the decision-making structure was in a constant state of flux. We stared gloomily out the window together. Washington seemed a cursed place to us all.

Not all of President Kennedy's appointees stood together or even with Robert Kennedy. The disparate officers of the U.S.S. *New Frontier* had been held together only by its captain and now their captain was gone. Some members of the Administration scrambled for position in the new power structure. Some wooed the new President with sickening sycophancy. Some pressed to take advantage of his unfamiliarity with their areas of competence, to rush through decisions on which JFK would have wanted other opinions to be heard, to undo decisions JFK had already made against them, or to invent JFK intentions that I knew he never had. Others sought to expand their domains, moving into areas already occupied by Kennedy men too grief-stricken to react. Intimate friends became quietly suspicious, then openly hostile with each other. There was ugly talk of who had too eagerly recovered from grief and who was drowning it in drink. A series of lobbies, factions, and cabals seemed imminent inside John Kennedy's once proud and harmonious ministry of talent.

Finally, Washington divided, not into many camps but into two. There was no declaration of war between the Johnsons and the Kennedys. There was no need for division. But it spread, from the bottom up and the top down. "Someday I'm going to write," Bob Kennedy told me later, more in humor than in bitterness,

about all the people who changed their attitudes as soon as Jack was killed, all the people in the Cabinet and in Washington who had been so nice until I no longer was the President's brother. I had the same position as before but they knew I no longer had the same power, and that the new President wanted them to choose sides. Most went where the power was. A few were in my camp. Bob McNamara was openly and genuinely in both camps, and two or three tried to make me believe that they were really in my camp while telling Johnson they were really in his.

Anti-Kennedy stories were circulated by Johnson partisans—that Bob had been rude to the new President, that Jacqueline was incoherent in her grief, that JFK's budget deserved to be cut, that the Kennedys had tried to embarrass the Johnsons on the trip back from Dallas. Kennedy loyalists replied in kind. There was condemnation of all Texans, insults about the new President's tastes, and cutting comments about his humor, his accent, and his speaking style. To add a note of partisanship to the picture, the House Republican Policy Committee rushed in with a statement that "the teachings of Communism" were to blame for the assassination and that Americans need not feel guilty.

For me to pass judgment on those times is still difficult. Some men had to end their mourning before they could resume full speed. But somebody had to run the government in a crucial and sensitive period and help the new President as he groped his way into the light. Some men were in Washington primarily because of the man who lay dead. Others had positions or programs to protect. Some men felt Johnson sat where Kennedy should still be sitting, that his state of Texas was responsible somehow, that he was not worthy to succeed to the office. Others felt the President is dead, long live the President. Emotions ran far ahead of reason. It was the worst of times even for the best of men. "None of us should be blamed," remarked one Kennedy intimate later, feeling remorse for some of his own bitter thoughts during those months about the Johnsons, Texans, the Secret Service, the FBI, and the world in general, "for anything we thought or said or did during that first awful year."

From the original Kennedy men in the Administration and White House, all of whom the new President convincingly asked to stay on, different reactions emerged. Some wished to stay in hopes of advancement. Some wished to stay at least through the 1964 campaign. Some were reluctant to return to an uncertain future in the private sector. Some wives wanted to stay in Washington. Some husbands were indispensable to Johnson. All were enormously flattered by his appeals. I resigned.

I was not motivated by the slightest ill feeling toward the new President. From my acquaintanceship with him in the Senate, to my work with him when he was Vice President, to his unfailingly considerate treatment of me after the Dallas tragedy, to his many kindnesses to my three sons and praise for my work, I had nothing but good will toward him and good wishes for his success. And neither Bob Kennedy nor anyone else suggested I resign. Bob planned to stay at least until the Civil Rights Bill became law and felt everyone else should choose for himself. He was grateful that I was willing to stay three months until the Kennedy program for 1964 had been translated into Presidential messages and transmitted to the Congress.

But the White House had become a sad and empty place for me. It was hard to walk into the Oval Office and find another man in the President's chair. It was hard to do my best for a new President when I could not in my heart want him to be *more* successful than his predecessor. It was hard to keep answering the question, from well-meaning friends as well as strangers, "Where were you when it happened . . . ?" momentarily bringing back all the trauma of that terrible day.

Particularly because my relationship with the late President had been personal as well as professional, because he had selected me for that position in the White House on the basis of our long-standing rapport as well as my qualifications for the job, it was clear to me that by definition I could not fulfill the same function for a new and very different man. President Johnson was entitled to have personal aides of his personal choosing—men who shared his background, thought his thoughts, and spoke his language. Once I had completed my work on the 1964 State of the Union message and legislation, and his own staff had moved in, I was likely to be left primarily with the function of speechwriter, not adviser. My approach to a speech had, over an eleven-year period, become both identical and identified with that of only one man; and I did not think that either the new President or I would be comfortable with my putting Jack Kennedy's words into his mouth.

From our first long, somber meeting on the evening of November 23 onward, President Johnson and I were extremely frank with each other. He acknowledged, for example, his difficulties in attracting top-flight men, in obtaining good speech drafts from his aides, and in determining which advice was motivated by the national interest and which by departmental or personal interests. I told him that, even when some of us resented it, he had to be the President—to lead, to command, to do what he thought after due deliberation was right without submitting it to a Cabinet vote or an expert's veto. On his post-assassination "Let us continue" appearance before the Congress, we had a friendly but frank disagreement on what portions of that final text represented changes his aides had made in my draft.

Although he was candid and considerate with me, I observed in his relations with his own personal aides an attitude toward staff considerably different from John Kennedy's. Some of his men, such as Bill Moyers, were immensely talented. All were as completely dedicated to him as our group had been to JFK (although their own internal rivalries and resentments were far deeper). But President Kennedy had regarded us as associates as well as assistants. President Johnson did not seem equally interested in receiving counsel from his staff, much less criticism. They were crew, not officers, and he could at times be patronizing and at other times mean and angry with them. When he urged me to stay on he assured me, "You'll find as you get to know me better that I treat my staff just as though they were my own children." I nodded my head in agreement.

I also left to write a book about John Kennedy. I knew that if I did not write it then, memories would fade, other interests would occupy my mind and time, and there might never be so appropriate an opportunity to drop everything else for so long a period. As I explained in the foreword of that book in more detail, I had never contemplated such a book. (Indeed, except for idle speculation with Mike Feldman and Arthur Goldberg about forming a law firm, I had never given thought to any post-White House activity.) But several JFK friends urged it, his family encouraged it, and publishers wanted it. I set out to write it. I made no pretense of being either an historian or detached. I attempted to be fair and factual, to betray no state secrets or personal confidences, and to attribute no views, motives, or intentions to President Kennedy that I did not know firsthand. In describing some controversial sessions of the President with his advisers, I omitted names to protect the guilty as well as the innocent. In using classified documents contained in my files, I omitted some sections, paraphrased others, and simply quoted without using quotation marks from others. Although there was some debate about whether a White House aide's files belonged to him, to the President he served, or to the government, I listened to the debate and wrote the book. No official clearance was sought or needed, although Messrs. Bundy, Gilpatric, Kaysen, and others reviewed pertinent portions with security sensitivities in mind. All chapters were in fact reviewed by those expert enough to catch any inaccuracy or omission, and the Kennedys, as well as my editors and a few friends, read the whole manuscript in draft. From all this came a variety of suggestions and additions, some of which I accepted and some of which I rejected. Neither the Kennedys nor I wished the book to be either censored or authorized by the family, and it was neither.

They liked my *Kennedy,* published in the fall of 1965. They liked Arthur Schlesinger's superb *A Thousand Days,* published later that fall, which justified JFK's decision to have his own historian in the White House. The controversy caused by published excerpts of Arthur's book that previous summer, the Kennedys felt, was unfair when viewed in the context of the entire book.

A much more bitter controversy, however, broke out more than a year later regarding a book entitled *Death of a President* by William Manchester. Jacqueline and Robert Kennedy had decided early in 1964 that it was important to history and America's conscience that all the facts surrounding the Dallas murder be set forth in a solid, careful book which could put to rest all the rumors and draw upon their recollections while still fresh. Understandably unwilling to relive those shattering hours repeatedly and motivated in part by her dislike for the style and tastes of author Jim Bishop, who was planning such a book, Jacqueline wanted one writer selected in whom she had confidence and to whom she and others would be required to unburden themselves only once. The author would write as he saw fit, but the final manuscript approval and the timing of publication would remain in her hands. After attempts to get Theodore White and other authors failed, Pierre Salinger recommended William Manchester, whom Jacqueline did not know but who had earlier written a short and sympathetic book about her husband. Manchester was selected and a hasty letter of agreement was signed. Intentions on both sides were good but ill-considered.

Inasmuch as my law partners represented Mrs. Kennedy in the litigation that was eventually required and then successfully settled, I will say only that all those early 1964 decisions on the Manchester book—like so many other things said and done during that period—appear today, with the invaluable aid of hindsight, to have been a mistake: the single-book idea, the written agreement, the stream-of-consciousness interviews based on the assumption of later editing, and the selection of Manchester. Not a professional historian, he became so personally involved in so emotional a subject, and there were such conflicting views of the roles of each player in the Dallas drama and so many inconsistent interests that required such a book, once written, to be altered or shelved or published without alteration, that an imbroglio seemed almost unavoidable, given the imperfections of human behavior and the imprecisions of the English language.

The poisonous fallout from this controversy did more than anything else to affix the image of ruthlessness on Bob Kennedy. He was accused of seeking censorship by injunction, breaching his contract, and using the book to spread derogatory views on President Johnson. None of this was true. It was Jacqueline Kennedy who instituted suit to enforce the contract, against Bob Kennedy's advice, when she wearied of the evasive and vacillating tactics of Manchester and his publisher. And it was Bob who had hoped for deletions that would amount to treating Lyndon Johnson less harshly in a book that RFK knew would be blamed on the Kennedys. He had been unaware of the author's emotional approach—which was more apparent to those who saw Manchester in Washington or received lengthy telephone calls from him—until he had had the manuscript read by friends. He had decided then, after lengthy discussions and futile attempts to make changes, that the only answer was simply an introductory disclaimer making clear that the Kennedys were washing their hands of the entire project. Once the lawsuit started, he fought hard for his sister-in-law and, like many lawyers in court, saw merit only in her side. A stronger stand by the book's publisher, he always felt, could have required Manchester to meet his obligations. Then at the peak of his popularity, Bob Kennedy suffered in silence the paradoxical accusation that he had sought to suppress a book that in fact was basically friendly to the Kennedys. Manchester, who publicly compared the Senator to Hitler in 1967, would support him for the Presidency in 1968; but by then permanent damage had been done.

Manchester's was not the only book on the events of Dallas that aroused controversy. The Special Commission under Chief Justice Earl Warren, appointed by the President to investigate all aspects of the slaying, filed an extensive report confirming the conclusions previously reported regarding a single assassin acting on his own. Its conclusions were repeatedly challenged by books and articles alleging a variety of conspiracies. The atmosphere was further clouded by the phony seers who said they had had premonitions of JFK's death in Dallas or had sent words of warning to him and by the scramble among Secret Service,

FBI, and Dallas police spokesmen to absolve their men of all blame.

Bob Kennedy refused to involve himself in this controversy. His brother was gone and no investigation or revelation could bring him back. But if he had known any grounds for legitimate suspicion suggesting that others were involved in his brother's murder, it is hard to believe that he would let such a matter rest. The author of one far-reaching conspiracy theory presented me with enough unfounded allegations to justify my calling Bob about them. He had his deputy, Nick Katzenbach, investigate those as he had many others and nothing substantial was found.

I have shared his reluctance to go into the subject. I realize that no one can prove a negative or rule out the unknown. I have no doubt that the Warren Commission, like most government commissions composed of busy officials, permitted staff compromises to meet deadlines. But I have read nothing that leads me to believe that any other commission proceeding in any other fashion would have produced any other names of individuals actually involved in the killing.

Nevertheless, as my law practice and lectures took me around the world, I heard the same three questions asked everywhere—by journalists and students, officials and citizens, in rich lands and poor, Communist countries and free. The first, to be discussed later, related to Vietnam. The second was the truth about Dallas, the possibilities of a conspiracy, the coincidence of its having occurred in Texas (which in many countries would have indicated a *coup d'état*), and the merit of all the theories attacking the Commission's conclusion, theories that continued to spread, just as they did for decades after the assassination of Lincoln and the death of his killer. So many people in the world had placed so much hope in President Kennedy that they refused to believe that his security could have been penetrated by one unknown assailant. Somehow his death would have seemed more meaningful and therefore more acceptable to them if he had been the victim of a right-wing, left-wing, racist, or political plot. I could only respond that this did not seem to be the case.

The third question asked everywhere was when the Kennedys would return to the White House. Already, Bob Kennedy was better known around the world than President Johnson. A self-appointed global constituency cheered his every utterance and overlooked any possible errors. They admired him for showing the same youthful idealism and energy his brother had shown; they sympathized with him because of his brother's tragic death. They were delighted by his stirring trips to Africa, Latin America, and Eastern and Western Europe. They respected his strong stands on peace and human rights. They preferred his style to the new President's, which was familiar to the citizens of Midwestern and Southwestern America but not to those in other lands. Above all, they believed in Robert Kennedy because he was a Kennedy.

RFK had picked up the fallen torch and carried it forward with renewed vigor. The early months of 1964 had not eased his spirit or answered his questions about his future. Passage of President Kennedy's Civil Rights Bill enabled him to bow out of the Attorney Generalship, which he had contemplated leaving for a State or Defense post in his brother's second term. He was willing to serve as Johnson's Ambassador to Saigon, away from the Washington scene, but the President, to his credit, recognized that that hazardous post made no sense. He wanted to be Johnson's Vice President, but that dubious honor was denied him. He was unwilling to run for Governor of Massachusetts—despite pleas from that state and advice that it was an easy stepping stone to the Presidency—because he had little interest in state administrative problems. He considered living abroad and traveling for a year or more, but decided that that was only escape. He had no desire to practice law, to take over his father's business, or to invent some kind of busywork.

The New York Senate race proved to be the answer. It also proved to be a tonic to his spirits and a major factor in his growth. He was no longer telling politicians how to help elect his brother. He was asking everyday citizens to cast their votes for him. He had to show to the general public the warmth and humor he had previously reserved for his family and friends. He had to ask for help from people he may not have liked, to take a position on issues not previously familiar, and to develop the techniques that come with speaking to mass audiences several times a day every day for several weeks in a row.

In the Senate he had to take a back seat as a freshman and to seek cooperation from his elders. But he recognized, too, that he had obligations and commitments as well as ambitions beyond that of other Senators. For in the eyes of millions—politicians, students, Catholics, blacks, intellectuals, Jews, women, liberals, plain everyday voters of every kind yearning for another dashing hero—he was the heir apparent to John F. Kennedy's legacy and "movement."

In his speeches on the Senate floor, across the country, throughout New York, and around the world, he revitalized that legacy and enriched it. He was no longer the leader's emissary; he was the leader. He talked of the special responsibility of all the world's young to continue the work of John Kennedy. He talked of pain—not the pain of his brother's death but the pains of poverty, prejudice, disease, illiteracy, war, and wasted hopes. Always the crowds turned out. The impassioned humanitarian pleas of a slain President's brother moved them; their impassioned responses moved him. Having seen more than his share of human violence and venality, he might have had contempt for mankind, but instead he loved it.

He devoted extra time and care to Jacqueline, who had also shaken off the cycles of gloom that recurred throughout 1964 and early 1965. He played the key role in establishing, in place of the usual memorials and bronze monuments, the John F. Kennedy Library and the John F. Kennedy School of Government at Harvard, and with both he refused, like his brother, to be satisfied with anything short of the best. He kept in touch with, and sought ideas and advice from, a large group of Kennedy followers and advisers in private and political life all around the country. This was not a "government in exile" or "shadow Cabinet," as it was sometimes termed, for it had no organized basis save our admiration of one man and no agreement on political strategy or major issues, including even Vietnam. Nor was this group as a group at war with the Johnson Administration, most of whose members to the end were John F. Kennedy appointees and many of whom were among those most often consulted by Bob.

To the Senate he brought an experience in national and international matters that JFK as a Senator had never really possessed. He had convictions on hotter issues that JFK as a Senator never faced. His experiences as Attorney General—laboring for civil rights, working with young delinquents, initiating programs for the poor, and contemplating the horrors of war—had revised his thinking as a public official and as a human being. His observations in Poland, South Africa, and particularly Latin

America made a deep impression. His brother's death and his own Senatorial candidacy had brought changes in his personality but not in his urgent need "to do more." He was still the fighting moral crusader he had been as a rackets investigator, but his priorities and interests had changed.

Having viewed my progressive tendencies with suspicion when I joined his brother's staff more than a dozen years earlier, he was highly amused by the suggestion of a New Left newspaper interviewer that I was more temperate on some topics than he was. "Can you imagine," he wrote to Jacqueline, sending her the clipping, "what you-know-who would say if he heard me described as more liberal than Ted Sorensen!"

He was clearly more liberal in his pronouncements and proposals than Lyndon Johnson. His growing constituencies and concerns as a Senator took him well beyond the limits staked out by the Democratic Administration—on civil rights and implementation of the Kerner Commission Report; on job creation, new housing, and other programs in the black ghettos; on more funds and new tools for the war on poverty, for those on welfare, for those hungry in Mississippi or despairing on Indian reservations or oppressed in the migrant-worker camps.

In 1965 he criticized President Johnson's decision to intervene unilaterally with American troops in the Dominican Republic—an intervention justified originally as a means of protecting resident Americans and later as a means of preventing a take-over of the government by Communist-inspired forces.

In 1966 he broke—somewhat tentatively but nevertheless irrevocably—with the President on Vietnam, and that issue dominated their public differences thereafter. But their earlier differences should be kept in mind. For while it is true that President Johnson's escalation and Americanization of the war in Vietnam clearly worsened RFK's attitude toward the President, it is my belief that his existing attitude toward the President influenced RFK's position on Vietnam.

Exactly when the difficulty between RFK and LBJ started is a matter of some speculation. In the traditionally humorous and off-the-record speech Bob delivered to the Gridiron Dinner in early 1967 he said,

All those stories about President Johnson and me not getting along during my brother's years in the White House simply do not square with the facts. We started out during the Kennedy Administration on the best of terms—friendly, close, cordial—but then, as we were leaving the Inaugural stands . . .

The trouble actually started even earlier than that. The Lyndon Johnson–John Kennedy contest in 1960 for the Presidential nomination pitted against each other two men who had worked well together in the Senate in an atmosphere of mutual regard and respect. Kennedy had supported Johnson for Senate Democratic Leader in 1953 and had helped him on some crucial votes. Johnson had helped put Texas behind Kennedy for Vice President in the 1956 convention fight with Kefauver. He had helped obtain for Kennedy in 1957 his coveted seat on the Senate Foreign Relations Committee. But the campaign introduced a few more jarring notes, as campaigns will.

Johnson told me later that he had no desire or intention to run for the Presidency in 1960 or any other time (the reader must judge the credibility of this statement for himself); that Speaker Sam Rayburn had told him he must do it to prevent the nomination from going to a Catholic; and that he did it not for any religious bias of his own (which all agree he never showed) but to satisfy Mr. Sam. Whatever his motives, his campaign in its final weeks became increasingly personal toward JFK. His attacks on Kennedy's youth and supposed willingness to apologize to Khrushchev (which he had forgotten by the time he told me all this), his top campaign aides' convention-eve assertion that JFK had Addison's disease and would not live out his term (which LBJ, usually master in his own house, told me he knew nothing about in advance), his own snide references to the Kennedy family's position on Joe McCarthy and the Ambassador's position on appeasement, and the vicious unattributed stories linking Joseph Kennedy to the Nazis (which we suspected to have come from the Johnson camp), all were regarded as blows below the belt by both of the Kennedy brothers. Jack's motto as a practicing politician was "forgive but never forget." Bob's general practice in those days was to do neither.

JFK was nominated. It was politically logical, shrewd, and necessary that he offer to the runner-up Majority Leader the Vice Presidential spot on the ticket. It was astounding to both Kennedys that Johnson accepted. In a day of confused and crossed communications, Bob Kennedy was dispatched that afternoon by his brother to see if LBJ, who had postponed a final commitment that morning, wanted the second spot badly enough to risk a convention floor fight with labor and liberal opponents. This episode angered Johnson, in the tradition of the ancient Orient where messengers with bad news were beheaded. He suspected, contrary to fact, that RFK had acted independently because he was personally opposed to the Texan being placed on the ticket. Bob Kennedy had in fact been opposed earlier; he had assured others it would be a Midwestern liberal in the Vice Presidential slot; he had not expected Johnson to reverse public statements he and his aides had made within the preceding month rejecting the Vice Presidency; and RFK was a fighter unaccustomed to joining forces suddenly with the enemy. But he would never cross his brother—so he had not lobbied against the decision and was concerned only with obtaining a winning ticket.

There will always be disagreement on that confused 1960 convention day's events. And there will always be disagreement on how the President regarded his Vice President during their 1961–1963 Administration, because John Kennedy refused to regard Johnson or anyone else as all good or all bad and was reticent about disclosing his innermost personal attitudes about other individuals. He tended at times to save his adverse comments on other people for those who particularly enjoyed hearing them. There was no shortage of people around him in the White House who enjoyed hearing whatever barbs he might aim at his Vice President. For example, protesting that I treated Johnson too kindly in my last book, one Kennedy confidant wrote to me:

You must know as well or better than I President Kennedy's steadily diminishing opinion of him then. . . . Lyndon Johnson's style always embarrassed him, especially when he sent him around the world. . . . As his term progressed, he grew more and more concerned about what would happen if LBJ ever became President. He was truly frightened at the prospect.

RFK, on the other hand, observed that Johnson served JFK "with the utmost loyalty"; and so he did. (On April 3, 1968, after removing himself from the Presidential contest, Johnson told his Cabinet that he had been a B+ Vice President to John Kennedy, compared to Hubert Humphrey's triple-A average.) Evelyn Lincoln's recollection notwithstanding, there was never at any time any question in the President's mind about renaming LBJ as his running mate in 1964. During the first several months of his Administration in particular, he was sensitive to Johnson's sensitivities and kept him in the spotlight as best he could in various ceremonies.

The President invited the Vice President to most of the formal decision-making sessions—the Cabinet, the National Security Council, the breakfasts with legislative leaders, and the breakfasts before each press conference. He did not invite him to the long legislative planning sessions in Palm Beach at the end of each year or to many of the smaller and more informal meetings where the final decisions were often made. This reflected no ill will on the President's part, only the fact—discovered by all Vice Presidents—that they have no real position from which to share in the exercise of Executive power.

At those meetings where Johnson was present, JFK would make a point of including him among those whose specific recommendations or approvals were sought. The purpose, he once told me, was not only to obtain LBJ's views but to get him on record in front of others so that the Vice President could not later complain, as some previous Vice Presidents had complained, that he had not been consulted or had not been in agreement. Occasionally President Kennedy grumbled (but only in private and never to the press) that LBJ was avoiding committing himself in most of these meetings, pleading insufficient information—but such pleas may simply have been the Vice President's own subtle way of complaining to the President.

I know of no instance of Johnson's complaining to anyone else, even off the record, while Kennedy was alive (and we usually would hear about his background press talks). Even impolitic remarks by his associates, when called to LBJ's attention, were brought into line by his direction. Yet he was no more happy in the job than any of his predecessors or successors. He was uncomfortable with the Kennedys and considered himself an outsider in the White House, but nevertheless felt better treated by JFK, as he later said, than JFK would have been had their roles been reversed.

A surprisingly large portion of the Vice President's time was devoted to Texas politics, on which the President had agreed to give him a free hand in terms of patronage and legislative liaison. He also presided with some pride over the President's committee to ensure equal employment opportunity for all races on government contracts; and he was angry and hurt when Robert Kennedy strode into the committee one day and demolished as meaningless a careful statistical presentation of the committee staff showing the *percentage* increase in nonwhite jobs. Johnson participated in the Cuban missile crisis deliberations but was away during the crucial meetings of the first week, when the basic decision was hammered out.

His voice was distinctly heard on three subjects—oil, Vietnam, and civil rights. Even before they were reviewed with the Vice President, those provisions in our working drafts of President Kennedy's tax-reform bill relating to depletion allowances and other preferential treatment given the oil and gas industry had been modified in the hopes of preventing a total revolt by oil and gas legislators against the rest of the President's program. Kennedy was outraged by the figures showing that multimillion-dollar oil companies and investors paid very little by way of taxes. Indeed, he would comment on this fact again to his wife in Texas on the last day of his life. But he saw the practical value of Johnson's argument that our staff proposals, without the slightest possibility of their ever emerging from the House Ways and Means and Senate Finance Committees, might nevertheless cost him the electoral votes of several states in 1964 and the seats of some basically friendly Congressmen in 1962. The Vice President suggested that the bill be studied for possible further modifications by a firm of Texas oil attorneys whom he recommended. It was not an unreasonable suggestion, nor were the modifications later suggested unreasonable. The oil provisions of the bill were still blocked by industry representatives, and the Kennedys had no reason to fault Johnson's role in the matter.

On Vietnam Johnson became more of an advocate than was his custom as Vice President. This stemmed from a mission undertaken in the spring of 1961 based on the often-practiced Kennedy premise (shared by other Presidents) that it was cheaper and safer to send to a troubled area of the world a Vice President, regardless of his experience in foreign affairs, than it was to send a few platoons of Army infantrymen or AID check-writers. The Vice President's task in 1961 was to show the Presidential flag to the sagging South Vietnamese government and to hear firsthand the fears of other friendly Asian governments who were complaining about Kennedy's reversal of Eisenhower's militant position on Laos.

Johnson returned from that trip a zealous convert to the all-out defense of Southeast Asia, to the domino theory, and to the Saigon regime of Ngo Dinh Diem, whom he termed the Churchill of Asia. "The battle against Communism must be joined in Southeast Asia," he told the President in his written report, ". . . or the United States, inevitably, must surrender the Pacific and take up our defenses on our own shores." He agreed that the primary burden should be borne by Asians but argued that they would do so only if they had confidence in American leadership and support. "We must decide whether to help Asian countries to the best of our ability or throw in the towel in the area and pull back our defenses to San Francisco and a Fortress America concept."

Robert Kennedy, as will be noted later, did not dispute this point of view at that time. But John Kennedy rejected all recommendations that he put American combat divisions in Vietnam. He sent the Vice President on many subsequent trips abroad and included him in major crisis and National Security Council meetings. But after his 1961 trip Johnson did not have a major hand in the formulation of the Kennedy Administration's Vietnam policy and cannot be blamed for its errors.

Johnson's role was more important with respect to the comprehensive Kennedy Civil Rights Bill of 1963. Whatever his inner doubts about its ability to pass the Congress and its adverse effects on Democratic politics and the Administration's program, Johnson loyally supported the President's decision—although reports of his uncompromising insistence to Kennedy on an all-out bill from the outset have been greatly exaggerated. Much to the consternation of Attorney General Kennedy, however, and to a lesser extent the irritation of President Kennedy, the Vice President insisted that public disclosure of the final package and its transmission to the Congress be delayed until the legislative atmosphere could be more carefully explored, until the South could be neutralized through a series of Presidential and Vice Presidential addresses, and until his own favorite proposals for a Conciliation Service (later changed to a "Community Relations" service to meet objections from Negro leaders) and for a supplemental job-training program could be added.

The Attorney General, who was anxious to press ahead

on the bill his department had drafted in view of the racial
crisis then spreading across the South, was skeptical about
"conciliating" anyone's Constitutional rights; and he felt
job training belonged in a separate bill. But the President
was enthusiastic about adding a job-training–vocational-
education–literacy-instruction section (provided I could
come up with a program over the weekend); and, in view
of the importance of LBJ's all-out support, he had no objection to the revised Community Relations Service. There
was no tour of the South before the bill's introduction; but
the delays for Congressional consultation also proved constructive. No continuing animosity between RFK and LBJ
was created on this issue, other than that stemming from
the aforementioned meeting of Johnson's Government
Contracts Committee.

When John Kennedy was killed in Dallas, the Civil
Rights Bill had already cleared its most difficult hurdle, the
House Judiciary Committee. Its necesssarily long, rocky
road to enactment had seemed certain in his mind to end
with success within a year of its introduction. If any of
the Southerners who cheered—as many did—the news of
JFK's assassination thought seriously that his Texan successor would dilute or delay the bill, Johnson proved them
wrong immediately. He included a ringing endorsement
for swift action on the entire bill as a part of his "Let us
continue" address to a joint session of Congress the following week.

The new President was true to his word about continuing. He kept as many Kennedy men as he could in the
Administration. He presented Kennedy's 1964 legislative
program, under preparation at the time of the assassination, in his own State of the Union message the following
January. He fought for Kennedy's controversial tax-reduc-
tion bill and other 1963 measures. With Congress more

subdued and softened as a result of the tragedy, and sympathetic to the burdens of the new President, virtually the entire Kennedy program—including civil rights—passed in 1964, just as Kennedy had predicted in his last press conference. Whatever items then remained unenacted were passed in 1965 through the new Congress elected in the Goldwater debacle of November 1964.

Although the leaders of both parties in both houses of Congress agreed that the program would have passed as well if JFK had lived, Johnson's skill in Capitol Hill leadership was fully devoted to the realization of his predecessor's legislative goals. He felt, he said to me more than once during the years after he assumed the Presidency, that he was obligated to carry on the Kennedy–Johnson partnership of 1960; that he could not therefore accede to the suggestions of John Connally and others that all Kennedy people be replaced and that some Kennedy programs be set aside; and that he hoped when his service was finished "Jack Kennedy will look down from heaven and feel that I have faithfully carried on the partnership in the interests of all the stockholders."

Robert Kennedy, first as Attorney General and then as Senator, was grateful for Johnson's fidelity to the Kennedy program and commended the President's follow-up efforts in health, education, and other areas. While his own leadership as Senator from an urban state often brought him to favor measures more far-reaching than the President's, his Senate votes were generally in accord with Administration policy. "Everett Dirksen," President Johnson told me in 1968, "makes a big thing of his friendship with me but almost never votes with me. Your friend Bobby makes a big thing of his differences with me but almost always votes with me." Senator Ted Kennedy had a similar record of support.

Thus the split between Lyndon Johnson and Robert Kennedy, which long preceded their split over Vietnam, did not grow out of many substantive differences. The origins were more personal and chemical, subtle but at the same time very strong. To some extent the split was inevitable in view of the circumstances of LBJ's succession: the assassination had occurred in Johnson's home state during a political peace-making trip undertaken by JFK at least in part because of Johnson's own internal difficulties in that state. Johnson moved with the strength and firmness the situation required of a new President while others were still shock-ridden and distraught. References to "the President" on November 23 suddenly meant not Jack Kennedy but another man seated at his desk in his office. Misunderstandings, inevitable in all the grief and confusion, arose during that sorrowful swearing-in ceremony and trip back from Dallas. Some Kennedy appointees eagerly genuflected in front of the new President before the old President was buried. Johnson simply was not JFK and did not have his same style of government or background and had not been one of his intimates. All of these facts, all beyond Lyndon Johnson's ability to influence or change and for which he cannot be blamed, nevertheless caused understandable resentment in the hearts of the grief-stricken Bob and Jacqueline.

It is hard to imagine a man more different from John Kennedy than Lyndon Johnson. His success in the ways of Capitol Hill had made him cunning where JFK was candid, secretive instead of open, preferring the process of maneuver to the substance of decision. Like JFK he was sensitive to public criticisms; but far more than his predecessor he tried first to please all his critics and then to punish them. It was more difficult for him to laugh at himself, to accept bad news and dissent from his subordinates, or to attract and retain the loyalty of intellectually talented men, much less change the traditions, illusions, principles, myths, and misinformation that had characterized Democratic Party policy in Washington since the days of his hero, Franklin Roosevelt. It was not his Southwestern State Teachers College style which displeased the Kennedy fans, for most of them were accustomed to many rhetorical and intellectual styles. It was President Johnson's style of government.

President Johnson "was extremely kind to me and members of my family in the difficult months which followed the events of November 1963," Bob later said; and indeed he was, going out of his way on more than one occasion to be considerate and helpful, even when spurned. While there were times when he might have been more perceptive of their feelings or chosen his emissaries more carefully, he was caught up in a vortex of pressure and responsibility for which no man can be adequately prepared. He had to demonstrate to the nation and world a strong continuity in the American Presidency and the Executive Branch of government. A sensitive man, he naturally countered the Kennedy's versions of disputed events with his own. A proud man, he began reacting in anger to constant statements about how JFK would have done something or what JFK had intended.

More important, in the same way that much of the Kennedys' resentment of Johnson was illogical but understandable in the circumstances, so also did Lyndon Johnson have fears of the Kennedys that were illogical but understandable. Because he had the power and security of the Presidency, it has been said, he had an obligation to get along with the Kennedys as JFK had gotten along with him. But he did not feel secure. He had a feeling that the Kennedys were against him, that the Kennedys were condescending to him. He wanted to emulate their graceful wit and intellectual elegance, to be loved as JFK had been loved, but he seemed at the same time to resent the Kennedys' Eastern polish. He had all the wealth, stature, power, and prestige any man could want; and his own enormous abilities had helped bring him to the Vice Presidency of the United States, from which he had succeeded to the Presidency. But until he had won the Presidency on his own, in recognition of his own convictions and capacity, he would not feel in 1963 and 1964 as secure as he had in fact every reason to feel from the start.

In this sense, his fear was political as well as psychological. After all those years, he had reached the Presidency. He was the first occupant of the White House from his part of the country. He held the one job that provided him with the power he cherished, with the maximum life of eating, breathing, and talking politics and public affairs seven days a week, fifty-two weeks a year. He knew that if his own party stayed united no Republican then on the horizon could take that job away from him in 1964. The only potential source of opposition was the Kennedys. Already there was talk of the restoration, of Bobby Kennedy for President. From November 23, 1963, onward, LBJ was convinced that RFK would someday run against him; and contrary to RFK's own expectations, that prediction turned out to be right for a brief two-week period in March 1968.

RFK never seriously entertained the idea of running against Johnson in 1964, despite the urgings of a few friends. He assumed Johnson would be the nominee in 1968 as well. But Johnson, like the "missile gap" theorists of the 1950s, looked at the potential enemy in terms of his capacities, not his intentions. He did not want his Administration to go down in history as nothing more than a brief interlude between two Kennedy Administrations. Even after 1964 he was not amused by Bob's joking references: "I have no designs on the Presidency, and neither does my wife, Ethel Bird. . . . I'd like to settle any disputes I have with the President by making it clear that I am willing to go more than halfway to the White House. . . ."

The gap was widened by the press—which always enjoys a good political feud—and by partisans, advisers, and aides of the two men who helped poison each principal's mind against the other with exaggerated slights and rumors. Long after the breach seemed irreparable, Johnson told me, when I visited the White House, that he had strictly instructed his associates not to utter or permit any unkind words about the Kennedys. But both he and I knew that this mandate had not been carried out. The gap was widened further by the Kennedys' feeling in 1964 that Johnson was using Sargent Shriver—a rumored Vice Presidential possibility and later Johnson appointee to head the War on Poverty—as a Kennedy foil, as a means of professing to the public his affection for the family in a way they could not challenge.

The gap beween them was widened still further by Johnson's rejection of RFK's Vice Presidential hopes, which were at best misguided. ("Hubert didn't like the job," LBJ said to Bob in my presence in 1968, "and you wouldn't have liked it either"—a masterpiece of understatement. Yet it is interesting to speculate how history might have been different had Johnson accepted RFK's bid for second place in 1964 or his willingness to serve as Ambassador to Saigon.) The gap was needlessly increased in that summer of 1964 when Johnson leaked to the press his version of their conversation on the Vice Presidency, which both had agreed to keep confidential. He then went to extreme lengths—including postponement of a JFK memorial film at the national convention—to make certain that no support developed for RFK as his running mate. (Johnson later told me that his personal preference for the Vice Presidency that year was Robert McNamara but that leaders of organized labor had vetoed the choice "because they didn't realize McNamara has a social conscience." Gene McCarthy had lobbied him hard for the job, sending many mutual friends to see him, he said, but some of those friends shared his own doubts about McCarthy's performance in the Senate.)

RFK needed and was grateful for Johnson's campaigning with him in the New York Senate race in 1964, and Johnson felt he had generously given of his time and assistance. But they rarely saw each other after that. Johnson's gracious attendance at the brief dawn ceremony consecrating John Kennedy's permanent gravesite early in 1967 was an exception. The President told me he had regularly invited Bob, along with other Senators, to both official and social functions at the White House. Bob, he said, unlike Ted Kennedy, never came and frequently never acknowledged the invitations. (When I reported this to Bob, he agreed he had never accepted but was sorry and surprised to hear that his office had not always communicated his regrets.)

Bob also resented the President's practice of timing dramatic White House activities and news announcements to overshadow the New York Senator's major speeches. Various department and agency heads, Bob was convinced, had been instructed to sabotage his housing, education, and other legislative proposals. The President, on the other hand, was convinced in 1967 that an abortive Vietnam peace rumor traveling from Hanoi through Paris to an RFK meeting had been leaked by the Senator to the press in order to embarrass the White House. Returning

home from that well-publicized trip on which he met with
several European heads of state, a journey not likely to
have warmed the President under any circumstances, Bob
found himself face to face with Johnson in a stormy White
House confrontation that came about more by accident
than the desire of either man. The meeting exploded in
anger and political threats. The President did not realize
that the State Department (*"your* State Department," each
termed it) had received the message from its Paris Embassy and leaked it without Bob's ever knowing about it.
A U.S. victory in Vietnam, said the irate President, would
soon end RFK's political future. "All you dove politicians
will be dead in six months," he thundered. "We had a long
serious talk," RFK later quipped to the Gridiron Dinner
regarding his visit, "about the possibilities of a cease-fire,
the dangers of escalation, and the prospects for negotiations. . . . And he promised me that next time we were
going to talk about Vietnam."

All communication was not missing. The Kennedys did
not feel that either McGeorge Bundy or Sargent Shriver
was an appropriate intermediary, but they liked Johnson
men Bill Moyers and Joe Califano and always welcomed
advice from General Maxwell Taylor, Averell Harriman,
and particularly Robert McNamara. Ted Kennedy remained on friendly terms with the President, and I also
saw him on rare occasions. ("Maybe," said Johnson to RFK
and me in their reconciliation meeting of April 1968, "all
this wouldn't have happened if *you"*—pointing his finger
at me—"had come here more often—or hadn't left in the
first place.")

But potential bridges became useless when escalation
of the Vietnam war widened the gap too far to be bridged.
I cannot believe that the war was anything but a bitter,
unwanted trial for President Johnson. His desire for world

peace had been clear to me since the day he had sent an olive-branch-bearing message (on which he had requested my help) to Khrushchev shortly after JFK's death. The war not only detracted from his own political standing but also interfered with the domestic programs of which he was passionately proud. It will be unfortunate if his massive accomplishments in civil rights, education, health, housing, conservation, and other domestic areas remain obscured by the bitter controversies over his Vietnam policy. Thus it must be said that on this issue he did his duty as he saw it; and so did Bob Kennedy. Each simply saw it differently.

Yet their personal feelings about each other could not have been irrelevant. Robert Kennedy at times, particularly in his early years as Senator, refrained from criticizing the war for fear it would be attributed to a Johnson–Kennedy feud. When he did speak out, his feelings about Lyndon Johnson no doubt added emphasis to his opposition to the war, once it became known as "Johnson's war" and not "McNamara's war." And President Johnson's refusal for three years to alter his course in Vietnam no doubt took into account the fact that the opposition was led by, among others, Robert Kennedy. Had there been no personal breach from the outset, Johnson's desire to end the war and to bring American forces home might have enabled him to listen more objectively to RFK's call for a bombing halt and a negotiated settlement. But they were working in isolation from each other, and the breach only widened.

As Johnson sharply escalated American involvement in the war early in 1965 through the deployment of massive military personnel and the heavy aerial bombardment of North Vietnam, Bob Kennedy was at first publicly restrained in his criticism. But he was privately skeptical and increasingly disturbed by what he regarded to be fundamental breaks with JFK's Vietnam policy. As will be noted in Part Two, his own views evolved gradually, influenced in part by the effect of the conflict on his late brother's hopes for a cold-war *détente* and domestic progress but constrained in part by the fact that his brother's hand-picked successor was in charge.

Bob and I discussed his dilemma in 1965 and early in 1966. He retained a deep respect for the judgment of Robert McNamara, Averell Harriman, and Maxwell Taylor, who played major roles in Vietnam decision-making. President Johnson, with whom he was in basic agreement on most domestic goals, was the leader of the Democratic Party, struggling with a growing problem in Vietnam. He had inherited the problem from John Kennedy, but the inheritance included no precise solution. The polls indicated a more negative public response to *Johnson's* conduct of the war than to *America's* involvement; and any RFK advocacy of an early disengagement under the terms of a risky diplomatic settlement might well have antagonized both party leaders and the general public. The press would accuse him of using the issue to attack the President personally; and inasmuch as he was operating on the assumption that Johnson would be the party's nominee in 1968 and that the Kennedys would have to support him, he felt it better not to say too much that might have to be swallowed later.

On a January morning early in 1966, after moving my admission to the Supreme Court bar, Bob asked me to review in his Senate office a memorandum from McNamara regarding the thirty-seven-day bombing pause then in effect. The memorandum and its attachments indicated that the bombing of North Vietnam had not been effective, that the American military position over the past months had deteriorated, and that fatalities in American ranks

alone could rise to the point of a hundred a week (unfortunately a gross underestimate). At the Senator's request, I drafted a brief memorandum urging, in effect, that
the United States unilaterally cease the bombing of the
North but maintain its freedom to retaliate against any
massive North Vietnamese attack on our forces. I pointed
out to him that the latter approach would be consistent
with the original rationale of the first bombing undertaken
after the Communist raid on the American base at Pleiku,
and that this act of de-escalation on our part could lead to
more on both sides. The Senator later told me that he had
passed on my memorandum, or his own version thereof,
along with the suggestion that an independent commission
of outsiders—for which he was suggesting Burke Marshall,
Roswell Gilpatric, and me as possible members—be appointed to examine all the alternatives before the bombing
was resumed. The suggestion was conveyed ultimately to
the President; but nothing came of it.

When the bombing was in fact resumed a few days
later, Bob decided the time had come to speak out. He prepared a talk stressing a settlement that would make possible
a National Liberation Front share in the political processes and power of South Vietnam. I agreed with his objective but raised the questions we had earlier discussed
concerning an open break with the President. Having
received similar advice elsewhere, he was mulling his course
when he received what he regarded as a "White House
pressure" call from Averell Harriman. "If I don't give the
speech now," he told me, "they'll think they've scared me
out." He may have been a new and gentler Bob Kennedy,
but threats and pressure were the surest way to make him
more determined than ever to go ahead. Go ahead he did,
although not without some ensuing confusion on both his
part and the Administration's as to how much they really

disagreed. During the remainder of 1966, he spoke out on the war with increased frequency but continued caution.

Then, early in 1967, a far more emphatic attack on the bombing of North Vietnam made it clear that the die had been cast. This time no effort was made by the White House to paper over differences. RFK's direct attacks on the Administration's Vietnam policy increased. He still avoided in them personal references to President Johnson. He still strongly disapproved of people calling the President a "baby-burner" or "bloodthirsty," just as he disapproved of Administration attempts to stifle dissent on the war. He saw no merit in forming a separate party. He still took steps—such as insisting on a rushed 1967 publication of his book *To Seek a Newer World*—to avoid giving any impression that he had political plans for 1968. And, until the 1968 campaign was already under way, he still thought it inadvisable for him to run against Lyndon Johnson.

Bob Kennedy and I discussed his possible candidacy for the Presidency many times after his brother's death. The question of whether he *should* run or *could* be a serious candidate was never mentioned. It was unnecessary. The question was wholly one of timing and tactics. As I have mentioned, 1964 was never seriously considered. Running against Lyndon Johnson in 1968 was not seriously considered for some time.

In July 1966 we reviewed the many possibilities. If Johnson declined to run in 1968, Bob would run. If anything should happen to Johnson before 1968 and Humphrey as President sought the nomination, it would depend on his policies. If Humphrey succeeded to the Presidency before January 20, 1967, he would be Constitutionally ineligible to run in 1972 (a fact realized by few). If Johnson were re-elected in 1968, he would be ineligible to run in

1972. If he died between January 20, 1971, and convention time, 1972, the new President (presumably Humphrey) could run in both 1972 and 1976.

These and others constituted so long a list of contingencies beyond Bob's control that fixing any kind of target date for his own campaign-planning purposes seemed meaningless. At the same time, our review of other potential candidates, if Johnson ran without changing running mates, left only Humphrey as a strong subsequent challenger to RFK among convention delegates, although we thought it possible that Johnson might try to name his own successor and pick a dark horse such as Governor John Connally of Texas or Robert McNamara. In no circumstances would RFK, four years wiser than in 1964, have wanted to replace Humphrey as Johnson's 1968 running mate.

Our talks always proceeded on two mistaken assumptions: first, that Johnson would run again in 1968; and, second, that Truman's experience in 1948 proved that even an incumbent President in trouble could dominate a convention composed of delegates from his own party if he were seeking renomination. But we did not take either assumption for granted. In a Princeton lecture and a *New York Times Magazine* article in the spring of 1967 I observed:

. . . of all the Vice Presidents who originally succeeded to the White House as Mr. Johnson did by virtue of their predecessor's death, not a single one has ever sought to be re-elected for a second full term. . . . If Mr. Johnson of his own accord chooses [not to run], no one can call that a retreat from the historical pattern when it would in reality be fidelity to it.

Some columnists—and, I was told, some irate White House aides—called it the first salvo from the Kennedy camp. In fact RFK knew nothing of it. But he had heard from a reliable source that the President had promised Mrs. Johnson not to seek re-election in 1968. Some of the wise Washington money, given sufficient odds, was betting that the Republican Congressional sweep of 1966 and the worsening Vietnam and racial situations would cause Johnson to find "health reasons" compelling his retirement. Bob Kennedy remained skeptical. Nevertheless, he recognized that his chances of being nominated by a less bitterly divided party would be substantially improved if LBJ were to announce his retirement without RFK's having entered the race against him.

Late in the summer of 1967 I suggested to Bob that, at least to canvass the contingencies and prepare for any opportunities, a meeting should be called of those friends who had some political "punch" and the discretion to keep such a meeting completely confidential. After thinking for a moment (under water, for we were in his back-yard pool in McLean, Virginia), he replied, "I know some people who have political punch, and I know some who have the necessary discretion, but I don't know anyone who has both!"

Nevertheless, on a Sunday afternoon in October, a meeting was held, convened by Pierre Salinger in his Regency Hotel suite in New York and attended by a wide assortment of former JFK associates and present RFK associates. Bob Kennedy stayed away. Except for Ted Kennedy and New York State Chairman John Burns, few of those present had much political "punch" in terms of our delegate influence. And subsequent reports in the press indicated that someone present did not have the discretion to keep it completely confidential. Although Bob was surprised and hurt that a leak could emanate from a group so close to him, the problem was sufficiently important that he met with somewhat the same group—actually broken into two groups of overlapping membership—on December 10.

The results of those largely disorganized meetings were inconclusive but basically negative. No one could count a majority of convention delegates against an incumbent President, even if RFK swept all the primaries (and no one was certain that he could). In fact, no one knew of a single important leader of the party who would be willing to endorse RFK's candidacy or urge LBJ even privately to step aside. All the Democratic Senators who felt as Bob did on Vietnam were reported to be pleading that his entry would sink their chances for re-election and accomplish nothing else.

While all of us felt strongly about the Vietnam war, the polls still showed a majority of Democrats favoring the President's position; and Johnson's ability at any time to halt the bombing, open negotiations, or otherwise undercut any opponent on that issue gave him a considerable advantage. His control of the military progress reports, his appeal as Commander-in-Chief in wartime, the sympathy he received when abused by militants, the many and divided factions in the antiwar camp, the inhibitions on criticism which either negotiations or all-out war would bring—all made less appealing the notion of running against the President on the war issue. "The Democratic slogan," said one man sourly, "will be 'Don't change horses, or any portion thereof, in the middle of the stream.'"

Bob's appeal, several noted, was limited primarily to minority and poverty groups in the big cities and to youthful liberals. Without compromising his principles or abandoning those groups, they suggested, he should broaden the scope of his speeches and travels to include other parts of the electorate (and cut his hair).

We agreed that political sentiment around the country should be explored, that the possibility of a test primary in some state where RFK's consent would not be required should be studied, and that we should all begin to keep in touch generally. We agreed that he should not campaign for Johnson, that he should devote the next several months to making friends and taking soundings in key spots, that he should not yet file affidavits under the Oregon and Nebraska primary laws declaring that he would not be a Presidential candidate in 1968, that RFK's friends should get themselves selected as delegates in all states, that hotel space and communications facilities should be reserved for the national convention in Chicago, and that one or more of RFK's aides and associates should spend full time making exploratory contacts. We also initiated a November 1967 poll of New Hampshire Democrats. It showed RFK well ahead of McCarthy but trailing LBJ substantially; and that result alone had an important deterrent and dampening effect on those few privy to it, including the two Senators Kennedy.

Somewhat earlier, during late summer 1967, a tireless and brilliant New York organizer, Allard Lowenstein, and other founders of the "Dump Johnson" movement had hoped Bob would be their candidate against President Johnson in the primaries in order to permit a "dialogue" on Vietnam. But the substance of every RFK speech differing with the Administration's Vietnam policy had been largely ignored in press and public comments which concentrated instead on his political or personal war with Johnson. Primarily with that in mind, RFK told Lowenstein, in effect, what he had told others—that his entering the Presidential race would not advance the cause of peace in Vietnam but would only submerge it under a wave of accusations that he was using the issue, wrecking the party, and ensuring the defeat of Democratic doves up for re-election merely to advance his own personal feud with the

President and his ruthless ambitions to regain the White House for the Kennedys. All this would accomplish nothing if he could not be nominated and elected; and one result might well be the election of Nixon over whatever Democrat was nominated.

All this was consistent with my own advice to him. Indeed, that was how I felt until the day he announced. It was not because I failed to feel deeply about the war and other issues but because I did feel deeply about them—and about him. As much as I shared his distress at the Adminstration's blind reaction to the Tet offensive, I feared that RFK, and other doves, would lose influence if he entered the primaries against Johnson and, win or lose, tore the Democratic Party apart. I saw no chance of his changing policy before 1972 if he entered the primaries, but some chance if he awaited further developments. On all the evidence available at that time, his decision not to run against his brother's successor and the party leader in the primaries made sense to me as both a dove and an RFK supporter.

RFK suggested to Lowenstein and his associates that they try instead an early opponent of the war, South Dakota Senator George McGovern. The latter, faced with a difficult re-election fight in 1968, referred them to Minnesota Senator Eugene McCarthy, who had made a speech calling for Rusk's resignation on the war issue, was not up for re-election, and had little to lose. McCarthy agreed to the request of the Lowenstein group and announced his candidacy, initially hinting, however, that he contemplated yielding his position in the race to RFK before the convention. Many young activists who had been angered at Bob's refusal to run soon moved in behind McCarthy; and their disillusionment with RFK deeply troubled the New York Senator, who had become their hope and inspiration during the preceding four years. He felt his position as leader of the Democratic opposition endangered, with all the consequences that implied for 1972 as well as 1968.

The entry of another dove candidate with growing support considerably complicated Robert Kennedy's own decision on whether to run. The fact that it was Gene McCarthy quadrupled that difficulty. For Senator McCarthy, for reasons never known or understood, had chosen for many years to align himself against the Kennedys. His vote in 1969 as virtually the only Senate liberal and dove to favor Russell Long of Louisiana over Ted Kennedy for Assistant Majority Leader (Whip) was simply continuing a pattern set years earlier. No one disputed McCarthy's understandable backing of Humphrey in 1956 and 1960, or his effort to be chosen by Johnson as his running mate in 1964. But both before and after the 1960 convention, where he had eloquently nominated Stevenson while supporting Johnson, McCarthy had made consistently derogatory remarks about John Kennedy, his ability, his Catholicism, and his integrity.

One of McCarthy's close Senate friends had told President Kennedy to "forget it, it's just sour grapes—Gene thinks he's a better Catholic." But Bob Kennedy was less likely to forget. In the 1964 conversation eliminating RFK from the Vice Presidency, Johnson had contemplated the possibility of Bob making the nominating speech for the ultimate choice for that slot. As Bob pondered this suggestion (which, like the simultaneous suggestion that he serve as LBJ's campaign manager, was never mentioned to him by Johnson again), he told me he would do it with enthusiasm if it were Humphrey but could not do it at all if it were Gene McCarthy. "No one in Washington respects that man," he said.

That judgment seemed to me to be too harsh, in view of McCarthy's intellectual attainments and voting record.

But at no time in 1967 or 1968 did Robert Kennedy ever believe that he could support Eugene McCarthy for the Presidential nomination, regardless of the alternative. "I just don't think he has what it takes to be a good President," he replied when some of us urged him—once he was in the race himself—to agree that he would support McCarthy if the latter knocked him out in the primaries.

When Senator McCarthy announced for the Presidency late in 1967, Kennedy said it was "healthy" for the party and indicated his basic agreement with McCarthy's anti-Vietnam stance. He even retreated from an earlier endorsement of the Johnson–Humphrey ticket to a posture of neutrality. But he did not campaign for McCarthy in New Hampshire. "If I am going to fight to unseat an incumbent President," he remarked, "I might as well start my own campaign instead of supporting someone who can't win whether I help or not, and who hasn't been in the forefront of this fight anyway."

With the exception of such McCarthy supporters as Dick Goodwin and Ken Galbraith, with whom he kept in close touch, his neutral position brought disappointment to those in the camp of the Minnesota Senator. But their disappointment turned to bitter antagonism when, in the midst of McCarthy's most triumphant moment—the day after he nearly defeated a write-in vote for Johnson in the New Hampshire primary—RFK stated in answer to press inquiries that he was "reassessing" his decision not to enter the Presidential race. It was one of those statements of utterly spontaneous candor that had gotten him into trouble before; and it stole the headlines from McCarthy before he had enjoyed more than a few hours of the glory fostered by his near triumph.

The RFK statement was assailed as a graceless example of ruthless opportunism. Certainly the timing was poor.

The White House naturally enjoyed the discomfiture of both men and circulated one good crack: "It took sixteen years for Bobby Kennedy to come out against McCarthy and then he came out against the wrong one."

In fact, Robert Kennedy had been reassessing his position for several weeks. What he had thought was a final meeting with Steve Smith and me in mid-January, accompanied by similar advice from his brother Ted, had led him to tell the press that he would not "under any foreseeable circumstances" run against President Johnson in the primaries. But almost immediately "unforeseeable circumstances" began to occur. McCarthy's near victory in New Hampshire was the least of these, although the attacks on the Minnesota Senator's patriotism by Johnson's managers, and the Minnesotan's youth-powered campaign, had helped to prove Bob's point that the split in the Democratic Party went well beyond any Kennedy–Johnson feud.

Two developments outraged him most. One was the President's refusal to endorse or implement the far-reaching recommendations to end racial discrimination, frustration, and violence contained in the March 1 report of a White House commission under Otto Kerner. The President's own housing and urban program for 1968, RFK felt, was totally inadequate; and he had not been reassured by a visit from White House aide Joe Califano which preceded Administration attacks on the Kennedy housing program.

The other—and prime—factor in his pre–New Hampshire reassessment was his conviction that the dangerously successful Tet offensive by the Vietcong early in 1968 had proven the sham of the Administration's claims of military success in Vietnam and its predictions of "victory just around the corner" but had nevertheless produced no change in the Administration's policies of escalation.

On the contrary, since Robert McNamara had been shuffled out of the Administration in a manner RFK regarded as "unconscionable," he felt the prospects for any alteration in the Johnson policy to be dimmer than ever.

When his sources within the Administration informed the Senator that the Pentagon's recommended response to the Tet offensive was to add 206,000 more American servicemen to the 500,000 already committed, he was deeply distressed. "I can't just stand on the sidelines and let this happen," he said to me on the telephone. "I've been a leader against all this, and now I'm not in it when it counts." I reminded him of our previous discussions to the effect that he could offer more effective leadership on this issue as a Senator with no immediate ambitions at stake than as a defeated candidate for President. It was not the answer he wanted to hear, and he glumly ended the conversation.

Later in February we met at his McLean home with California Democratic power Jesse Unruh, the first Democratic leader in the country who wanted him to run and who was anxious to have him enter that state's Presidential primary with an Unruh-led slate. Bob's wife, like his sisters Pat and Jean, urged him to do it. Other advisers were divided or said only he could decide. His brother Ted and I remained opposed, pointing out that McCarthy's entry had complicated matters, that Johnson still might step aside, and that, if the President did not step aside, winning the primaries was neither enough by itself nor necessary to oust him at the convention. As we walked about Hickory Hill after Unruh left, RFK seemed unhappy about his choices. "Philosophically I wish I could do it," he said; "realistically I know I should not do it."

He was determined, however, not to complicate the picture by having his own name entered in the New

Hampshire primary without either his consent or his campaigning. At his request, I undertook to remove it, and I
found in an unrelated luncheon with Johnson aides that
they, too, were anxious to have it done. On a flying trip to
New Hampshire, I persuaded the understandably irate
RFK backers to dissolve their effort and advised New
Hampshire residents through a press conference that the
Senator would regard one vote for him as too many. Upon
my return, RFK called to express his gratitude. Within
minutes the White House called to express the President's
gratitude! The President, it was added, hoped I would
come by and see him the next time I was in Washington;
and subsequently the date was set for Monday, March 11,
coincidentally the day before the New Hampshire primary.

I visited Bob Kennedy in his office before going over to
the White House. The previous week, in a long meeting
with his brother and Fred Dutton, he had virtually made
up his mind to run but did not want to make an announcement that would interfere with the New Hampshire vote.
Oregon and Nebraska primary statutes required an almost
immediate decision, as did Jesse Unruh if he were to have
enough time to circulate petitions in California. Through
his brother Ted and Dick Goodwin, Bob had sent a message conveying his intentions in advance to McCarthy;
but he was uncertain whether his message had been delivered to the Minnesota Senator precisely as he sent it—
or at all.

A real change in direction in U.S. Vietnam policy, he
told me that Monday morning, could be the only deterrent to his entering the race. I said that, if given the
chance, I intended to suggest to the President an independent commission on Vietnam policy, as earlier suggested by *The New York Times*. Bob said that Chicago
Mayor Richard Daley had told him he had made the same

suggestion to Johnson, saying, "When you have a losing hand, throw your cards in." RFK added that replacing Dean Rusk with a dove as Secretary of State would also signal to the war's opponents that a real change was forthcoming.

What began as a brief, friendly visit with the President turned into a two-hour session. Johnson was in top form: warm, gracious, humble about his mistakes, acknowledging he did not know the answer to Vietnam, and talking candidly about members of his Cabinet and about the Washington press corps. In backing all Senate doves for re-election, he was imposing no loyalty test, he said, and he regretted both the attacks on and the attacks by McCarthy in the New Hampshire primary, then drawing to a close.

Repeated references to the national campaign indicated that he was a candidate for re-election. But in explaining his willingness to let McCarthy have Massachusetts by default in order not to force Ted Kennedy into a choice, he recalled FDR's advising him in 1940 not to split the Democrats in Texas by fighting Garner before the convention. Then he added, "If this convention is going to be so close I can't give up one state, then maybe I won't be a candidate." "On my word of honor," he said later in the conversation, he would not "favor Hubert or oppose Bobby" as his successor.

He was somber on Vietnam. He thought that Kosygin had agreed at their Glassboro, New Jersey, conference in 1967 to reconvene the Geneva Peace Conference but that Hanoi and Red China had vetoed it. Perhaps you could undertake a mission to change the Kremlin's mind, he said to me, although their attitude in general had been colder since the replacement of Khrushchev. He had decided to ask Congress in 1964 for the Gulf of Tonkin resolution, despite Rusk's opposition to the idea because as Majority Leader he had persuaded Eisenhower to make similar requests for authority regarding the Middle East and Formosa. He did not then dream that his troop commitments would exceed half a million men. Although his new Secretary of Defense, Clark Clifford, had earlier opposed the thirty-seven-day bombing pause, he was not the hawk the press had reported him to be. Clifford, he said, had strongly opposed extension of the war into Cambodia and was hoping to get RFK's and Senator Fulbright's suggestions.

I mentioned RFK's likely candidacy only in passing and in fact said very little. But when the President asked what possible steps could be taken to heal the bitter divisions over Vietnam in the Democratic Party and the country, I replied that there were two. At least one of them, I added, was presumptuous and out of place for me to suggest, since I admired Dean Rusk's dedication. Johnson replied that it had not been his policy to request anyone's resignation (here he launched into a long story of Mc-Namara's departure) and that Rusk had offered his resignation only when his daughter was about to marry a Negro, which was not the time to accept it. I made no mention whatever of RFK's feelings regarding Rusk.

My second suggestion was a national commission of independent status to evaluate what had gone wrong in Vietnam and to recommend a new policy. He said that Dick Daley had made the same suggestion (positing RFK as a member) and that it might have merit, even with RFK as chairman, provided it did not appear to be undermining Rusk or indicating incoherence in our policy. He said he had already consulted with men like Edwin Reischauer, General Matthew Ridgeway, McGeorge Bundy, and George Ball, who were not in agreement with his policy, but that he would think over the commission proposal. He asked me to submit a list of possible names, including my own. Contrary to the reports subsequently leaked from the White House, I did not indicate that the commission was an RFK proposal, much less a condition of his noncandidacy.

The following evening the returns from New Hampshire startled the Kennedys as well as the nation. The next afternoon, Wednesday, March 13, RFK's friends gathered in Steve Smith's Manhattan apartment to re-examine our position. By then, Ted Kennedy and I had become virtually alone in our opposition, and Ted had no heart for opposing his brother's obvious desire to run. McCarthy's showing had only strengthened my conviction that intervention against him in the primaries would be unnecessary in terms of ultimate convention strength against Johnson and undesirable in terms of splitting the liberal and anti-Vietnam forces against Johnson.

As much as anyone in that meeting, I wanted Bob Kennedy elected President at the earliest possible date. But I could not see how simultaneously embittering both the Johnson regulars and the McCarthy liberals would help him win California and Oregon, raise money, or find the necessary majority of delegates outside the South. McCarthy still had no chance of winning the nomination; and whatever loss of standing RFK had suffered among the young by not entering in November would not be offset by his entering in March.

His options were limited, however, by his inability to believe in McCarthy's capacity to be President—and McCarthy's new belief in his own prospects. RFK could not endorse McCarthy or otherwise team up with him, as Arthur Schlesinger urged, in the hope that their unity would produce a Kennedy victory at the convention.

Moreover, our deliberations that afternoon seemed confined to the question of "how," not "whether," in view of the reassessment statement Bob had spontaneously made in Washington. Then we watched him on television in an effective interview by Walter Cronkite. He spoke movingly of his obligation to undertake a campaign he knew was uphill. That, commented his brother Ted, "was Bobby at his best."

As I left to fulfill a speaking engagement in Rochester, New York, I received, to everyone's amusement, a message to call the White House. The President, I was told, liked the Vietnam commission idea and wanted my list of suggested names immediately. I promised an answer in the morning.

When I reached RFK at one a.m. after my return from Rochester and his intensive round of conferences and phone calls, he told me that Mayor Daley had told him of the President's decision to alter his Vietnam policy with a commission "as soon as Sorensen gives him the names." Daley had advised RFK not to run against a policy about to be changed. Clark Clifford had been designated as the appropriate intermediary and RFK had already made an appointment with him for that morning; he asked me to join him.

We met at the river entrance to the Pentagon and paced up and down the sidewalk discussing his position. He was unwilling to offer a "deal"—his not running in return for a truly independent commission. On the other hand, he said, he really did not want to run against Lyndon Johnson for President. While there were many issues to be raised in a campaign, it was the Vietnam issue which had taken him past the dividing line between not running and running. If he could be convinced that that policy was truly to be changed, he would stay out of the primaries. We drew up, both before and after the meeting, lists of names for the commission, most of whom were known to be opposed to Administration policy. It is interesting that a somewhat similar group of men—including Bundy, Ball, and Ridgeway, who were on our list—was convened eleven days later in a secret "commission" of wise men Johnson called into a two-day session at the White House.

Our effort on March 14, however, was an exercise in futility, much to RFK's disappointment. The meeting with Clifford was cordial; the new Secretary showed sympathy with our approach, and he promised an early decision by the President. Bob left the Pentagon hopeful that he would not have to run and hopeful that Vietnam policy would be changed. But when the President's decision came late that afternoon, it was negative. The last barricade of doubt having been removed, RFK decided to announce his candidacy two days hence, on Saturday.

The following day, with RFK traveling in New York and in constant contact by telephone, we compared the map with the calendar. Some urged that he run only in California because of the limited time left. Yet Oregon and Nebraska laws required the listing of all candidates, and he was unwilling passively to accept the outcome in those states without a campaign. Most of us urged him to stay out of conservative Indiana with its notoriously reactionary Indianapolis newspapers. But, concerned that he might lose in Nebraska and receive no credit for winning in the District of Columbia primary, he wanted an early win. "Indiana's a gamble," he said, "but so is this whole campaign, and we don't have a chance if we don't take every gamble." He explored the New Jersey primary and a write-in campaign in Massachusetts and decided that time and resources were insufficient, particularly when a private poll showed him losing decisively to Mc-Carthy in Massachusetts. While he was still weighing whether to enter the South Dakota primary, a first-rate slate pledged to him was entered without his consent. McCarthy blocked efforts to form coalition slates and efforts in several states.

A brief talk Bob had with McCarthy the day after the New Hampshire primary had not gone well, each reportedly feeling the other to be arrogant. "He's certainly changed his tune from our last meeting on the basis of one good showing," RFK told me. "He now says I can succeed him after he serves one term!" Dick Goodwin proposed a pact between the two men not to enter the same primaries, but Nebraska and Oregon laws made that impossible. Nevertheless, Goodwin arranged for Ted Kennedy to see McCarthy late that Friday night in Wisconsin. We hoped that the Minnesotan would agree that the two antiwar candidates should not attack each other but aim for a common goal. McCarthy, however, was uninterested; and the discouraged younger brother returned to Washington before dawn.

Walking into Bob's home, where aides slept on couches all about, Ted awakened me to say that it looked as if McCarthy intended to fight us all the way. I dressed and went downstairs, with gloomy spirits for such an important day. For one incredible minute there was a panicky discussion around the breakfast table—two hours before the press conference at which he would announce his candidacy—as to whether RFK should run in the primaries or at all. But he was firm, his announcement statement was completed and approved, and the two brothers and I (and a dog) piled into a car to drive to his Senate Office Building press conference. It was clear that both the liberal and the conservative wings of his party were wedded to other candidates. It was unclear how he could possibly obtain a majority of convention delegates. Yet he could no longer ignore the moral imperative. He felt compelled to try to save the country from four more years of Johnson's foreign policy, regardless of what happened to the party or himself. As JFK had said of the time his little brother kept jumping off the sailboat, "It showed either a lot of guts or no sense at all, depending on how you looked at it."

Except for two later press-conference statements, following the President's withdrawal and the Oregon primary (and his speech in Cleveland after Martin Luther King's death), Bob's opening announcement was virtually the only writing I did for the campaign. That night at dinner Bob asked me to devote full time in Washington, with Ted Kennedy and Steve Smith, to running the campaign. I replied that it was a bit ironic, in view of my previous opposition to his candidacy. But I had actually told him at the Unruh meeting weeks earlier that I would give him full time should he ever decide to run and so request. I returned to my New York law firm for one day to clear the way with my understanding partners and clients, and then signed on once again to work in a Kennedy Presidential campaign.

But what a difference from the last one! Bob Kennedy had none of the time Jack Kennedy had to build an organization, to prepare his team, and to test the possibilities in each state. On the other hand, Jack had started out far less known with far smaller crowds and with the serious handicaps of religion and youth that were nearly nonexistent in 1968. Bob's pace was necessarily more frantic and even frenzied from the start, trying to make up for lost time and capitalizing on his enormous prestige. Bob's speaking style was more impassioned and sometimes strident; Jack's approach to issues was less heated. Bob held highly controversial views on the deeply divisive problems of race and war, to say nothing of such special-interest issues as cigarette smoking and gambling. He faced an incumbent President. Jack had run with no clear-cut issues of this kind in a party that had no single leader. JFK led all Democrats in the polls throughout 1960. Bob trailed LBJ in the polls of 1968.

But there were many similarities. Both were forty-two years old. Both began with the suspicion or outright hostility of the best-known organization Democrats, the party's liberal intellectual wing, the South, most of organized labor's leaders, the business establishment, and the leading publishers. Neither had much announced support from his fellow Senators. Although Bob had far more black support than Jack and far more college-student activists, many of the best students had already committed themselves to McCarthy. Both overcame their shyness to plunge into crowds to touch swiftly all the hands that reached, clawed, and pressed toward them. Yet both disliked politicians' placing their arms around them. Both spent large sums of money, although Bob—it turned out, after all the press attacks on his spending were forgotten—spent no more than McCarthy.

Both also worked harder in their Presidential campaigns than any other candidate. Each day Bob spoke, toured, shook hands, and spoke again from breakfast to midnight, drawing in March crowds unlike any JFK had seen until October, and using spare moments to place telephone calls to the lists of party leaders we continually supplied. He was more informal and fun-loving about the campaign than Jack, often campaigning with his jacket off and tie loose and engaging the crowd with more banter and self-deprecating humor. JFK, as 1960 drew nearer, had sought to avoid talk of his immaturity by trimming the bushy hair style in which cartoonists had previously delighted. Bob's hair was more shaggy than bushy, often because he failed to find time to get it cut. The more its length had become an issue even among intelligent men who knew better than to judge Presidential potentials by their hair, the more stubborn he had become about cutting it. Finally, to run in conservative Indiana, he bowed to political necessity and emerged from the barber's chair feeling half naked.

Their campaigns also had in common an air of determined confidence that others attributed to arrogance. Bob Kennedy believed he was the only dove who could defeat Johnson, given the incumbent's considerable advantages over a Kefauver-like McCarthy effort; and he believed he was the only Democrat who could defeat Nixon, given the gaping divisions in the Democratic Party which New Hampshire had only symbolized. These realities troubled many top McCarthy supporters whose real goal was peace in Vietnam. As old-time Kennedy haters moved more actively into the McCarthy camp, other McCarthyites quietly switched to Kennedy. Others, in frequent touch with Kennedy, such as Al Lowenstein and Ken Galbraith, stayed to keep the lines of communication open for eventual merger.

Despite a growing pattern of sniping and snide remarks from McCarthy—including an unguarded admission to a newsman that Humphrey might well be his next choice— Bob continued to turn the other cheek. He offered to campaign for McCarthy in Wisconsin. He eliminated from his own literature and speeches (until he lost in Oregon) all statements that even by implication compared him favorably with McCarthy or exposed McCarthy's Senate voting record (although he could not even know of all the versions of McCarthy's record soon to be circulated by various adherents without his authorization). He rejected the advice of those who wanted him to run "against" McCarthy as well as Johnson and Humphrey. Until defeat in Oregon made him realize that it was all or nothing in California (and that McCarthy was indeed a serious contender), he refused to debate McCarthy unless Humphrey also appeared, in order not to emphasize the notion that they were opposed to each other. He took pains in the debate to make clear his basic agreement with McCarthy and to show warmth toward him, even while adhering to his own programs and policies. He did not—he could not, for it was not in his nature—match McCarthy's talk about firing Dean Rusk, J. Edgar Hoover, and General Lewis Hershey. But he wanted to do or say nothing that would deter McCarthy delegates from ultimately switching to him, for he could not win the nomination without them.

The Kennedy 1968 campaign has been previously reported by numerous other writers. It is important here chiefly as it related to the development of the Kennedy legacy. In his writings, speeches, and activities as a Senator and national leader, Bob Kennedy had already staked out those areas where he was to expand and develop the legacy of his brother. Stump speeches in a political campaign, hastily prepared by aides usually on the basis of previous speeches and then hastily reviewed by the candidate, do not ordinarily add much to the policy positions of one who has previously voiced his views on so many subjects.

But Bob Kennedy's campaign in 1968 was not ordinary. The statements he made were important—because he felt obligated to define his positions on many issues and not base his campaign on Vietnam alone; because he recognized the necessity of broadening his appeal to voters other than those sharing his concern for racial and urban problems; because a man opposing an incumbent President who had enacted most of his late brother's legislative program was required to produce a new list of priorities for the future; because he was deeply moved by the campaign crowds, particularly by the look of hope on the faces of otherwise angry or despairing blacks and other dispossessed citizens; and because the climate of his brief 1968 campaign was constantly altered by sudden, drastic, dramatic changes in the political atmosphere: the assassination of Dr. Martin Luther King, the ensuing riots in major cities, the withdrawal of President Johnson, the reversal of our policy in Vietnam, the student riots at Columbia and elsewhere, the peace demonstrations in many cities, and the Poor People's Campaign march which ended in "Resurrection City," Washington.

In his haste and passion, he made at the outset occasional charges against Washington and Saigon that were not in keeping with his own high standards of integrity. But these errors were small and few, beside the sweep of his major statements. Bob himself wished that he had more time and opportunity to develop reflective and positive Presidential themes, instead of limiting his campaign largely to criticisms and the usual four-point programs. But none of us realized the extent to which his whirlwind efforts did engrave the needs of the downtrodden and dispossessed on our national conscience and consciousness.

No doubt his courageous championing of the underprivileged and unrepresented groups in American society alienated more voters than it won him, for those groups were largely unregistered and—except for California, the District of Columbia, and parts of Indiana—not present in important numbers in the primary states. No doubt he disturbed the minds of many voters by giving voice to his own anger and agony over such unpleasant topics as depressed young Indians committing suicide on their reservations or the bloated bellies of hungry children in the Mississippi Delta. But at the same time many whites, frightened by the terror and turmoil that followed the murder of Martin Luther King, were impressed that only Robert Kennedy (and Mayor John Lindsay of New York) could walk unafraid into the ghettos at that time, to urge angry blacks to cool it, and to tell them that violence was self-defeating and self-destructive.

Some whites, to be sure, reacted to the new wave of Negro violence by increasing their hostility toward the black man's favorite candidate. On March 28, police in Salt Lake City received an anonymous telephone threat about a bomb in the hall where Kennedy was to speak. When we talked somberly by telephone the night of Dr. King's assassination, one week later, I told the Senator that his own life could be in danger in such an atmosphere. "I can't care about that," he replied. The following week police spotted a possible roof-top sniper in Lansing, Michigan.

The President's withdrawal from the race on Sunday night, March 31, astonished RFK as it did us all. He sent an immediate wire to the President commending his "magnanimous" decision and requesting an early conference "in the interest of national unity." His press conference the following day began a new policy of exercising caution on precise developments in Vietnam, avoiding criticism of the President, and stressing even more heavily the need for reconciliation in our own country. I do not agree with the published assertion that his campaign lost direction and purpose after Johnson withdrew and Vietnam talks began. He had not—as he had stated in his opening press conference, to the dismay of some advisers—been running merely "against" Johnson or the war. The King assassination and rioting that would follow only a few days after LBJ's withdrawal would make clear the remaining mission which RFK alone could fulfill.

An example of the national reconciliation he sought was the hundred-minute meeting he and I had with President Johnson two days after the latter's Sunday-night withdrawal. Most of the talking was done by the President, and most of it was on Vietnam. He had achieved only with the greatest difficulty, he told us, a three-to-two vote from the Joint Chiefs of Staff favoring the partial bombing halt he had announced in the same Sunday-night speech. A total halt would have been four-to-one against him, he added. A dispatch from Hanoi radio shortly before the meeting gave the President hopes of negotiations and further de-escalation. He said he had removed himself from the campaign to prevent his bid for peace from being politically suspect to those groups whom he seemed unable to win over: the Kennedy and McCarthy followers, the blacks, the students, and the academics ("after all I've done for civil rights and for higher education!").

He was frank but even-toned in discussing the gap that had risen between him and Bob. Both men expressed regret that it had occurred and each accepted a share of the blame. At one point, when the President spoke of putting his efforts for peace ahead of his own political career, the Senator interrupted to say emotionally but still with difficulty, "You are a brave and dedicated man, Mr. President." He swallowed it and had to repeat it a second time before the President heard him.

Johnson, once prodded, expounded at length on his posture of neutrality and nonintervention in the campaign. Hubert Humphrey had been loyal, he said, but "if I were going to get involved I might as well do it on my own behalf." He had no intention of being another Truman, he added, making a spectacle of himself trying to nominate his successor. He agreed to inform RFK should his position change, to keep his appointees neutral, and to maintain contact through his aide Charles Murphy and me. The room was glowing with friendly expressions of sentiment all around as we closed, having run some forty minutes overtime, with Vice President Hubert Humphrey waiting outside to see the President.

In a way, we felt sorry for Humphrey when he entered the race. The spectacle of Southern Governors (who later switched to Wallace) and Wall Street bankers (who later switched to Nixon) teaming with George Meany to stop Robert Kennedy, the man disliked by the liberals, by supporting this former ADA champion from Minnesota would all have seemed ludicrous had it not had such serious implications for the future of the Democratic Party, the AFL-CIO, and Robert Kennedy himself. But RFK's enemies were not limited to racists, reactionaries, and big businessmen. Because most Americans (there are always a few Victor Laskys around) bury with the dead whatever antagonism they held toward them, it is easy to forget today that Bob Kennedy was not the beloved figure, even outside the South, that he seemed to be on the day of his funeral train. "I'm the only candidate," he said, "who has ever united business, labor, liberals, Southerners, bosses, and intellectuals. They're all against me!"

Many liberals who would later invoke RFK's name with fervor were among the bitterest of his assailants. Their attacks were sometimes subtle, sometimes sanctimonious, and sometimes uninhibitedly vicious and almost irrational. His record of compassion was ignored, his sense of pity was jeered, his record as Attorney General was distorted, and his obvious growth and changes were forgotten. Liberals who had supported Stevenson in 1952 after Kefauver swept nearly all the primaries argued that only McCarthy was entitled to the nomination in 1968 because he had been the first to enter the primaries. Other liberals who had condemned Bob's earlier refusal to run as selfish opportunism condemned his decision to run as selfish opportunism. Had it been Kennedy vs. Johnson, they would have termed "determined" what they now called "ruthless." He was accused of claiming the White House by inheritance when he was in fact going the hard, risky route of the primaries. "I am not asking anyone to hand anything to me," he said. "I am going to the people. . . ."

In each state whose primary he entered, he became the central figure. Regardless of the other candidates, voters divided according to whether they loved or hated Bobby Kennedy. We were urged by some to confront the "ruthless" issue in the same way that JFK had confronted the religious issue—but no one could suggest a method by which the circulation of such attacks would be halted more than they would be dignified and increased. Like LBJ's problems with the "credibility gap," only the evidence of time and action—not new words—could change people's minds once this fixation had taken hold.

At times Bob would wonder aloud about the hatred aimed at him. But, with the exception of Oregon, he kept winning in spite of the hostility—in Indiana, in the District of Columbia, in Nebraska, in California, and in South Dakota. A myth that he depended on nonwhite, left-wing, and ethnic-group votes was perpetuated by those ignoring his two largest victories outside the District of Columbia—in Nebraska and South Dakota. In every state he won the votes of union members whose national chieftains were against him; he carried many supposed white-backlash neighborhoods that after his death would move in part to George Wallace; he carried black, Puerto Rican,

Mexican-American, and Indian precincts by margins no Democratic primary candidate of his race had achieved in modern times; he won the votes of those under thirty by margins up to two-to-one over McCarthy; he carried those farm counties and small towns in which he campaigned in person to offset his unfavorable public image; he won increasing support from the peace groups, academics, church groups, and others who had first leaned toward McCarthy; and he took pains not to alienate the professional liberals and other McCarthy supporters, most of whom he was hopeful would eventually come over.

It was a broad spectrum, a winning spectrum even without the South; and we had by no means written off all the South. We were placing friends on Southern delegations who would be freed if the unit rule were broken, helping organize counterdelegations to oppose the credentials of lily-white regulars, and paving the way for adding more delegates and neutralizing others. Robert Kennedy, in short, while far too controversial a figure to achieve national reconciliation through consensus, was the one national figure in his party who could, through the strength of his personal charisma as well as his program, reach not the bloc leaders but the individual voters in every walk of life, and particularly those most at odds with each other and their society.

Largely because of the late start, RFK's campaign generally was not as well planned or well organized as JFK's. Far more staff members were on the road with him. The schedule was too often disregarded or impossible to fulfill. Waste and duplication were particularly severe in the area of TV commercials. In California in particular local politicians resented the Eastern invasion while the invaders accused Unruh's men of helping only themselves. In many states the old JFK network was revived for lack of a readily available alternative. But many of its members were not as influential, as well-informed, or as energetic as they had been eight years earlier.

Bob recognized what a severe handicap he suffered from starting so late—feigning (I hope) a ferocious glare at me whenever the subject came up but maintaining that his late start was his own decision for valid reasons. (Interestingly enough, those who have most criticized his refusal to enter the race earlier seem surprisingly certain that he would have been nominated anyway.)

There were some internal differences in our campaign effort as well. It suffered no shortage of foot soldiers, but there was a surplus of generals. Sargent Shriver had recently been appointed Ambassador to France and decided, after some negotiations regarding his possible campaign title and role, to continue on to Paris. But his wife Eunice and all other members of the family campaigned in full force. No agreement was ever reached on titles for Ted Kennedy, Steve Smith, Larry O'Brien, Ken O'Donnell, Fred Dutton, or me, nor were functions and lines of authority ever clearly drawn. This was partly because we were all too rushed and partly because of some sensitive personality problems that the candidate was too busy to settle (although he had foreseen some of them in his talk that first night with Ted, Steve, and me).

His strategists varied and his strategy veered almost from day to day on the subject of crowds. We weighed the stimulus of excitement, enthusiasm, and popular appeal against the appearance of frenzy and the danger of injury. He frequently complained to Dutton and me that his speechwriters were concentrating too much on the war and race issues instead of broadening his appeal to moderates. Yet he not only continued to use their material but extemporized along similar lines when he lacked it.

The meshing of JFK, RFK, and EMK staffs was never complete. The old politics and the new often differed. But reports of a bitter and continuing age- or ideology-based struggle among his aides have been considerably exaggerated. His decisions on whether to run and when to debate involved no such division; and the normal jealousies of a few rather than any large differences of principle caused the only dissension drawn to my attention.

The final difference between RFK's campaign for the nomination and JFK's was the difference in the primary states themselves. Unlike Jack, Bob entered the race too late to run in the New Hampshire, Wisconsin, and West Virginia preferential primaries, where JFK had won impressive victories (as he did in Maryland, which had later abolished its primary). JFK had bowed out for favorite sons in the District of Columbia, California, and South Dakota primaries, where Bob won impressive victories. Both ran and won in Indiana and Nebraska, but RFK scored major victories over his opponents in those conservative states, whereas JFK had been in effect unopposed. Both ran in Oregon, where by law all contenders were on the ballot, JFK facing opposition chiefly from favorite son Wayne Morse and winning, Bob facing opposition chiefly from Gene McCarthy and losing.

In each primary RFK's stiffest opposition in terms of numbers of Democratic voters seemed to come from well-off, well-educated, white suburbanite and upper-middle-class voters. They were sufficiently liberal to be registered Democrats and were attracted to McCarthy's quiet, anti-war progressivism. But they were not quite ready to welcome such revolutionary fervor on behalf of black ghetto dwellers and white slum dwellers or to view with approval such adulatory mobs on their television sets as those associated with RFK. These voters formed a broad base of

early McCarthy support in Oregon, and he steadily enlarged it.

RFK's Oregon campaign was too long taken for granted
because of a favorable poll, was too late in getting under
way, and was run too much in accordance with the old
political standards. He was hurt by his failure to debate
and chided for an impromptu swim in his undershorts.
Key political and labor leaders in Portland had special
reason to resent RFK ever since his probe of that city as
Rackets Committee Counsel more than ten years earlier.
National labor leaders who were out to "stop Kennedy"
in order to help Humphrey concentrated money and manpower in this contented, virtually minority-less, North-
western state. Opponents of RFK's stand on strict gun
controls heckled him from the audience. McCarthy
shrewdly analyzed the Oregon electorate and mood when
he told one crowd that surveys showed Kennedy strongest
"among the less intelligent and less educated . . . bear that
in mind as you go to the polls here on Tuesday."

The defeat in Oregon, the first in his generation of
Kennedys, was a terrible blow to Bob. His strategy had
depended on a sweep of the primaries, not to knock out
McCarthy, whom he believed never had a chance to be
nominated, but to confront the party leaders with a clear
mandate from rank-and-file Democrats. He was making
considerable headway in the small and medium-size states
outside the South and had hopes of doing well with those
McCarthy delegates who were primarily issue-oriented
once their candidate released them. But McCarthy's victory in Oregon clearly heightened the Minnesota Senator's
determination to stay in the race at least until the convention. Moreover, in addition to his own state of New
York, RFK needed a sizable majority of delegates from
Pennsylvania, Ohio, New Jersey, Michigan, and Illinois

in order to win a convention in which the South was nearly unanimous in its opposition to him. He had reason to believe that a sweep of the primaries would bring in Illinois under Richard Daley and other large blocs as well. But, once he lost Oregon, the combined power of Administration influence, big-city machines, and AFL-CIO forces, all of whom supported the war and feared his independence, made his prospects in the big states much more difficult.

After effectively but indecisively "debating" an ill-prepared and seemingly diffident McCarthy on national television on June 1, he returned to his San Francisco hotel suite in a contented but philosophical mood. "Well, we've done our best," he said to me while changing clothes for a fund-raising gala, "and if we keep on doing our best until the convention, whatever happens after that will be all right; even if we don't make it."

On the night of June 4 he was more exuberant. Had he lost California or even South Dakota, he would have promptly withdrawn from the race, remained silent on the other candidates, refused the Vice Presidential nomination, and promptly endorsed whatever ticket was chosen at the convention. But he did not lose. On June 4 he carried California, the largest urban state in the nation, and South Dakota, one of the most rural states and Humphrey's home territory. The possibilities for gains in the nonprimary states looked better. His campaign alone of all the contenders' had real momentum. He had won five out of six contested primaries; McCarthy had won only two (including Wisconsin, from which Johnson had withdrawn) out of nine; and Humphrey had won none.

"We can win this thing now," he told me. "I never should have lost in Oregon. . . ." He was too much of a realist to be confident of the nomination at that point.

We could not then know that Humphrey's strength would ebb during the summer as the war dragged on. But the Senator was hopeful that the McCarthy forces would move his way and free him to concentrate on the big states.

In the bathroom of his Los Angeles hotel suite we talked to Goodwin about an immediate approach to McCarthy through Lowenstein, Galbraith, and others. Bob talked with me about a planning session with all of his top campaign aides scheduled for the following day. We contemplated the intensive effort he would make in New York before the June 18 primary if McCarthy remained in the race, the visits to dozens of nonprimary states, a trip to Europe, then invitations to Eastern state delegates to visit with him at Hyannis Port before the convention. In Los Angeles, he was full of hope, energy, and enthusiasm, full of life, as he left his Ambassador Hotel suite to thank his followers in the ballroom. I stayed in his bedroom to watch it on TV until he returned. But he never returned.

PART TWO

Performance

To KNOW THE KENNEDY LEGACY fully, one must read the collected speeches and books of the two deceased brothers. To understand it fully, one must have viewed it in action. When I realize that most of today's college students were in elementary school when John Kennedy began his campaign for the Presidency and were not yet sophomores in high school when he was killed, I wonder whether any words from me or from anyone else can convey to them a feeling for those remarkable years.

This is particularly true of the much-discussed Kennedy style. There is a tendency now to separate the style from the substance—to regard the "Camelot" flavor of elegance and sophistication as a world of glittering parties, pageantry, and press repartee wholly apart from the grim world of international crises and the daily grind of political campaigning. But they were not separate. The Kennedys sought out intellectuals not merely to stimulate White House parties but to advise or work directly for the Administration. Laughter not only pervaded the

White House dining room but was heard in the Cabinet Room as well, in the President's crisis conferences as well as in his press conferences. His ability to view his own actions with detached amusement and to puncture the pomposity of others was an important factor in the success of our deliberations.

Good taste and finesse governed not only their selection of clothes and their refurbishing of the White House but also the Kennedys' visits with foreign leaders, appointments to Federal office, ceremonies for signing bills, and conduct of political campaigns. They shunned cheap fakery and hokum in their public policies and proposals as they did in entertainment and art. They inspired the same sense of zest and excitement in the decision-making process that they did in the Washington atmosphere. They insisted on the same high standards in national affairs as they did in cultural affairs, in advancing the interests of the nation as they did in advancing its civilization. Their programs for education, conservation, urban redevelopment, aid to the arts, and public television reflected the same concern for quality in the life of our society as the Kennedys displayed in the quality of their own social life.

My use of the plural in talking of President Kennedy's style refers not only to Jacqueline but also to Robert. For he enlivened the musty halls of Justice with his wit and his candor, his constant prodding and probing, his almost daily sessions with streams of young visitors to his cavernous office, and his informal, coatless travels through the halls often trailed by one or more children or dogs. The monthly "seminars" at his Hickory Hill home added to the intellectual ferment of the New Frontier.

If some of it seemed contrived, some of it was contrived —in the sense that John F. Kennedy deliberately set out with the aid of all the image-making media to make his

Presidency stand for excellence in all aspects of American life. He had been elected by an exceedingly narrow margin. He was taking on the bitterest of controversies. Any elevation in his personal standing in the country meant an increase in his political power with the Congress. Within three months of his Inauguration—despite clashing with the medical lobby, the real-estate lobby, the billboard lobby, the truckers, the publishers, the retailers, and others, including his own Church—he had become a nationally admired figure, his televised press conferences had become household institutions, and his religion, his youth, and his narrow margin of victory were no longer objects of suspicion.

The Presidency and campaigning were hard work. Contrary to the popular notion about politicians, the Kennedys did not prefer endless rounds of speechmaking and handshaking to quiet weekends with their families. The work and weariness were tolerable only if the work was fun, with some variety, some humor, and some interesting people mixed in with the pressures of the moment. JFK had more patience with pushy or boring people than RFK, but both of them preferred the company of those who, like them, possessed style—not only people with glamour, fame, or heroic achievements but also those who could think precisely, speak concisely, give and take humor, and talk about something other than themselves, their jobs, and their money. Thus one of their most important legacies even today is that group of men of unusual quality whom they attracted into politics and public service at all levels —some of whom they did not even know but many of whom will be influencing public affairs in this country for many years to come.

All this was carried on by Robert Kennedy after his brother's death. He, too, had that ever curious, ever critical mind that plumbed all sides of American society. He, too, developed widely imitated political techniques and up-lifted the spirit and quality of American politics and gov-ernment. He was an idealist like JFK but a moralist as well, with an even more rigid intolerance of imperfection and impropriety in public affairs. This earned him the enmity of the power brokers and manipulators in business, labor, and politics who were fearful of his reaching the White House. "He'll even have our tax returns checked!" one leading lobbyist was overheard wailing early in 1968.

He continued and developed John Kennedy's concern for the quality of American life, his concern for our na-tion's "poverty of purpose" as well as material poverty. A favorite RFK theme was the absurdity of measuring American life by the size of its Gross National Product. GNP, he said,

counts the destruction of redwoods . . . napalm and nuclear weapons . . . television programs which glorify violence to sell toys to our children. Yet the Gross National Product does not allow for the health of our children, the quality of their educa-tion, or the joy of their play. It does not include the beauty of our poetry . . . the integrity of our public officials . . . neither our wit nor our courage, neither our wisdom nor our learning, neither our compassion nor our devotion to country. It meas-ures everything, in short, except that which makes life worth-while; and it can tell us everything about America—except why we are proud to be Americans.

As this passage makes clear, Bob had excellent speech-writers—particularly the brilliant if dogmatic radical, Adam Walinsky, who was aided in the campaign by such other gifted men as Jeff Greenfield, Peter Edelman, Mil-ton Gwirtzman, and others. (I did not write speeches for RFK.) But even without speechwriters, RFK could inspire his listeners by virtue of an unusual gift of empathy—

an ability not only to sense how an audience felt but also to see the world through the eyes of those totally different from him, *not as he would see it were he they but actually how they saw it.* He urged his comfortable white audiences to put themselves in the migrant worker's shoes or in the black child's skin, to view the United States "through the eyes of the young slum dweller—the Negro, the Puerto Rican, the Mexican-American," not because most members of that audience would but because he could. He also liked his facts to pierce home: "Our citizens this year will spend three billion dollars on their dogs and less than two billion dollars for the War on Poverty. . . . Fourteen thousand American children are treated for rat bites every year."

It was natural that his campaign speaking style was like his older brother's, not only because they came from the same background and were so close in the 1960 campaign but also because Jack Kennedy was to Bob Kennedy the hero he hoped to emulate. He quoted him frequently, particularly in the first post-Dallas years. Moreover, it was good politics to use the same staccato phrasing, the mass of statistics, the self-deprecating humor (which came naturally to him anyway), the stabbing finger, and soaring idealism. But he did not have his brother's gift for understatement, for using apt quotations naturally, or for editing out the occasional romanticized exaggerations or oversimplifications of his speechwriters.

Bob had not always been an effective speaker. He began his 1964 Senate campaign by reading texts prepared by others in a dull, flat monotone. His extemporaneous talks tended at first to surround a problem with words, with elongated sentences that left a listener uncertain of their structure and ending. His voice was higher than JFK's and more nasal in quality, particularly when he spoke with passion and excitement. But that passion—often at its best in answer to hostile or skeptical questions or when exhorting young people to act—could rouse an audience in a way that polished syntax never could. His brief Presidential sprint contained, as I have mentioned, an unusual amount of meaty material for a political campaign which is always crowded with stump speeches to mass rallies or dry accounts of specific programs. Although it could not offer the kind of dramatic forum offered JFK in the 1960 campaign by the Houston ministers or the Nixon debates, Bob Kennedy's campaign nevertheless revealed that he, like John, had an inner eloquence which evolved more articulately and manifested itself more openly with each additional year of experience. He was particularly powerful when excited by an overflow youthful crowd. If anything, there was during the first weeks of that 1968 campaign a danger that Bob (and his writers) would be too carried away by the frenzy or the crowds, that he would lapse into unaccustomed demagoguery or make a mistake comparable to his 1966 statement, later regretted, which approved of America sending blood plasma to the Vietcong. Yet he demonstrated in conservative Indiana and Nebraska that he could adjust his style and emphasis without compromising his principles.

John Kennedy's reputation with the spoken word was heightened in the White House because it was the White House. No nationally televised Presidential address on the Cuban missile crisis, for example, could possibly have been superficial or boring, no matter who was President. Even a superficial or boring speech, when delivered by the President of the United States from his Oval Office, is invested with a certain majesty and dignity. Beauty in public speaking is partly in the ear of the listener. John

F. Kennedy, however, consistently rose to great occasions
with great speeches; and as his public standing and private
confidence increased, he was by 1963 less cautiously restrained in his public utterances and more boldly idealistic
and farsighted. His written speeches—rarely more than
twenty-five to thirty minutes in length—followed the formula he had developed with me over a period of years. They
consistently featured a numbered sequence of major points,
a preference for short sentences, and a penchant for occasional alliteration. Quotations from the Founding Fathers
reflected his deep sense of history. A combination of humor
and candor reflected his deep sense of confidence. When he
deviated from a released text, he stood by the original.
When he was unwilling or unable to release it in advance,
he secured an immediate transcript for the press. His major
speeches were tools of policy, not mere public relations.

His famous *"Ich bin ein Berliner"* speech illustrated
both the spontaneous eloquence an aroused audience
could arouse in him and the dangers of stump speeches
on foreign policy. He sounded as though he were rallying
opposition to the very kind of collaboration with the
Soviets he was then seeking on the Test Ban Treaty and
other matters. He recognized immediately that he had
been carried away and sought to correct in his next speech
the impression he had left. But the incident illustrated
JFK's dilemma: He was at his most forceful best when
discussing extemporaneously as an individual those world
issues about which he cared the most; but those were the
very issues which required him to speak as President from
a carefully prepared and distributed text.

What he could not do well, and would not do often,
was summon a nation-wide television audience to hear
him "educate" the public in "fireside chat" fashion from
prepared texts dealing with economic or philosophic ques-

tions about which he did not have the same passion. The combination of his crisis addresses and formal appearances before the Congress or UN provided, in his view, all the television lecture time he could hope to use effectively. He had no way of compelling people to listen, of compelling those who listened to agree, or of compelling those who agreed to act accordingly.

Bob Kennedy's public speeches invariably exhorted action—especially action by the young or for the young. It was with the young that both men enjoyed a special rapport. John Kennedy was the youngest man ever elected President. He surrounded himself with young aides and young advisers. He offered youth an opportunity to serve —in the Peace Corps, in Washington internships, in the ghetto. His programs stressed the next generation and his style as well as his age appealed to them and made them feel represented, that someone was listening to their gripes. His death created a vacuum that only RFK could fill.

"There was," Robert Kennedy told Japanese college students in 1964, "a special feeling between President Kennedy and young people. He was more than just the President of a country—he was the leader of young people everywhere." Because Bob Kennedy was even younger than Jack Kennedy, because he felt his brother's death obliged him to carry on this special leadership, because he had worked with so many young groups in civil rights and other efforts as Attorney General, because during his four years in elective politics the number of young activists grew even larger and their voices even louder than ever before, and because, most of all, his speeches voiced their own frustrations and aspirations, he became long before 1968 the one public figure most trusted and admired by American youth.

He did not cater to their every whim. He was aghast

at the use of drugs by college and high-school students unaware of the horrors of addiction. He spoke to me with fervor about the need for legislation to regulate cigarette advertising that appealed to children not yet old enough to decide wisely whether to start smoking.

While favoring a more equitable revision of the Selective Service System, he opposed draft deferments for college students as unfair and undemocratic compared with random selection. He reproved in shocked tones a student questioner suggesting that Selective Service was a boon to Negroes seeking escape from the ghettos. He refused to favor amnesty for those who had fled to Canada to evade the penalties of noncompliance. Those who invoked the doctrine of civil disobedience, he said, should be as prepared as Thoreau and Gandhi to accept the consequences, and those who faced up to serving in Vietnam, or in prison, or in the alternative-service program for concientious objectors should not now be told that others with the money or morality that enabled them to flee their country would pay no price for that action. As much as he disliked the element of compulsion, he was skeptical of the feasibility of an all-volunteer army attracting largely men denied access to the civilian labor market. "I don't want an all-black army fighting white middle-class wars," he told me. (The draft, it should be noted, was not a major issue during the John Kennedy Administration, despite some grumbling by mobilized reservists. It was the escalation of America's intervention in Vietnam, the enlarged Selective Service quotas it required, and the moral and political denunciation it received that focused attention on the draft by 1968.)

Nor was RFK willing to condone destructive student acts in the name of dissent. Harassed by militant hecklers shouting "fascist pig" during a campaign speech at a San Francisco college, he deplored audiences' interfering with the free-speech rights of those with whom they disagreed. Like his older brother, he believed dissent should be encouraged, not simply tolerated and protected. "But that dissent which consists simply of sporadic and dramatic acts . . . which seeks to demolish while lacking both the desire and direction for rebuilding . . . which casts aside the practical instruments of change . . . that kind of dissent is merely self-indulgence," he said, and can accomplish nothing.

He urged society and its leaders to listen to the young dissenters, to seek the causes of youth alienation, to recognize the absurdities and remedy the inequities that fed the youth rebellion. RFK knew the vacuum that young people felt when JFK was gone, when a miserable war they did not want and a massive society they did not respect slowly crushed their dreams and suffocated their individuality. "Bobby," said a college student after he was killed, "was our companion, though we never met him."

Bob regretted that some of those students who had previously adored him scorned him by the time he entered the Presidential race. But he did not desert his belief that their spirit was the world's hope. Despite warnings from his advisers that he was addressing too many college audiences and not enough voting audiences, he wanted his campaign in 1968 to help mobilize that spirit. He called upon students to act as well as to complain, to devote their summers to working in a ghetto or on an Indian reservation, to organize a campaign to feed the hungry.

This youthful vigor and vivid style characterized the Kennedys' actions as well as their words. Both were men of action, uninterested in theories they could not apply, impatient with those who wasted time and words, and intent on finding specific solutions instead of vague generalities. Although Bob had more executive talent, as will be discussed later, neither brother was as enthusiastic about the details of administration as he was about policymaking. Both excelled at making concrete decisions on concrete problems. The word frequently applied to the Kennedy Administration was "pragmatic." But pragmatic, in their case, meant more than an absence of ideological rigidity or sweeping theoretical criteria and more than an emphasis on problem-solving. It also meant a willingness to innovate and experiment, a government that intended to get things done because its leaders were concerned and compassionate men.

JFK's style of administration seemed dangerously loose to outsiders (and some insiders), but it was not as informal or helter-skelter as some believed. "My experience in government," he said, "is that when everything is beautifully coordinated, not much is going on." While he was criticized for taking too many problems under his own wing at the earliest stages, he in fact did so only on major decisions—primarily in foreign policy—when he knew any other course would limit his choices prematurely. He appeared to terminate meetings without making hard decisions, but in fact he based his decisions on a series of meetings, consultations, and staff reviews, making them sometimes in private and never before they had to be made. Because he insisted on cross-examining the advocates of both sides of a question, because he insisted on retaining until the final moment as many options as possible, and because he insisted on hearing divergent, unofficial, and inexpert points of view, some thought he was indecisive when he was in fact facilitating better decisions. Because he personally controlled from his White House office all crisis operations after the Bay of Pigs, because he used White House aides in wide-ranging assignments traditionally reserved for departmental representatives, and because he seemed inordinately accessible to so many subordinates, some thought he was abusing the authority of his office when he was in fact protecting it.

His desire for conciseness did not mean hasty decisions or an inadequate consideration of the alternatives but, on the contrary, made possible sufficient time for them. He fed in his own suggestions to the early stages of the decision-making process without any insistence that they outrank all other suggestions before the final decision was made. He had an unusual ability to compartmentalize his mind and move rapidly from major to minor to public to personal questions without either confusing his positions, ignoring any links between them, or becoming preoccupied with one to the exclusion of others. On the same morning that he had convened his top advisers in our first meeting on the Cuban missile crisis, for example, he had also met with his Panel on Mental Retardation, proclaimed storm-ravaged portions of Oregon eligible for disaster assistance, and met with astronaut Walter Schirra and his family.

Like RFK, he should have made more time available for meditation and long-range planning but would not have particularly enjoyed it. He delegated extensive authority to those in whom he had absolute confidence but, like RFK, needed more men in whom he had absolute confidence. It is true that the White House under Kennedy "interfered" with Executive departments, as charged, for he viewed that his responsibility. It is also true that he could have organized his time better, but not without interfering with his flexible mode of operation. One fact should always be borne in mind: confronted during his first eight months in the White House not only with a national recession but also with a series of urgent international crises—involving the Congo, Laos, the Bay of Pigs, Berlin, nuclear testing, the United Nations, the Dominican Republic, Vietnam, the race in space, and other critical problems—John Kennedy found himself in 1961, far more than Eisenhower in 1953 or Nixon in 1969, launched pell-mell into orbit before he had time fully to chart his course or even master the controls. By the time of his first major personnel reshuffle on Thanksgiving weekend of that year, he was getting his hands on the right levers.

Bob Kennedy excelled at organization and implementation. As Attorney General, he showed real executive talent. Whether he was reopening public schools in Prince Edward County, Virginia, or ransoming Bay of Pigs captives from Castro's prisons, he had a gift for the imaginative and tireless use of whatever funds, laws, and other resources could be suggested by the highly talented, dedicated, and loyal team he had assembled. He was a doer, a practitioner of power for public purpose, a believer in what he termed, on the last night of his life, "the politics of reality." For all his moral standards, he was not above politics in any sense, including all the compromises and accommodations that had to be made. For politics was respected by both brothers as the means by which the nation could get things done. They preferred, where necessary, working with hard-nosed politicians who could reach decisions and abide by them to engaging in endless discussions with liberal amateurs too critical of each other and everyone else to be effective.

Both men had a tendency to personalize issues in terms of those who were involved in them. JFK once said that political personalities more than programs were discussed by his father at that celebrated family dining table; and personalities continued to fascinate both brothers, not only in politics but in all fields. Their meetings with unemployed miners in Appalachia or black sharecroppers in Mississippi increased their interest and understanding of those problems. When young blacks whom they had personally met were beaten in the midst of protests, their sympathy for the civil-rights movement increased. When a Senator such as George Smathers or Tom Dodd presented them with a proposal, they were inclined to be more questioning of its merits because they could not always respect the motives of its author. Their enthusiasm for space exploration was heightened by their admiring friendship with John Glenn and other astronauts. Their hostility to the steel price increase was heightened by a lack of rapport with Roger Blough.

Both men applied this same personalization to foreign affairs. Because John Kennedy personally liked Harold Macmillan, felt befriended by him, and understood his domestic political problems after the collapse of the Skybolt missile program, he agreed to Polaris missiles for Britain in conjunction with the ill-fated MLF (multilateral force). Partly because both Kennedys came to know and admire individual heroes among those Cuban exiles whom they ransomed from captivity after the Bay of Pigs, their attitude toward Castro remained adamant. Because Bob Kennedy admired Willy Brandt's "firm will [and] tenacious spirit," he believed more deeply in the preservation of West Berlin.

John Kennedy had a way with foreign leaders. He could teach Chancellor Ludwig Erhard to wave at the crowds in West Germany, discuss the Irish revolution with President Eamon De Valera, and appreciate Indonesian President Sukarno's interest in semipornographic art. He shook Pope Paul's hand instead of kneeling to kiss his ring and learned to embrace Latin American heads of state with gusto. He quoted Mao Tse-tung to Nikita Khrushchev, stopped in the middle of the Cuban missile crisis to keep a long-standing appointment with Uganda's Prime Minister Milton Obote, and woke his daughter, Caroline, to introduce her to King Saud. He could respect France's Charles de Gaulle without agreeing with him and agree with Canada's John Diefenbaker without respecting him. When he admired the unusual ornate watch of President Lopez Mateos of Mexico, Lopez insisted that he take it, in accordance with Mexican custom. But a minute later, when Jacqueline appeared in a stunning gown and Lopez expressed his admiration, JFK said, "You had better take back your watch."

Above all, he understood, as in the Macmillan case, that, whatever their system or tenure, these were all politicians who had to consider their own domestic political problems. He studied in advance of each meeting the internal pressures each man faced, the economic and geographic differences that made his interests different from our own, and reports on their personalities and personal traits.

Bob Kennedy's meetings abroad as envoy extraordinary were not so uniformly smooth. He clashed with Cambodia's Prince Sihanouk and heatedly with Indonesia's Sukarno, for example, to say nothing of a stuffy American Ambassador to Poland who resented RFK's barnstorming appearances. Nevertheless, his trips were generally great successes. Both brothers were effective with foreign audiences, including Bob's encounters with radical, near-riotous student groups. The warmth of JFK's reception throughout West Germany provided him, he later said, with some "political capital" that he could draw on in negotiating the Nuclear Test Ban Treaty over Bonn's misgivings. RFK's eloquent lecture tour of the universities of South Africa, a liberal leader of that country later told me, "did more than anything else in the lifetime of these English-speaking students [and others battling apartheid] to give them hope . . . just to know that someone on the outside cared."

Prior to my service in the White House, I had regarded Presidential travel abroad as largely pageantry. After all, complete information should be available to the President without his leaving the White House. But my travels abroad with President Kennedy, and my travels since leaving the government, have convinced me otherwise. The special meaning of West Berlin, the isolation of Isreal, the struggle for progress in the Congo, the mixture of poverty and hope in Costa Rica—these are all better understood when they are seen and felt. Both Kennedys had this view. Both acquired new insights and developed new approaches to the problems of the nations they visited. Both listened more than they talked.

A striking example was RFK's trip through Latin America late in 1965. President Kennedy had given special priority to Latin America promptly after his Inauguration, launching only six weeks later the Alliance for Progress, a mammoth ten-year plan for economic progress and social justice within a framework of democratic institutions. It was revolutionary in spirit and concept; and, said JFK, aiming his remarks primarily at that two per cent of Latin Americans who controlled more than fifty per cent of its wealth and political institutions, "those who make peaceful revolution impossible will make violent revolution inevitable." He stressed the need for self-help and self-reform —tax reform, land reform, education reform, political reform—the need to end social injustice and inequality as well as poverty and illiteracy, and the need to push ahead with economic development and diversification. Despite setbacks, failures, and discouragement, it was one of his most important long-range initiatives. It was by far the brightest spot in his foreign-aid program, which made ever less headway in its struggles with increasing populations and decreasing living standards in the developing countries and with a recalcitrant Congress and wooden bureaucracy here at home.

Two years after his brother's death, RFK found the *Alianza* stalled and the United States disliked. The middle class had progressed but not the poor. A new educated elite had joined the hereditary elite. Ninety per cent of the land was controlled by less than ten per cent of the landholders. Up to eighty per cent of the people in some areas could not read or write. Poverty and disease still stalked most of the continent. The United States, he was told everywhere, had intervened with its forces in the Dominican Republic to crush a popular democracy. Most students were certain that the giant corporations of the United States wanted only to bleed Latin America dry and that Wall Street controlled Latin American economies while the Pentagon controlled their armies, overthrowing any governments that disobeyed Washington.

It was a turbulent trip. The Senator was shouted down and pelted with garbage by leftist students and cold-shouldered by military governments. He traveled by dugout canoe in remote parts of the hinterland. As always, he talked with Peace Corps volunteers as well as ambassadors, with heads of state and *campesinos,* workers and intellectuals. He urged youngsters to stay in school. He urged affluent students to devote their energies to helping those countrymen who needed it most. He met villagers who had never seen anyone from their own central government. One said he must be their king. Many spoke tearfully of his brother.

When he returned he made extensive, scholarly reports on his findings to the Senate and State Department. He urged more U.S. assistance to Latin American programs to limit the rising birth rate, redistribute land, and assure educational and economic development. Then he convened a meeting of New York business executives with Latin American interests. Their initial suspicion gave way to admiration, if not always agreement, as he warned them of the revolution that was coming if American business and government did not work together to improve our relations with the many as well as the few throughout Latin America.

But RFK was frustrated. The State Department resented his suggestion that the Dominican intervention might have awaited more reliable information from sources other than our embassy, more multilateral action by the OAS, and a better rationale than the need to protect Americans. The President ignored his charge that the United States was not willing to break off relations with a Latin American military junta that overthrew a democratically elected regime but was willing if American oil fields were seized. The Senate rejected his proposed increases in Alliance for Progress funds. And a few months later at a private dinner meeting I attended, a business leader declared, "What we need to preach in Latin America to these young radicals is an acceptance of the free-enterprise system and a respect for property rights. And we can't do it if Bobby Kennedy is going down there and upsetting everything we've been saying."

None of this deterred RFK. Upon his return from South Africa in 1966, he asked both the State Department and American corporations with major investments in that country to re-examine the extent to which they were contributing to the maintenance of the apartheid system or to the easing of the black citizens' lot. He had little to show for that either; but he remained too much a man of action to be content with simply speaking on the Senate floor or introducing meaningless resolutions.

He was well aware of the conservative viewpoint on foreign affairs that concentrated on maintaining the *status quo,* the cold war, and the domination of foreign resources and populations by American enterprise. He had heard more of those views than any other during his youth and had expressed some of them himself. Although in an address to the Americans for Democratic Action late in 1967 he criticized what he termed "a foreign policy . . . built on the rhetoric of anti-Communism" and "imprisoned in that rhetoric," he had engaged in such rhetoric himself, even as late as 1962 in an address to the American Legion.

The difference between the two speeches was not the difference between the ADA and the American Legion. Bob Kennedy's views had changed. As a United States Senator, he voted against the very kind of amendment to cut off aid to nations shipping goods to the Communists that he had urged in his brief service with Joe McCarthy. His reflections on the 1962 Cuban missile crisis, written in 1967 and published posthumously in 1968 under the title *Thirteen Days,* indicate even stronger reservations about the military mind and method than either brother had felt at the time of the crisis itself. Their reservations then, however, had been stronger than three years earlier.

Part of the evolution in Bob's thinking on foreign policy had resulted from an evolution in his thinking on domestic policy. As his concern for the black and the poor in our own country grew, as he urged more Federal funds for jobs, housing, health clinics, schools, and the War on Poverty, he recognized more clearly the enormous drain on the budget represented by military spending in general and the Vietnam war in particular. It would be difficult enough in peacetime to persuade Congress to commit the resources necessary to meet our domestic needs; but a series of Vietnams, another round in the strategic arms race, a policy that unnecessarily made too many world problems our problems would clearly deter Congress from acting on the priority tasks this country faced. For the same reason he urged cuts in the space effort he had proudly boasted of only a few years earlier.

His thinking was influenced also by his exposure to the penetrating questions of hostile students around the world. Attempting to defend and explain American foreign policy made him realize that "blanket moral statements cannot determine all strategic judgments." It was foolish, for example, to try telling African students that our Vietnam intervention was justified by our commitment to "self-determination" when we were not supporting with equal vigor independence for Angola and Mozambique. "It is less our intention than our *pretension*," he said, "which is objectionable." He began to see, too, how American moves in Asia and elsewhere could logically if inaccurately be interpreted in Moscow and Peking as preparation for American aggression, encirclement, or domination.

Just as he could see the world through the eyes of a young black in an American ghetto, so he learned to see through the eyes of the young Latin American or Asian who resented American affluence instead of admiring American progress, who equated this country not with democracy and diversity but with a new form of imperialism. President Kennedy said in 1961 that it was a mistake to credit the Communists with every revolution in the world. To this Bob added his own judgment that it was equally mistaken to assume that all revolutions were harmful to the interests of the United States, even all revolutions exploited by the Communists. The forces of change in the world, the conditions of chaos in the world, he reasoned, made inevitable a number of revolutions and reversals which this nation simply could not and sometimes should not prevent or suppress.

It was in this context that he spoke out, as others had earlier but with less prominence, against the concept of the United States as "world policeman." The subsequent sharing of that sentiment by Nixon, Rusk, and others led him to hope that this country might examine its international commitments with more care. He was not for a return to isolationism or his father's concept of a Fortress America. He was not for unilateral disarmament or for capitulation in our competition with the Soviets. His own humanitarian instincts for the desire of others to be free reinforced his recognition that the United States needed both friends and allies. He recognized, too, that our allies would necessarily include some regimes which did not share his devotion to political democracy, social justice, and economic opportunity.

We need not, however, give such regimes military support, said the Senator. "It makes an enormous difference when the United States withholds its favor from corrupt, autocratic, aggressive regimes. It makes an even bigger difference when the United States favors regimes that are honest and democratic, and imbued with social purpose. . . ." He knew that the United States, contrary to its critics, had in fact backed governments not wedded to the *status quo*. Chile, Venezuela, Colombia, Mexico, and Costa Rica were outstanding examples. He also knew that this choice was not always easy to implement, as JFK had discovered in Latin America in particular. Refusing to recognize junta governments rarely solved anything. Excluding them from *Alianza* aid programs might

only destroy all hope for their citizens. Forcing land reform and political equality on other nations in the name
of self-determination was a contradiction in terms. If with-
holding our aid had enabled Castro agents to overthrow
a Latin American government of which we disapproved,
other hemisphere leaders might well have deserted the
Alianza altogether to ally themselves with that seemingly
irreversible wave of Communist power.

In short, each case had to be weighed separately. But
after JFK's death, it seemed to RFK that this nation was
edging toward a blanket approach to Latin America and
other developing regions—an approach under which we
backed the *status quo,* opposed all far-reaching reforms and
revolutionary aspirations, and used less and less of our
influence to encourage land redistribution, education and
free speech.

The United States, he realized, could not abandon all
forms of competition with the Soviet Union for power and
position in the world. But neither could we prevent other
peoples from choosing their own system. JFK was willing
to use overt and covert means to prevent a new Guyana
from going Communist, but he was also willing, as he told
Khrushchev, to live with a Communist regime in Guyana
if its electorate so decided. For "democratic ideas," as
RFK said, "are almost incapable of export." That is why
the best hope for America and mankind, he said, was his
brother's goal of "a world made safe for diversity"—with
each nation "developing, according to its own traditions
and its own genius, each solving its economic and political
problems in its own manner, and all bound together by a
respect for the rights of others. . . ."

Thus Bob Kennedy's thinking on foreign policy evolved
swiftly over the last seven years of his life, building during the last four from the level to which JFK had evolved at

the time of his trip to Dallas. John Kennedy's own evolution in this area had been remarkable. He, too, had begun with strongly orthodox views of America's role in the world. As a young Congressman, he had voiced belief in military solutions, denounced the "betrayal" at Yalta, sought cuts in foreign trade and aid, and blamed the Truman Administration for the Communists' gaining control of China. But in the decade or more that had passed since those initial foreign-policy speeches as a Representative, both he and the world had evolved radically. Despite the continued bipolarity of destructive and political power, the globe was no longer neatly divisible into three camps, or characterized simply by great powers and colonies, or amenable to much influence from any one source. Once he was inside the White House looking out, required to provide solutions instead of suggestions, that world looked even more complex. In devoting his entire Inaugural Address to foreign policy, he spoke in many overlapping and conflicting roles: as the champion of the Free World and a seeker of one world, as a believer in the United Nations and a leader of NATO, SEATO, and the OAS. The United States, he knew, could not achieve its goals relying only on the force of its example, although that needed strengthening, or only on the force of its arms, although they needed strengthening, or only on the United Nations, which also needed strengthening. There was no single or certain answer.

John Kennedy, knowing this, undertook to make certain that the American people knew it. One of his major foreign-policy contributions was to take off the shackles of anti-Communist sloganeering which had handcuffed the flexibility of American diplomacy since the days of Dulles and to some extent Acheson. The United States had never been willing to go to war to "roll back" the

Iron Curtain or to "unleash" Chiang Kai-shek against the mainland of China, to cite two well-known examples. We were not even prepared to insist upon such a posture in our negotiations or diplomatic pressure plays. But by repeatedly proclaiming such goals, we made it impossible for either allies or adversaries truly to know our policy. The repetition of slogans also obscured our own perception of major changes in the world, such as the Sino-Soviet split. By substituting unusual candor for the usual cant, Kennedy closed the disparity between our incantations and our intentions and at the same time made those less belligerent and grandiose intentions acceptable to all but the extreme right wing.

From his first week in the White House he was skeptical about military men, military solutions, and military spending. From his first Defense budget onward he cut out a host of misbegotten plans—including a nuclear-powered aircraft that could not fly, a jet-powered flying boat that always crashed, a space plane, an obsolete missile system, and others. He told Congress that he would not spend its appropriation for the B-70 aircraft even if it so ordered. He resisted Pentagon pressure for an antiballistic missile system (ABM) because he knew it could not offer meaningful protection.

The frailties of military power and wisdom were made quickly and unmistakably clear to him in humiliating fashion at the Bay of Pigs. The story of that sadly mistaken operation, how it came about and how President Kennedy was misled into it, has been previously told. It was not, as some have suggested, a moral failure on his part. "Permitting a group of freedom-loving exiles to return to their homeland and recapture it from a foreign-controlled despot without involving the United States," as some of its defenders termed it, would have been no more immoral than similar plans to help free Ireland or others in the past. That it was in fact a very different kind of operation taught Kennedy not that his moral principles were lacking in authorizing that venture but that his critical powers had been. He never revealed the deficiencies in judgment and operation on the part of the CIA and Joint Chiefs which were uncovered by the specially commissioned study that followed under RFK's and Maxwell Taylor's leadership. Consistent with his concept of Presidential power and responsibility, he assumed full blame for the fiasco. This alone astounded those Foreign Service and Civil Service career officials who had long grown accustomed to seeing the onus placed elsewhere. He did not overreact. His decisions on Southeast Asia, which some attribute to post-Bay of Pigs trauma, were distinct in thought and timing. To a remarkable degree he retained his self-confidence and balance. He looked not for scapegoats, not for compensating opportunities to prove his toughness or his skill, but for better ways of making decisions and for better decisions to make.

JFK realized that he had been too deferential to Allen Dulles, Lyman Lemnitzer, and the other renowned military and intelligence chiefs he had inherited from Eisenhower. He realized, too, that a more critical examination of their premises and promises would have called a halt to the plan much earlier. Had he been less influenced by the specialists, he must have mused, and more open to the views of two generalists—Fulbright and Schlesinger, who were not professional soldiers but had broad judgment and experience—he might never have been persuaded by the CIA and the military to let this operation go ahead. He had not fully known until he read the RFK–Taylor post-mortem that impressive official documents from these agencies could contain so many unproven assumptions and biased conclusions. In politics he had never placed his full trust in the experts, having learned that his own intelligent amateurs provided a logical, common-sense balance. After the Bay of Pigs he moved similarly to check specialists with generalists in national-security matters. He increased the role of his brother and his White House and budget aides. He brought Maxwell Taylor back to Washington to provide an experienced supervisory eye over military and intelligence activities. And he encouraged from Bundy, RFK, and me a more forceful role in challenging new proposals and old assumptions.

In the weeks that followed, Bob Kennedy, hurt by the setback to his brother, conferred with us at length on ways to prevent similar blunders. In time changes were made in the personnel of the Joint Chiefs, the CIA, the State Department, and the White House. Changes were made in the procedures preceding decisions to assure a more careful and comprehensive examination of the alternatives and the consequences. Changes were made in our Latin American policy to promote a healthier Alliance for Progress as the best means of isolating the Castro virus. But the most important changes were in John Kennedy's own thinking. The Bay of Pigs plan had resembled an intricate offensive play in football chalked out on the blackboard with little regard as to how the defensive team would respond. Kennedy, realizing too late that such planning ignores the fact that defensive players do not stand and watch in open-mouthed amazement and admiration, thereafter calculated for each foreign-policy move what each other nation's reaction would be, how we would then respond to their reaction, and how they would reply to that.

He had been assured before the Bay of Pigs that the scheme could not really fail, inasmuch as a contingency plan for the men to escape into the mountains guaranteed no real cost or loss to the United States. That assurance was groundless; and he thereafter calculated more carefully the consequences of failure, the price that would have to be paid in bloodshed, humiliation, or other coinage if once again premises proved wrong and plans aborted. Although he was irritated by those Latin American governments which had urged intervention against Castro because they feared the Cuban leader and then denounced the attempt (after it failed) also because they feared him, President Kennedy recognized more clearly than ever that America's massive military superiority did not guarantee her success, much less respect, around the world.

These were all valuable lessons. "Thank God the Bay of Pigs happened when it did," he said to me later, "otherwise we'd be in Laos by now—and that would be a hundred times worse." There had been strong pressures for American military intervention in Laos. Eisenhower told him the day before the Inauguration, "You might have to go in there and fight it out." But by the time these pressures reached their peak, in May 1961, John Kennedy had become more skeptical of military advice and military solutions. His request for separate appraisals of the prospects for our military intervention in Laos from each of the Joint Chiefs produced inconsistent papers full of unanswered questions—including specifically his own questions about the reactions of others and the consequences of failure.

No one could assure him that serious allied support would be forthcoming in Laos or that an overwhelming Chinese response would not be. The Chiefs' basic premise was simply for America to go all out or get out. Kennedy found both choices unacceptable. Finally, the President— who as a young Congressman had condemned the Truman

Administration for threatening to discontinue aid to Chiang Kai-shek unless he accepted a coalition government with Mao Tse-tung—opted for a neutralist coalition regime in Laos. It was a remedy that failed in practice. Yet it succeeded in helping to achieve his basic aim of avoiding both a Communist take-over of the country and a major war to prevent such a take-over.

The Central Intelligence Agency's deep involvement in both the Cuban and Laotian problems caused him to keep a closer check on that agency's activities. So long as the Soviet Union and the United States were competing among men and nations in many parts of the globe, the President saw no reason why helpful covert and unconventional means could not be used by our side as well as theirs. But he wanted to make certain that such means were at all times subject to Presidential control and kept consistent with his own foreign policy.

Except for a transfer to the Pentagon of responsibility for all operations large enough to be considered paramilitary, studies of the various CIA functions after the Bay of Pigs did not result in the kind of major reorganizational changes JFK and RFK had first contemplated. But they did result in a closer Presidential eye on all CIA activities through Taylor, Bundy, and a revitalized Intelligence Advisory Board. The President still felt hampered by an inability to know personally the extent of CIA operations in countries not on his crisis agenda. Time permitted him to know the details of such activities only in those nations whose problems were on his desk. But Bundy's office referred questionable practices to him and he often reversed the agency's plans.

CIA specialists were regarded by the President as simply that. He had learned to become wary of accepting the broad policy judgments of specialists of the military,

diplomatic, scientific, or any other variety. He was a faithful reader of the daily flow of estimates he received on
the world scene from the intelligence community; but he
noted that it varied in quality. Satellite photographs of
troop maneuvers, for example, were not surprisingly
more meaningful than forecasts of political and economic
developments, which to him seemed little different from
the information available to any careful reader of *The
New York Times*. For official information not covered by
the daily intelligence booklet, he used his press-conference
preparations to stimulate a steady stream of reports and
memoranda. With all agencies he refused to rely solely
on governmental sources and channels. Secret cables and
official firsthand observations, as he learned too late in
Vietnam, were often less objective and factual than the
published reports of those newsmen whose editors would
permit no equivocation, irrelevancies, or undocumented
opinions.

His early experiences in Laos and the Bay of Pigs also
confirmed the convictions he had expressed in the 1960
campaign regarding the futility of relying solely on our
mammoth powers of nuclear retaliation. War could never
be deterred by this nation's threatening in advance to use
nuclear devastation in response to any act of aggression,
no matter how small or local it might be and no matter how
capable the Soviet Union was of paralyzing us in return.
That was simply an invitation to be nibbled to death.
Thus he increased the flexibility and mobility of American
forces to discourage any attack.

Bob Kennedy's special interests in this effort lay in the
area of counterinsurgency. Reading, as did his brother, the
works of Che Guevara and Mao Tse-tung, he recognized the
folly of attempting to deal with guerrillas, terrorists, subversives, and wars of liberation—which posed the chief threat

to the peace in the 1960s—through reliance on nuclear weapons or even massed armies. Eisenhower had failed in Southeast Asia, the Kennedys felt, because he thought conventional forces could stop unconventional attacks. Bob became the President's chief arm-twister for obtaining more support for the Army's Special Forces. That effort at least reflected the Kennedys' recognition that the threat in Laos, Vietnam, and elsewhere was more political than military. But the program was not a success. The unofficial Cabinet-level counterinsurgency committee that Bob sparked was too military-minded and repeatedly wrong in its assessments.

The Kennedy Administration initiated the largest and fastest military build-up in the nation's peacetime history —not only counterinsurgency forces but also nuclear forces and conventional ground and naval forces. In hindsight, much of that build-up appears now to have been unnecessary; and the questions asked by JFK of his Pentagon budget-makers in the fall of 1963 indicated his growing awareness of this fact.

Fortunately, he increased at the same time our "unarmed forces"—the Peace Corps, Food for Peace, the new Disarmament Agency, and a variety of efforts in aid, trade, space, overseas information, and the United Nations. All these measures had their effect in helping convince other peoples that the United States intended to meet its responsibilities in the world community and to meet them with peaceful means if possible. But these were all minor advances for the cause of a peaceful world, compared to John Kennedy's handling of the Cuban missile crisis.

The Berlin crisis of 1961, to be sure, had been a tough test of Kennedy's mettle. Faced with a dangerous deadline which would have required him to abandon a commitment vital to our interests, confronted with a threatened squeeze too subtle for nuclear response but too serious to ignore, he found that he had inherited a "Berlin Contingency Plan" and a military capability in that area which gave him a choice of either nuclear holocaust or abject humiliation. He found as well that his allies and advisers were divided. Some said, in effect: Refuse to talk and fight if pressed. Others said, in effect: Refuse to fight and yield if pressed. Still others said, in effect: Refuse to fight or talk or yield, but think of something. Kennedy, making clear what we would and would not talk and fight about, shrewdly engaged Khrushchev in a long correspondence and other diplomatic exchanges on the issue, meanwhile building the deterrent power of our conventional forces (and mistakenly inspiring a national civil defense craze) and permitting the deadline to pass without notice.

Soviet long-range missiles in Cuba, however, represented a sudden, immediate and more dangerous and secretive change in the balance of power, in clear contradiction of all U.S. commitments and Soviet pledges. It was a move which required a response from the United States, not for reasons of prestige or image but for reasons of national security in the broadest sense. JFK's obligation as President in October 1962 was to find some way of effecting a removal of those nuclear weapons without either precipitating mankind's final war or trading away anyone's security. It was in a very real sense the world's first armed confrontation between two nuclear superpowers.

Ever since the successful resolution of that crisis, I have noted among many political and military figures a Cuban-missile-crisis syndrome, which calls for a repetition in some other conflict of "Jack Kennedy's tough stand of October 1962 when he told the Russians with their missiles either to pull out or look out!" Some observers even attributed

Lyndon Johnson's decision to escalate in Vietnam to a conviction that America's military superiority could bring him a "victory" comparable to JFK's. That badly misreads what actually happened. Kennedy himself took pains to point out to Adenauer and others that the Cuban outcome was not a "victory," that it was not achieved solely through military might, and that what success we had in this instance —with the Soviets at a geographic and world-opinion disadvantage—could not be counted on in instances, such as Berlin, which more directly affected Soviet security.

It is true that American military force—namely, a barrier of naval vessels around Cuba—before its effectiveness could be rendered less meaningful by the delivery of all missiles to the island, interposed itself against a potential Soviet force on its way to Cuba. It is true that our superiority in deliverable nuclear power, as well as our superiority in naval power, undoubtedly made the Soviets more cautious than they might otherwise have been about physically challenging our naval quarantine or retaliating with a blockade of West Berlin. It is also true that JFK's address sternly warned that any nuclear missile launched from Cuba against any nation in the Western Hemisphere would be regarded as a Soviet attack on the United States "requiring a full retaliatory response upon the Soviet Union." But these facts should not be taken out of context.

Kennedy in fact relied not on force and threats alone but on a carefully balanced and precisely measured combination of defense, diplomacy, and dialogue. He instituted the naval quarantine without waiting for diplomatic efforts, because once such efforts failed (and he was convinced they would fail), it would be too late to prevent completion of the missiles or get them out without more belligerent and dangerous measures. He chose the quaran-

tine in preference to an air attack because it was a measured, limited step, it offered the Russians both room to
maneuver and a peaceful way out, and it did not make
armed conflict inevitable. He deliberately called it a
"quarantine" rather than a "blockade," which is an act
of war. He took no action that would risk civilian lives.
He authorized no surprise attacks and no needless risk
of American lives. He posed the issue as one between
two powers restrained by mutual deterrence, instead of
making the unpredictable Castro his opposite number.

Despite his anger at being deceived and his awareness
that one misstep meant disaster, he remained cool at all
times. He refused to issue any ultimatum, to close any
doors, or to insist upon any deadlines, noting only that
continued work on the missile sites would "justify" (not
necessarily insure) further U.S. action. He made clear
to the Soviets both in writing and through his brother
that the United States was prepared to talk about peace
and disarmament generally and about the presence of
our missiles in Turkey specifically, once the Soviet provocation to peace had been withdrawn. He placed the dispute before the United Nations and corresponded with
Khrushchev about it almost daily. He was careful to obtain sanction for the quarantine under international law,
procuring unanimous authorization from the members
of a recognized regional defense group, the Organization
of American States (OAS), obtaining its members' multilateral participation, and invoking the self-defense provisions of the UN charter.

Even as Soviet ships and work on the missile sites proceeded, he avoided a confrontation that might force the
Soviets to attack. Even after an American plane was shot
down, he withheld retaliation in the hopes of an early
settlement. On the final crucial Saturday night before the

missiles were withdrawn, he adjourned our "Ex Comm" meeting as the hawks began to dominate the discussion and to urge an immediate air strike. He achieved a resolution that was in effect negotiated by mail, one that treated both powers as equals and restored the *status quo ante* instead of destroying Castro. Then he refused to crow or claim victory. He was at each step firm but generous to his adversaries and candid with his major allies, with the American public, and with the Congressional leaders, although he gave advance information to no one and sought advance approval from no one.

While oversimplified comparisons of drastically different situations are dangerous, it is interesting to take each of the above standards and apply it to this nation's role in Vietnam. My own view is that we might have avoided the disastrous escalation of that war had Presidents Kennedy and Johnson followed these same standards. I also think it highly possible that, had each of these standards not been followed in the Cuban missile crisis, this planet might now be in ashes. The medium-range missile sites under rapid construction in Cuba would all have been operational within a few days, according to the intelligence estimates, and some may already have been prepared to respond to any American attack by firing their deadly salvos upon the southeastern United States.

Some ask: What if Khrushchev had not backed down? Others say: Why did we settle for so little? The real question is: Where would we be if JFK had not pursued the above course and accepted Khrushchev's offer in a way that avoided the need for anyone to back down? It was indeed eyeball-to-eyeball, and fortunately both men blinked. Dean Acheson is right in crediting Kennedy with considerable good luck on this awesome occasion; but there was considerable good judgment as well as luck involved in the President's rejection of alternative recommendations, including the recommendation for bombing the missile sites which came from Acheson himself. (In short, among the ways in which JFK was lucky was in not taking Dean Acheson's advice!)

While some have since accused him of taking action to influence the Congressional elections, JFK at the time was convinced his course would hurt his party in the elections. It seemed clear on that fateful Saturday afternoon, October 20, when he made his decision for the quarantine, that an air strike would be a swifter and more popular means of removing the missiles before Election Day, and that a quarantine would encourage a prolonged UN debate and Republican charges of weakness in the face of peril. Yet he never contemplated changing that course for political reasons. Others have since accused him of overreacting for reasons of personal or national prestige to a move that did not really alter the strategic balance of power or pose an actual threat to our own security. But Kennedy recognized that appearances and reality often merge in world affairs; and if all Latin America had thought that the U.S. had passively permitted what was apparently a new threat to their existence, and if all our Western allies had thought that we would not respond to a sudden, secret deployment of missiles in our own hemisphere, then a whole wave of reactions contrary to our interests and security might well have followed.

Throughout this period the role of Robert Kennedy was unusually important. The President confided to me his concern that his Secretary of State in particular had been disappointingly irresolute during the few days preceding JFK's final formulation of the quarantine policy and too fatigued after guiding a brilliant execution of that policy during the following few days; that the Joint

Chiefs of Staff had been dangerously inflexible in their insistence on an all-out military attack as the only course the Soviets would understand; and that sooner or later everyone involved would reflect what both Macmillan and McNamara termed the period of most intense strain they had ever experienced.

But brother Bob displayed not the "emotional dialectics" suggested by some but hardheaded and cool judgment. He was a leader without designation when our little "Executive Committee" group—Rusk, McNamara, Dillon, Bundy, Ball, Taylor, McCone, and a half-dozen others, including me—met with the President. He used his full powers of presence and persistence to extract specific suggestions and objections instead of generalities and to produce concrete progress instead of anxieties. He was instrumental in the early days in rejecting the proposal for surprise attack. He was instrumental in the final days in conveying to the Soviet Ambassador the position that finally prevailed. He helped shape, organize, and monitor the entire effort that remains a standard for all time.

Never before had the Soviets and the Americans peered so clearly at each other down the barrels of their nuclear cannons and contemplated the meaning of attack. The effect was to purge their minds, at least temporarily, of cold-war clichés. If nuclear war were suicidal, if nuclear blackmail were futile, if an accidental nuclear war would be disastrous, surely there had to be a more sensible way of competing against each other than building still more exorbitantly expensive nuclear weapons. The chief lesson learned from this first nuclear crisis was not how to conduct the next one—but how to avoid it.

Thus the air was cleared for John Kennedy's speech on June 10, 1963, at American University, the single most important foreign-policy speech in the entire Kennedy legacy. It summed up his views on peace, "a process, a way of solving problems . . . the sum of many acts." It reminded Americans that "enmities between nations, as between individuals, do not last forever." It offered friendship to the Russian people and admiration for their many achievements.

And if we cannot now end our differences, at least we can help make the world safe for diversity. For in the final analysis our most basic common link is that we all inhabit this planet. We all breathe the same air. We all cherish our children's future. And we are all mortal.

That speech, Khrushchev indicated later, helped pave the way for the Nuclear Test Ban Treaty aimed at ending the radioactive poisoning of the atmosphere. Obtaining the Senate's consent to the ratification of that treaty was JFK's proudest moment, fulfilling one of his first priorities—but it was also the result of Kennedy at his educational best. The treaty was opposed by the chairman of the Senate Armed Service Committee, by the Senator who became the next Republican nominee for President, by three former Chiefs of Staff, and by other notables. Such a combination would normally have been enough to block the necessary two-thirds vote. Kennedy, fearing a repetition of Wilson's experience with the League of Nations, worked on his Joint Chiefs, on Minority Leader Everett Dirksen, on the Armed Services Preparedness Subcommittee, on the Joint Atomic Energy Committee, on every individual Senator he could, and on public opinion directly and indirectly. He was eminently successful.

Nor was he content with that one treaty. Like his brother Bob, he wanted his speeches remembered not for the words he used but for the action that resulted. In a period of a few months, he reached agreement with Moscow on a "hot line" for emergency communications, on banning weapons of mass destruction from outer space, on the first sale of surplus American wheat to the Soviet Union, on joint efforts regarding weather and communications space satellites, and on a cooperative program in nuclear studies. Earlier he had expanded cultural and scientific exchanges with the U.S.S.R., proposed mutual increases in consulates, removed at least one major trade restriction, offered a specific plan to implement the Soviet slogan of general and complete disarmament, conferred and corresponded with Soviet Chairman Khrushchev, and spoken directly to the Russian people via a front-page interview in *Izvestia*.

In his address to the United Nations two months before he was killed he urged still further steps, one of which— a treaty against the proliferation of nuclear weapons— became the subject for Bob Kennedy's first major speech as a United States Senator. The treaty was signed under Johnson's Administration and ratified under Nixon's.

John Kennedy did not do all this because he thought that all conflict or even danger had suddenly disappeared from Soviet–American relations. He recognized that two very different but very large and powerful nations, each necessarily concerned with events all over the world and each possessing a capacity to affect but not control those events, were bound to have conflicts of interest as well as ideology. Much as he understood and was fascinated by Khruschev's rough ways, he sensed in him an air of recklessness which —combined with a national inferiority complex—could drag us all into war. But he also recognized that the two great powers had a common interest in devoting their resources to peaceful pursuits instead of stockpiling arms and that those common interests could maintain treaties more effectively than any international police force.

He did not share the view of some that the Americans and Soviets would ultimately form an alliance against the Chinese. But he did believe that both nations could co-operate in reducing the risks of detonating the entire planet. As a student of modern history, he regarded the greatest danger of all to be the danger of war by miscalculation—by a nation mistakenly not expecting the other to respond, by a nation mistakenly fearing it is about to be attacked, by two nations mistakenly going to war over an issue that could have been equitably settled, by a nation not accurately distinguishing the other's vital interests or not accurately evaluating the other's commitments or capability. In the modern age, the first such mistake could be the last.

Thus his prime objective since taking high office had been "to get the nuclear genie back into the bottle," as he put it in an early press conference. That is why his proudest moment was not the day Khrushchev took his missiles out of Cuba but the day the Test Ban Treaty was ratified. For that one limited step symbolized much more that was then developing—including a general recognition that the prospects for a Soviet–American nuclear war, which a few years earlier most people had thought to be ultimately inevitable, were largely diminished.

It was this atmosphere of hope that Bob Kennedy sought to nourish and expand after Dallas. Supporting his brother's search for *détente,* he had come a long way from the RFK of the middle 1950s, who had assailed even Soviet–American agricultural exchanges as a means of enabling the Communists to catch up. He had returned from a 1955 mountain-climbing trip in the Soviet Union with Justice William O. Douglas condemning, in a *U.S. News & World Report* interview, those who trusted the smiles of godless Communists bent on our destruction. Now he had become a personal friend of Soviet diplomats in Washington because he recognized there was no acceptable alternative to the two great powers' living and working together. Progressive political programs, not guns and containment, were the key to besting Communism.

It was thus with dismay that he watched the Vietnam war escalate in 1965, the harsh cold-war language on both sides return, the prospects for new clashes arise, and the strategic arms race continue. He sought the Presidency in 1968 not only to end the war in Vietnam but also to "look beyond that terrible conflict to insure that it is not repeated, and to insure that the world's inevitable conflicts of interest and belief do not become irrepressible conflicts of death and global destruction."

This genuine devotion of both Kennedy brothers to peace clearly reached those on the other side of the Berlin Wall. Averell Harriman found that on his trips back to Moscow. I found it on my business visits to the Soviet Union and Rumania. Bob Kennedy found it on a trip to Poland in 1964. Ignored by the Polish government, acclaimed by the Polish people, he told them—as JFK had told the West Europeans a year earlier—that the objective of all who seek peace must be "the reconciliation of Eastern and Western Europe in association with the United States."

That objective faced obstacles in Western as well as Eastern Europe. The intransigence of General Charles de Gaulle had slowed political integration in Western Europe, as had resistance to JFK's ill-conceived multilateral force and his pressure for British admission into the Common Market. The suspicions of Chancellor Adenauer, encouraged by De Gaulle, had handicapped John Kennedy's search for *détente*—although after his death both De Gaulle and the West Germans, the Berlin issue having been largely muted by then, began their own efforts at rapprochement with the East. President Kennedy had patience with the restless nations of Western Europe and understood their resentment of American domination of NATO and Atlantic markets. His Administration showed little initiative and imagination in this area that was effectively implemented. But his ultimate hope was a truly reconciled Europe of independent and integrated states in place of an American-dominated half glaring at a Soviet-dominated half through an unnaturally divided Germany. Understanding the fear of all Germans that still persisted in Eastern Europe, he sought to strengthen the integration of West Germany into NATO and into a united Western Europe and to discourage West German hopes for an independent role, for a finger on some nuclear trigger, or for a quick route to reunification.

His *"Ich bin ein Berliner"* speech from the steps of West Berlin's city hall in June 1963 stirred the hearts of all who heard him and focused the attention of the world on the will of the brave West Berliners. But equally important though little noticed was his address that afternoon to the Free University of Berlin, in which he stated frankly that "the peaceful reunification of Berlin and Germany will not be either quick or easy," that it will be attainable only "in the context of the reconstitution of the larger Europe" and that "when the possibilities of reconciliation appear, we in the West will make it clear that we are not hostile to *any people or system,* providing they choose their own destiny without interfering with the free choice of others." (Italics added.)

President Kennedy conveyed the same message to the people of Communist China. "We are not wedded," he told his last press conference, "to a policy of hostility to Red China." Unfortunately, the government of Mao Tse-tung seemed far more wedded than did the Kremlin to a policy of hostility to the United States, spurning with vituperative denunciations any olive branch he proffered. JFK felt imprisoned in an American attitude toward China shaped for more than ten years by reactions more political and emotional than rational, by admiration for the brave Generalissimo Chiang Kai-shek and his beautiful wife, by attacks on the depraved Red Chinese who had ousted Christian missionaries, by Nationalist Chinese influence in Washington, and by myths and fears still lingering from the Joe McCarthy–Pat McCarran investigations. He no longer believed the charges he made as a young Congressman that China was "lost" to the Communists by the State Department. Nor did he believe the Dulles concept that Communism was merely a passing phase in China that we should hurry along its way. Nevertheless, he found it difficult to feel reassured by those scholars who reported China too weak economically to pose a serious threat for years to come. That the most populous nation in the world, under a Stalinist war-minded regime, was equipping herself with nuclear weapons and was accustomed in the past to dominating most of the weak nations adjacent to her, impressed him as "potentially a more dangerous situation than any we have faced since the end of the Second World War."

He made no effort to end the two negative touchstones of American policy: exclusion of mainland China from the United Nations and a denial of U.S. diplomatic recognition. Such moves at that time, he felt, would only encourage the Red Chinese to feel that their unremitting belligerence toward their neighbors, the U.S., and the UN had paid dividends. Both of those moves seemed inseparable, moreover, from the question of Formosa (Taiwan), where the exiled Nationalist Chinese government ruled some thirteen million inhabitants, was recognized in the

United States as the government of China, and represented all China in the United Nations. JFK knew that Chiang Kai-shek would never again rule or represent the mainland, and his 1960 campaign statements had in effect so indicated. But neither did he feel he had any legal or moral right to declare or support a UN action in effect declaring that Mao Tse-tung represented the inhabitants of Taiwan or could rightly change its status by force.

He recognized the need to alter American public opinion and policy on China to a more realistic view of the choices, and he initiated a State Department examination of this objective that bore some fruit in policy pronouncements after his death. But he was still too sensitive to the "soft on Communism" charge that he had avoided throughout his formative years in politics, too conscious of the narrow margin by which he had been elected, and too concerned about Congressional hostility to try bold innovations in China policy. "Let's face it," he said to me about grain shipments to China in particular but including the whole China question in general, "that's a subject for the second term."

The first term was not free from incident. He indicated America's interest in sending wheat to China at a time of famine; but he may not have phrased it with sufficient regard for Chinese sensitivities and, whatever the reason, met only the same hostile response. The Nationalist Chinese resented his refusal to back a reinvasion of the mainland (the Bay of Pigs all over again, thought Kennedy), resented his attempt to recognize the independence of Soviet-leaning Outer Mongolia (blocked by a China-lobby threat to wreck his foreign-aid program), and resented the visa his Administration granted to lecture in this country to a spokesman for Taiwan independence.

In 1962 he experienced an almost ludicrous example of the "mirror image" in foreign policy. Red Chinese troops, to his consternation, massed for what appeared to be an invasion, if not of Taiwan, then of the offshore islands of Quemoy and Matsu that the Nationalists had foolishly never abandoned. The President solemnly warned the Red Chinese and readied our forces, only to receive solemn warnings from Peking that its troops had been deployed to prevent an invasion *from* Taiwan. He replied that the United States would oppose any use of force by either side in the Formosan Straits.

In the fall of 1962 a Chinese attack against Indian troops in a prolonged border dispute brought new threats of a wider conflict. The Indians, not only ill-prepared despite some provocations on their part but also panicky, sent urgent pleas for help to Washington and London as well as Moscow. Kennedy's response provided more than enough help to assure a quiet border; but it was not nearly all the help requested, for that might have escalated into a real war as well as permanently alienating Pakistan. Because the brunt of this Chinese–Indian fighting broke out in the midst of the Cuban missile crisis, JFK's advisers were more concerned about its implications and less reflective on them than they might otherwise have been. Receiving a call from the Secretary of State at midnight for an emergency meeting on the matter, Kennedy patiently listened to an excited recommendation that in his view would have taken us to war with China, thanked his visitor, bade him good night, and never mentioned the proposal again.

He knew patience and firmness would be required before Red China would, as he hoped, "indicate a desire to live at peace with the United States [and] with other countries surrounding it." He rejected completely those urging him to risk a final showdown then before Chinese nuclear power grew. That was inconsistent, he knew, with our historic role in the world as well as our immediate safety. But he was never lulled by the fact that China would not become a full-fledged nuclear power for a decade or more. "We are going to be around in the 1970s," he said, "and we would like to take some steps now which would lessen that prospect that a future President might have to deal with."

Robert Kennedy picked up this part of the legacy and converted it into a more explicit framework for a new China policy. As with so many other issues, his own thinking evolved past JFK's of 1963, just as JFK's had evolved past his own earlier beliefs. In one of his best speeches on foreign affairs, addressed to the University of Chicago Conference on China in 1967, RFK attacked the substitution of fear, hostility, and wishful thinking for American policy. We should face the fact, he said in effect, that the Nationalist Chinese are not going to liberate the mainland ("a dangerous illusion"); that time and internal progress may not ameliorate Chinese malevolence; and that mere good will on our part is not enough for a reconciliation without resolving conflicts of interest. Finally, he said, we should put aside all the unprovable assumptions about the inevitability of Chinese military expansion, about the Chinese controlling all Asian Communists, much less all Asian revolutions, and for that matter about all Asian nationalism rejecting Chinese control.

Every extension of Chinese influence does not menace us, said RFK, pointing out that, without our intervention, the Chinese had been ousted from Indonesia and most of Africa. Despite their hostile words, we should not discourage economic, diplomatic, or tourist contact or any effort to reach agreements. We must, in short, recognize that "we live in the same world and move in the same continent with China" and treat her "as a potential danger and a possible opportunity rather than as a certain enemy and a lost cause."

He was not yet as precise in his recommendations as

Senator Ted Kennedy would be two years later, but he had earlier criticized our condoning the domination of indigenous Taiwanese by the Nationalists and our rejecting out of hand Chou En-lai's offer for a Sino-American pact outlawing the use of nuclear weapons. He called for "wider discussions and negotiations" with the Chinese and a total reassessment of this nation's policy—which he said in effect was no policy at all.

This speech was a direct outgrowth of RFK's evolving views on Vietnam. For he came to realize that the defenders of our deepening commitment in that quagmire were exaggerating the extent of Chinese inspiration and assistance behind Hanoi. By equating Chinese Communism with Asian Communism with North Vietnamese Communism, despite all evidence to the contrary, these military interventionists were seeking to place America's stand in that little nation in an undeserved global context. But it was not the threat of China that overshadowed all of American foreign policy, and even our domestic progress and politics, during those last years of his life. It was the war in Vietnam.

Particularly after RFK's open break with President Johnson on the issue of escalation, but long before as well, I was asked by every audience I addressed, both at home and around the world, whether President Kennedy, had he lived, would have pursued the same course in Vietnam as President Johnson. The constant reiteration of that question—not only by students and newsmen but also by foreign government officials, lawyers, businessmen, friends and strangers—was itself revealing. Because such speculation on a dead man's intentions was sought primarily as a means of blaming President Johnson, I always felt it would be unfair to answer that question directly so long as the

Johnson Administration remained in office. The question implied a control of events in that area that neither President ever fully possessed. Moreover, my past association with President Johnson and Messrs. Rusk, McNamara, Bundy, Taylor, and Harriman, all of whom he had inherited from President Kennedy, as well as my desire not to deepen the divisions betweeen the Johnson and Kennedy wings of the Democratic Party, all constrained against my answering that particular question publicly at that time.

I feel compelled now, however, to answer in the context of this book a crucial question worded slightly differently: Was the important Vietnam portion of Robert Kennedy's contribution to the Kennedy legacy a repudiation or contradiction of his older brother's? Was he, as so many critics said when his dissent became pronounced, seeking—in the words of one—"to promote his own personal career by undermining faith" in his brother's approach to Vietnam? To put it another way: Setting aside the greater limitations governing Presidential power and the fewer inhibitions governing Senatorial speeches, would John Kennedy, had he lived, have sought the general direction of the Lyndon Johnson route in Vietnam—particularly the route toward massive escalation begun in 1965—rather than the general direction of the Robert Kennedy route? The question, however worded, must, in my opinion, be answered in the negative.

This is not because Kennedy was smarter than Johnson, or more peace-loving, or more farsighted. But they were very different men, and they brought very different backgrounds and qualities to bear upon this question—differences which may well, if circumstances had permitted, have produced very different answers. I do not ignore the fact that President Kennedy not only reaffirmed but enlarged this nation's commitment to South Vietnam and passed that problem on to President Johnson. Historians will argue, after all the facts are in and viewed in perspective, whether in early 1965 the United States was in fact faced with a choice between large-scale combat intervention and unacceptable humiliation. But I am convinced that JFK would have acted during 1964, as he had in West Berlin and elsewhere and as his strategy on Vietnam clearly intended, to avoid being confronted with so limited a choice. By developing diplomatic as well as military alternatives not unlike those forced upon President Nixon in 1969, he would not have permitted this country to be placed in a bind where it had no acceptable alternative to massive escalation in 1965.

He was faced during his Presidency with a much lower level of Communist activity in Vietnam, largely guerrilla action in the South without large-scale intervention from the North. Having learned in Berlin, in the missile race and elsewhere that the other side invariably matches our increased military build-ups to such an extent that we are in a sense in a race with ourselves, I believe he would have kept our participation at a much lower level, sending no combat divisions to South Vietnam and no missions to bomb North Vietnam.

There were fifteen to sixteen thousand American military personnel in Vietnam the day John Kennedy died, with more on the way. That was a large increase in our commitment, and the men who were not in logistics or supply were in the field with the South Vietnamese forces they were training and advising. But these were not combat missions and he sent no combat divisions. The key statistic illustrating this distinction is that only sixty-nine Americans were killed in Vietnam during the entire Kennedy Administration. While JFK deserves his share of the blame for increasing our stake in Vietnam, the difference between

16,000 men and 550,000 men, the difference between sixty-nine killed in three years and several hundred killed every week, is more than a difference of degree.

It was simply not John Kennedy's nature to stubbornly throw division after division into a bloody, worsening struggle without re-examining the balance between cost and gains, without measuring the effect on our power, prestige, resources, and society compared with the realistic prospects for success. He was willing, as President Johnson was fond of quoting, to "pay any price, [and] bear any burden . . . to assure the survival and the success of liberty." But he made clear in the same speech that he wanted new nations "supporting their own freedom," and that he would "never fear to negotiate." I believe, in the words of that same speech, that he would have made certain before he "unleashed . . . the dark powers of destruction" that they would indeed "assure the survival and the success of liberty."

By the fall of 1963, he was aware of the need for new policies and personnel in our Vietnam effort, replacing those who had sought Saigon's cooperation by unconditionally pledging our backing with men he hoped would more realistically assess the state of that nation and our stake, if any, in it. He was increasingly aware that Vietnam was more of a political problem than a military problem. He had placed little confidence in most military solutions and military advice since the Bay of Pigs. He had found the Joint Chiefs wrong again when he succeeded in resolving the Cuban missile crisis by ignoring their recommendations; and he was turning as never before toward peace—with the Test Ban Treaty, the sale of wheat, the hot line, and all the rest. Had he lived, he would not have responded to Goldwater's charge that a negotiated settlement was a sellout by escalating the rhetoric of commitment, by demonstrating his toughness in the Gulf of Tonkin incident, or by postponing all serious attempts to negotiate.

In 1961 he had ridiculed the CIA's solemn assurance that Diem was a popularly elected dictator who had just been re-elected with nearly ninety per cent of the vote. In that same year he had expressed grave doubts about the so-called domino theory. Despite some subsequent statements adding to that theory, he clearly had no desire in the fall of 1963 either to Americanize or internationalize South Vietnam's civil war. He made it plain that he did not want Americans battling Asians on their continent. When Canada's Lester Pearson, asked for his advice during a visit to the White House, suggested that the U.S. "get out," the President softly replied, "That's a stupid answer. Everybody knows that. The question is: How do we get out?" I believe he would have devoted increasing time to that question in the winter of 1963–1964 and found an answer.

I am not impressed by the reply that JFK would have relied, as Johnson relied, on Rusk, McNamara, Bundy, Taylor, Harriman, Henry Cabot Lodge, and Walt Rostow, as well as our military commanders in the area. For JFK listened also to Ball, Gilpatric, Kaysen, Mike Forrestal, and, of course, his brother on Vietnam policy; he welcomed the views on Asia of Galbraith from India and Reischauer from Japan; and all these men, as well as virtually every one of his former White House aides who knew and shared his thoughts—O'Donnell, Schlesinger, Salinger, Goodwin, Dutton, myself, and others—dissented from the subsequent Vietnam policy of the Johnson Administration. Even McNamara and Bundy in time expressed views at variance with the Johnson approach. Other war critics such as Fulbright, McGovern, George F. Kennan, and James Gavin had earned JFK's trust. What matters most is not to which advisers Kennedy and Johnson listened but what they did with that advice, when they accepted it, how they weighed it and whether they altered it.

Nor am I impressed by quotations from JFK regarding our commitment to stay in Vietnam. Robert Kennedy did not deny our commitment nor did he recommend unilateral withdrawal; but he could refer his critics to one of JFK's last comments on the war:

> In the final analysis, it is their war. They are the ones who have to win it or lose it. We can help them, we can give them equipment, we can send our men out there as advisers, but they have to win it, the people of Vietnam against the Communists. (September 3, 1963, television interview)

Quotations can be used by both sides in this game. No doubt the speech delivered by Senator John F. Kennedy on the Senate floor in 1954 is one indication of how he would have felt about the large-scale deployment in 1965 of American troops and bombers:

> . . . unilateral action by our own country . . . without participation by the armed forces of the other nations of Asia, without the support of the great masses of the peoples [of Vietnam] . . . and, I might add, with hordes of Communist troops poised just across the border in anticipation of our unilateral entry into their kind of battleground—such intervention, Mr. President, would be virtually impossible in the type of military situation which prevails in Indochina . . . an enemy which is everywhere and at the same time nowhere, "an enemy of the people" which has the sympathy and covert support of the people.

Even earlier, upon his return from Indochina as a young Congressman in 1951, he had warned that the southward drive of Communism required its opponents to build "strong native non-Communist sentiment within these areas and rely on that as a spearhead of defense rather than upon . . . force of arms."

The real test, however, is not what John F. Kennedy said, or to whom he listened, or what he might have been thinking in November 1963. The real test is what he did and what he did not do. He did not authorize, despite a strong recommendation from several advisers, the sending of American combat divisions to Vietnam. He did not heed Pentagon requests for blank-check authority to seek a military victory. He did not accept Walt Rostow's recommendations in 1962 for bombing North Vietnam, as well as making a major combat-troop commitment to the South. (And it ill becomes Rostow, whom Kennedy removed from the White House, to claim now that he knew Kennedy's thinking on this subject "in a way that no other living person probably does" and that Kennedy would have escalated even earlier than Johnson.) JFK never regarded Vietnam as an end in itself to be preserved whatever the cost. He did authorize, as an indication of his goal, the October 1963 statement by McNamara and Taylor predicting a withdrawal of most American military advisers by the end of 1965, beginning late in 1963. He did tell the Saigon government that our continued assistance was conditioned on its adoption of political, economic, and social reforms. He publicly criticized the repression of Buddhists and others in disfavor with that regime. And instead of premising our presence among the Vietnamese on an effort essential to our own security rather than one undertaken at *their* request to help *them,* he made it very clear that any suggestion from the Saigon government that our forces were unwelcome would start them "on their way home . . . the day after it was suggested."

This was a crucial difference. In a long and impassioned answer during a 1967 television interview, Robert Kennedy indicated that the United States had gone originally to help the South Vietnamese secure their own self-determination but had apparently decided, under Johnson, when they seemed little interested in making the effort required, that we were instead fighting for our own security.

Our whole moral position, it seems to me, changes tremendously. One, we're in there, we're helping people. We're working with them. We're fighting for their independence. . . . Now we've changed. . . . Maybe they don't want it but *we* want it. So we're going in there and we're killing South Vietnamese, we're killing children, we're killing women, we're killing innocent people, because we don't want to have the war fought on American soil . . . because they're twelve thousand miles away and they might get to be eleven thousand miles away. Our whole moral position changes, it seems to me, tremendously. Do we have the right here in the United States to say that we're going to kill tens of thousands, maybe millions, of people, as we have, refugees . . . women and children . . . ? There are thirty-five thousand people without limbs in South Vietnam. There are one hundred and fifty thousand civilian casualties every year. . . . Do we have the right . . . ?

I have already set forth at length the important distinctions between this nation's conduct of the Cuban missile crisis and its escalation of the war in Vietnam. Other Kennedy crises also provide analogous clues to what he would and would not have done in Vietnam. JFK preferred the risks of a neutral coalition government in Laos to the risks of being sucked into a wider war on the Asian continent. Instead of inflating the importance of our stand, he told Khrushchev at Vienna that Laos was frankly not worth a war between superpowers. He was willing to acknowledge error in the Bay of Pigs and cut our losses before they grew larger. He avoided incidents and did not retaliate to affronts in the Berlin crisis because, he said, quoting Churchill, "to jaw, jaw is better than to war, war." He preferred UN intervention to U.S. intervention in the Congo. He authorized aid to the Chinese Nationalists for their self-defense but refused to support or even permit any offensive operations. He insisted on British participation in any aid to India's defense of her China border. Neither as Senator nor as President did he see the necessity or wisdom of blank-check, Gulf of Tonkin type of Congressional resolutions.

In all cases he stressed the value of negotiations, of making a start on the exchange of diplomatic proposals, even by mail. He stressed the need for multilateral and nonmilitary responses and the use of limited steps that made clear our intent without forcing the other side to the wall. He wanted any conflict to be confined, not widened or escalated. He was protective of the lives of American troops and hostile foreign civilians; he was unwilling to devote the bulk of our global forces to a single area; he sought the approval of our allies when he acted; and he did not insist on "victory" in the traditional sense. The way he handled problems in Berlin, Cuba, Laos, and elsewhere led his critics to accuse him of following a "no win" policy; and in the sense that he was willing to settle for a preservation of our basic interests without attempting to crush our adversaries, the critics were wholly justified in the use of that label. It hardly seemed consistent, therefore, for those same critics to charge in later years that Robert Kennedy's "no win" posture on Vietnam was a betrayal of his brother's legacy.

All this is not to suggest that John Kennedy should have recognized the immorality and futility of any U.S. role in Vietnam as soon as he took office: nor is it to suggest that his Administration can be exonerated for the downward drift in our Vietnam policy during his years in the White House.

To abandon in 1961 those South Vietnamese to whom President Eisenhower had given this nation's solemn promise of protection from a Communist military take-over, President Kennedy felt, would have shaken confidence in America's word throughout Asia and the world. Charles de Gaulle was already proclaiming the necessity of independent nuclear forces on the grounds that America, when the going got tough, would never risk its own youth to meet its overseas commitments. The Red Chinese were already warning weaker Asian nations that their future lay with Peking because America was a paper tiger. In addition, the doctrine of self-determination argued that we should help the South Vietnamese buy the time they needed to establish a more viable political and economic structure capable of withstanding any externally inspired revolt. South Vietnam's neighbors needed similar time.

Thus John Kennedy's motive in Vietnam was not, as some have suggested, an overcompensation for looking weak at the Bay of Pigs, Vienna, and Berlin. He was not weak in those cases; and he did have positive reasons to maintain and enlarge our Vietnam commitment. His failure was in not recognizing the point at which the scales were tipped the other way, the point at which the negative factors outweighed the positive, the costs outweighed all possible gain, the immoral outweighed the moral. By deferring hard choices to preserve his options while permitting each marginal step forward in the meantime, he made a reversal of course still more difficult.

He should not have been lulled into turning his full attention to Cuba, Berlin, Latin America, and elsewhere during 1962 and early 1963 by the optimistic reports of his commanders and Ambassador; for he had specifically criticized as a Senator the misleading optimism of French and American military and diplomatic personnel reporting from Indochina in the early 1950s. The best of the American correspondents in Saigon were writing the same thing in 1963, but he was more irritated than responsive.

He should have determined the extent to which each incremental increase in numbers of U.S. personnel and effort ("Just this one more step, Mr. President," to do what the last step was supposed to have done) was being offset by increases in Vietcong numbers and activity. He should have stopped and looked hard at our basic long-range policy, prospects, and premises in that conflict instead of concentrating on specific, separable, and seemingly manageable problems of operation.

JFK should have encouraged the inclusion of neutralists in the Saigon government who were willing to negotiate a settlement under which both sides would cease violating the Geneva accords of 1954. He should not have permitted the Saigon regime to evade the political and economic conditions and reforms he had attached to any increase in our role. Since he had no way to enforce these conditions upon a sovereign state, he should have cut back earlier on our economic aid to the regime and to its personal military force.

To be sure, this was not an easy choice. If the purpose of America's presence was to defend South Vietnamese self-determination, he could not logically impose his will upon its government. If our presence was to defend America's interests, we could not withdraw our forces. If Ngo Dinh Diem was as irreplaceable, dedicated, beloved, and successful in his "strategic hamlet" relocation program as the top American officials in Saigon reported, then there was no alternative to the policy aptly summed up as "sink or swim with Ngo Dinh Diem." Indeed, the very act of increasing American aid weakened Diem in the eyes of those who termed him an American puppet, thus requiring him to call for more aid.

But by never being certain which rationale to follow, by accepting several of the inconsistent explanations offered by State and the Pentagon from time to time, President Kennedy ended up with the worst of both worlds, with an unpopular regime whose weaknesses involved us more deeply but hampered our efforts at the same time. It was his growing recognition of this dilemma late in 1963 that would, in my view, have altered his course. If the Saigon government, he had said at that time, "doesn't make those changes . . . in policy and perhaps in personnel . . . I would think that the chances of winning it would not be very good." He did not connive in or request, but neither did he act to prevent, the military coup that overthrew the increasingly despotic and fanatical Diem regime. No doubt he could have prevented it, and his hands-off policy may even have implicitly encouraged it.

Robert Kennedy, as Roger Hilsman has reported, suggested inside the councils of government at that very time that the United States ascertain whether any Saigon regime would ever be strong enough to resist a Communist takeover. If not, he said, let us consider whether we should not get out of Vietnam entirely. He also urged his brother to initiate the same kind of careful and comprehensive study of this problem by all his top advisers that had served the President well in the Cuban missile crisis—an effort that, by bringing others of us in, might have made a difference. It was never launched because of Dallas.

But both before and after that fateful autumn, RFK's own role—as he fully acknowledged later—was one of complete support for the U.S. commitment, although in truth he was little involved in Vietnam planning before 1963. "The solution," he said in 1962, "lies in our winning it. This is what the President intends to do. . . . We will remain here [in Saigon] until we do." He placed full blame on Hanoi rather than regarding the conflict as a civil war.

His enthusiasm for counterinsurgency, his natural bent toward "winning" and "seeing this job through to the finish," and his undeviating support in public of all Kennedy Administration policies combined to produce an open-ended commitment on behalf of the American people "to do what is necessary . . . [to] see Vietnam through these times of trouble. . . ." He was even willing in 1964, as I have mentioned, to serve as President Johnson's Ambassador in Saigon.

But President Johnson's decision to escalate heavily in February 1965 with troops and bombing of the North fundamentally altered John Kennedy's Vietnam policy. The move shook RFK as it did so many other Kennedy men who had left the Administration (and some who had stayed). The first large-scale commitment of combat divisions, Bob prophesied privately, was a disastrous step that would end up tearing the country and Democratic Party apart. He was troubled, questioning, encouraging dissent, not yet an open dissenter himself, but edging each month closer to that role. Calling an enlargement of the war contrary to our interests and hopes for peace, he urged in May 1965 "that our peace efforts continue with the same intensity as our efforts in the military field." "Vietnam admits of no simple solution," he said in June. "Victory in a revolutionary war is not won by escalation but by de-escalation," he said in July. To postpone action on our pressing domestic needs because of the war, he said in December, "would be a terrible mistake." A week later he urged the President to extend the Christmas cease-fire.

Then in February 1966 came Robert Kennedy's first break with the Johnson policy. His hesitancy to make that break caused a confusing series of clarifications and reclarifications, but his basic analysis was clear: We could not abandon Vietnam nor could we obtain a total military victory within a reasonable period and a reasonable risk. Therefore a negotiated settlement, while risky, was necessary to halt the loss of life, both military and civilian, and to halt the war's adverse effects on our relations with China and on our efforts to meet domestic needs. Just as we could not turn South Vietnam over to Hanoi, he said, neither would Hanoi ever agree to leave "in the South a hostile government dedicated to the final physical destruction of all Communist elements . . . [and] dependent upon the continued presence of American military power." That meant that the "discontented elements in South Vietnam, Communist and non-Communist, who desire to change the existing political and economic system of the country . . . [must be admitted] to a share of power and responsibility. . . ." That also meant the risk of a compromise government fully acceptable to neither side, the risk of an adverse election on reunification, and the staged withdrawal of all foreign forces.

Essentially, that is what President Nixon proposed in 1969. But it was radical doctrine in 1966, when Hubert Humphrey termed it "putting a fox in the chicken coop." Had Robert Kennedy's suggestions been accepted and implemented then, before an additional third of a million American men were thrown into battle, history might well have been different. But his stand found little support in the country at that time, less in the Congress, and none in the Administration.

In March 1967 he spoke at length again, calling for a halt in the bombing to test Hanoi's intentions to negotiate. He cited the failure of the bombing to do more than harden resistance and reflected on the horror of the war to individual mothers and children, refugees and survivors, scarred homes and desecrated villages. "This horror is partly our responsibility," he told his fellow Senators, "not just the nation's responsibility, but yours and mine."

After that second major speech he began to speak out

constantly, mobilizing public opinion against the continued bombing, questioning the morality of the greatest power on earth warring against a tiny peasant nation, questioning the defensibility of our burning the very villages we were supposedly there to save, and gradually changing the climate of opinion that in turn would help bring about the March and November 1968 changes in Administration policy. He challenged the credibility of optimistic reports from the field about combat progress and pacification. He exposed misleading statistics on the numbers of Vietcong supporters killed or defecting and on the proportion of civilian population under allied jurisdiction. He knocked down old clichés about the domino theory, containment, and comparisons to Munich. As Winston Churchill had warned the British that they were not preparing realistically to face up to the unavoidable requirements for war in Europe, so RFK warned Americans that they were not preparing realistically to face up to the unavoidable requirements for peace in Vietnam.

He still did not think Vietnam admitted of easy solutions. But he wanted to "transfer the present conflict from the military to the political arena," to insist upon reforms in the South, to negotiate with all the parties involved, to shift more of the burden to South Vienamese troops. Time and again his speeches in 1967 and 1968 returned to the moral questions involved, for they troubled him as they had his brother in considering the whole question of force and wars:

Can we ordain to ourselves the awful majesty of God—to decide what cities and villages are to be destroyed, who will live and who will die, and who will join the refugees wandering in a desert of our own creation? . . . I am concerned that, at the end of it all, there will only be more Americans killed; more of our treasure spilled out; and because of the bitterness and hatred on every side of this war, more hundreds of thousands of Vietnamese slaughtered; so they may say, as Tacitus said of Rome: "They made a desert and called it peace."

Finally, he was concerned because Vietnam—a terrible waste of lives and resources—stood in the way of all that needed to be done at home. In civil rights, in housing, in education, in health care, in rebuilding our cities, and in alleviating poverty, John Kennedy had started the nation "moving again." Bob Kennedy wanted to carry on and go beyond this work. The domestic legislative programs of the Johnson Administration had been faithful to the legacy of John F. Kennedy in these and other areas. In a very real sense, most of the Johnson legislative program is an important part of the Kennedy legacy, and I do not demean Mr. Johnson by thus crediting him with a major contribution to the legacy of the Kennedys. But the cost of the Vietnam war was deterring the Congress from adequately funding these programs. It was slowing the addition of new programs. It was monopolizing the attention and energy of the government. It was increasing the bitter resentment not only of the young who faced military service but also of the poor and the black whose expectations had been aroused but unfulfilled.

It was ironic that fate pitted Robert Kennedy against Hubert Humphrey for the Presidency in 1968 as the result of the former's split with the Johnson–Humphrey Administration. Humphrey's battle for progressive legislation and particularly civil rights had begun more than twenty years earlier. The Kennedy brothers had, by comparison, only lately come to the forefront of the civil-rights fight. They had not been hostile to the cause or even indifferent to it, but simply to a great extent removed from it. Their speeches invoked comparisons to the discrimination suffered by their Irish grandparents, but they did not really experience in their own lives the agony or prejudice that Bob would later feel in the lives of others. On the contrary, they had grown up listening to the ethnic distinctions and derogatory phrases of their father's era and developing no particular sensitivity to them.

As a Congressman and Senator facing occasional civil-rights bills, Jack Kennedy cast all the right votes and said all the right words. But he took the lead on other issues. The "civil-rights problem" in the late 1950s to him meant largely the political problem of a Presidential candidate winning Negro votes without writing off all prospects for Southern support. He was against discrimination and segregation and was increasingly concerned about the economic problems facing the Negro, but he had given little thought to the moral imperatives involved. He was so clearly free from any prejudice or stereotyped responses and impressions himself that he was liked by black voters as the 1960 campaign got under way. It was by no means fervent or overwhelming support on their part and was motivated in large measure by their preference for any liberal Democrat. But as their enemies became his enemies, as he spoke movingly about their needs, aspirations, and denial of opportunity, he rose gradually into a favored position in their eyes.

John Kennedy was saddened by Georgia's jailing of Martin Luther King on a minor traffic charge and quietly called Mrs. King to express his sympathy. Bob Kennedy was angered and indignantly called the authorities to obtain Dr. King's release. "Each of us behaved in character," the President observed later. Their simultaneous but uncoordinated actions helped swell the tide of Negro votes to the Kennedy camp. While all kinds of statistical anomalies can be produced from an election result as narrow as

1960's, JFK never forgot that a majority of whites had voted against him and that an overwhelming majority of blacks had voted for him.

The first two years of the Kennedy Administration were marked by Executive action considered unprecedented at that time but mild by today's standards. The appointment and promotion of Negro officials, judges, White House aides, and ambassadors gave some hope but no help to the average black citizen in the ghetto. The progressive elimination of barriers to Negro registration and voting in the South offered the prospects of long-range changes in the political climate of those states but no immediate relief to their black inhabitants. The easing of discrimination in Federally financed employment, housing, social, and economic programs and in the armed services benefited only a small portion of black families. More important to improving the Negro's lot during 1961 and 1962 were Kennedy's housing, welfare, job-training, area-redevelopment, minimum-wage, food-stamp, unemployment-compensation, and other new laws. But there were no new civil-rights laws. During his first hundred days he outlined the nation's needs and the Administration's goals in major economic, health, tax, conservation, agriculture, housing, highway, foreign-aid, and other messages. But there was no civil-rights message.

Kennedy knew legislation was needed. He also knew it had no chance of passage. In 1961 he tried to give the Civil Rights Commission a long-term extension as well as renewal, and the extension was killed in the House Judiciary Committee. In 1962 he tried to eliminate discriminatory literacy tests, and the Senate could not even muster a majority, much less the necessary two-thirds vote, to shut off a Southern filibuster.

As President, he realized that at times he would have

to fight losing battles simply to make the fight. He was sensitive to criticism from liberal quarters that he was being too timid. But he argued that alienating the Southern moderates whose votes he needed and provoking an unbeatable filibuster in the Senate would only block action on those social, economic, and antirecession measures that the Negroes needed immediately. As in foreign policy, he had to consider the consequences of failure instead of merely launching new initiatives. The most optimistic count of votes in both houses of Congress in 1961, as well as the fate of all civil-rights proposals in 1960, made clear that failure was certain on any major new civil-rights bills, that the Republican–Dixiecrat coalition against his entire legislative program would have been revived, and that the country would have been divided in vain. His only course, he felt, was to step up the use of Executive powers in this area until public opinion could force Congress to act.

Most of the Executive effort—as well as the responsibility for supervising any legislative effort—came under the jurisdiction of Attorney General Robert Kennedy, who was fast being educated in these matters. "I have not had a chance to study the situation," he had said upon being named Attorney General. "My general philosophy is that we have to move strongly and vigorously. . . . I do not think this is a matter that can be solved overnight, however. . . . I would wait for my instructions and guidance from President Kennedy. . . . He is the one that is going to make the decision, not me."

That was a far cry from the Robert Kennedy of 1968. But his instructions, in view of the legislative stalemate in this area, were to *go,* and the more Bob learned about the facts of racial discrimination, the more shocked and indignant he became and the more he pressed forward. Ignoring warnings that his predecessors had proceeded more cautiously on Federal enforcement suits in the states of powerful Congressional committee chairmen, he initiated action throughout the South to enforce the Federal voting-rights statutes and, to the extent authority was available, the nondiscriminatory use of Federal funds and the Supreme Court's decisions on nonsegregation in education and interstate transportation.

In speeches to Southern audiences he made clear that the law would be strictly enforced. In Washington and points north he assailed the hypocrisy of those practicing discrimination in their private clubs and schools while deploring it in the South. In his travels around the globe he came to realize the size of the stain on this nation's honor created by its treatment of black citizens.

He shared his brother's reluctance to send heroic-sounding legislation to the Congress that had no chance of passage. That might help in the newspapers, he said, but "what we want to do is actually accomplish something." Still a moderate, he added, "We're not interested in pushing [things] down people's throats . . . we're trying to work these matters out."

Because RFK's department, under the quietly effective leadership of Assistant Attorney General Burke Marshall, had achieved widespread success in voting-rights cases, and because the one JFK bill to pass the Congress that was related to Negro rights sought the repeal of the poll tax in Federal elections by Constitutional amendment, both Kennedy brothers placed more hope than most on the gains to be achieved by Negroes through voting. Through mid-1963 the Attorney General continued to stress that "once the Negro obtains the franchise the situation will be far different. . . . All other rights for which they are fighting will flow from that . . . the most important area is the field of voting. . . . I think if they can . . . register and vote . . . they can frequently remedy their problems themselves in their own areas."

But Martin Luther King, important Negro leaders in the South, and students and other activists from the North were pursuing different means of remedying these problems themselves—nonviolence, sit-ins, demonstrations, and the physical testing of facilities where segregation was legally prohibited. When Federal court orders or Federally protected rights were affected by these actions, so necessarily was the Federal Department of Justice. Bob's first major involvement with the growing civil-rights revolution came with the Freedom Riders, whose peaceful challenge of segregation in interstate bus terminals in May 1961 brought violence from Southern mobs and Southern law-enforcement officials alike. Bob did not like anyone forcing his hand, and he grumbled to me privately that a second wave of riders had needlessly rushed to join the publicity and provoke violence. But personalizing issues as always, he saw in the defiant idealism of these young people, willing to risk death for their high principles, something of himself.

The freedom rides and similar events tested his ingenuity to find alternatives to litigation whenever that traditional Justice Department tool was insufficient, inappropriate, or ineffective. He devised new techniques of sending Justice Department aides to negotiate with Southern officials and whole squadrons of Federal marshals and agents to prevent violence. He used pressure as well as litigation on Federal commissions and private corporations to bring about the desegregation of railroad, airline, and bus terminals. More important, he became deeply, personally involved in the fight for human rights.

Then, in the fall of 1962, John Kennedy crossed his own racial Rubicon by undertaking to assure the entrance of James Meredith into the University of Mississippi. Foreign diplomats and visitors in the months that followed never failed to ask me how a government representing nearly two hundred million people could devote several hundred thousand dollars and thousands of troops to getting one lonely black man into a university. The answer lay in the Kennedys' adherence to that concept of law in which the least must be afforded the same protection as the most; in their adherence to that concept of the Presidency which could not permit the racial malice and political machinations of a state Governor to block the Federal Executive's responsibility for Federal court orders; and in their growing adherence to their own responsibilities for promoting and protecting human rights.

Two men died in the University of Mississippi riot; more would die in Birmingham; others would die in this struggle in the months to come. Throughout their lives it was always the episodes marked by death or near death that remained etched most deeply in the minds of the life-loving Kennedys. To John Kennedy, who lived by reason, the violent response of Southern mobs and officials brought increased conviction of the rightness of his course. To Bob Kennedy, who lived by feeling, the suffering of the innocent brought renewed determination to end it.

The Kennedys did not start the civil-rights revolution. They do not deserve so much credit for its remarkable growth in 1963 as Birmingham Police Commissioner Bull Connor and his police dogs or George C. Wallace and his sheriffs. The contribution of John and Robert Kennedy in 1963 was to assure not only the strength but the dignity of the new movement, to recognize not only its full legislative dimensions but its full moral dimensions. In February 1963 the President had finally sent a package of civil-rights bills to Congress, which completely ignored it. In

May and June 1963, as violence spread from Birmingham to Shreveport, north to Cambridge, Maryland, and nearly a thousand cities, the problem could not be ignored. The Justice Department and White House prepared sweeping new legislation commensurate with the new size of the problem, attacking all racial barriers to voting, employment, education, and service in public accommodations.

President Kennedy's televised address to the nation on the evening of June 11, 1963, fully committed for the first time the power and prestige of the American Presidency to the drive for black equality. My draft, hastily prepared because of his belated decision to speak that evening, drew heavily on material from the Attorney General and from previous JFK statements as well as my own convictions of a lifetime. The President's basic argument could not have been simpler:

It ought to be possible . . . for every American to enjoy the privileges of being American without regard to his race or color . . . to treat our fellow Americans as we want to be treated. . . . This nation, for all its hopes and all its boasts, will not be fully free until all its citizens are free. . . .

The speech outlined his legislative proposals, mild-sounding today but considered far-reaching in 1963. He stressed that it was not simply a legislative or legal issue, much less a sectional or partisan matter. "We are confronted primarily with a moral issue. It is as old as the Scriptures and is as clear as the American Constitution."

In the 1956 Democratic National Convention much of John Kennedy's support for the Vice Presidency had come from the South. In the years preceding the 1960 convention, he often sent his brother Robert to speak for him in the South, knowing that RFK's reputation for labor-rackets busting had made him a popular figure there. In

1960 JFK could not have been elected President without the South. In 1961-1962 Bob Kennedy's success in obtaining passage of the Justice Department's legislative program would not have been possible without the cooperation of key Senators from the South. But in 1963, by irreversibly insisting upon full equality for the Negro, both brothers knowingly cut themselves off from this traditional Democratic source of electoral votes without obtaining—in view of their already commanding political position among black and other liberal voters—offsetting gains elsewhere.

Not content merely to *propose* a bill, both toiled throughout that year to move it through the Congress, to build public opinion behind it, and to improve private actions and attitudes as well. In a series of White House meetings, they enlisted the aid of business, labor, lawyers, educators, clergymen, and others. More important even than the Civil Rights Act was the change they labored to effect in the nation's moral atmosphere which no future Congress could ever repeal.

RFK's prolonged testimony and public addresses helped guide the bill through Congress. With his flair for apt illustrations, he cited the tourist guidebooks which listed four accommodations in Danville, Virginia, for dogs accompanying whites but no accommodations for Negroes. He cited the case of the Negro walking down the street, with FREEDOM NOW written on his shirt, who was arrested for parading without a permit. He cited the rejection of Negro graduate students by voter registrars who were accepting barely literate whites. "Time is running out fast for this country," he warned in 1963. "The troubles we see now, agitation and even bloodshed, will not compare to what we will see a decade from now unless real progress is made."

He did not yet have the understanding of black bitterness and pain that he later would. A meeting with Negro intellectuals arranged by James Baldwin, in which he was dismayed by their criticisms of both the Administration and the nation, broke up with both sides more antagonized than sympathetic. He understood better than his critics that passage of the Kennedy Civil Rights Bill would not be enough, that Federal as well as state and local bureaucracies would evade their duties, and that Negroes needed more than legal rights. He had set out to do something about all that. But he felt, perhaps too cautiously, that there was little he could do to meet complaints from civil-rights workers that Federal troops and marshals were not sent into the South on all occasions; and he realized that explanations of the strict limitations placed by the Constitution on Federal intervention in state and local police matters fell on ears largely deafened by the howling of segregationist mobs. Student civil-rights workers, he said, assumed the existence of some kind of national police force that could protect them against the local authorities; and he winced when a group picketing his office booed him for being too legalistic.

He was sensitive as well to complaints about some of the Federal judges selected for Southern districts. But no district judge could be appointed without the approval of the Senators from that state, who would not consent to men hostile to the prevailing attitudes in their state. While he was disappointed in much of the subsequent records of at least three of his selections (the Hon. Messrs. Cox, Elliott, and West), RFK had undertaken in all judicial appointments, including those three, to obtain advance assurances of a willingness to uphold the Constitution as interpreted by the Supreme Court regardless of personal views. The fact that Cox was Senator James Eastland's former law partner illustrated RFK's desire to get Adminis-

tration legislation through a balky Congress, not his desire
to boost obviously prejudicial judges.

Nor did Bob Kennedy ever veer from his belief that
voting rights, if exercised, were essential to achieving the
long-run change in the political climate necessary to secure
other rights. Black student leaders who once scoffed at
this approach have since concentrated heavily in the area
of political organization. The rapid increases in the number of Southern Negro elected officials and in the number
of sympathetic white mayors, ever since an additional one
million Negroes were registered in the South, indicate
that the Kennedys' hopes in the franchise had not been
entirely misplaced.

RFK's commitment to the black man's cause seemed total
in 1963; and yet it had only begun. He understood the
grief, the fear, and the loss of hope that overcame many
Negroes upon John F. Kennedy's assassination. He was
deeply touched by the tributes he received from the black
community upon his resignation as Attorney General in
1964, especially one from the school children of the District of Columbia who thanked him for giving them "both
by personal example, and by the strength of his interest
and affection . . . pride in themselves and hope in their
future." Then, as a Senator from New York and a resident
of New York City, he saw and smelled and felt, really for
the first time in his life, the terrible force of a large ugly
ghetto with overcrowded tenement apartments so filled
with the stench of rats that he found it difficult on his
walking tours to linger in some houses. He saw that equal
rights laws were not enough—that massive public and
private efforts would be required to achieve real equality.

As RFK moved to the forefront of the political scene
in 1965–1966, the race issue did as well. Those blacks whose
approach was to reject all whites opposed him. "I would

not want to see your man run for President," Stokely Carmichael once told me, "because he can get the votes of my people without coming to me. With the other candidates, I'll have bargaining power." RFK in turn told black-nationalist leaders to their faces that their rejection of interracial cooperation had "set the civil-rights movement back considerably." But he developed an unusual bond with black men and women. They saw that he had soul, that he understood, that he really cared and would do whatever he could do to end their anger and agony. He not only spoke frankly and directly, he also did more than give speeches. He had JFK's conviction, compassion, and courage; and even without JFK's desk in the White House, he, too, provided the leadership the times demanded.

Somehow he understood. He understood how it must feel for a young Negro, denied a decent job because he is denied a decent education, denied a decent home because he is denied a decent income, "to live in the shadow of a multimillion-dollar freeway, to watch the white faces blur as they speed by . . . returning to the pleasant green lawns of the suburbs. . . . If we try to look through [his] eyes . . . the world is a dark and hopeless place indeed." In 1968 Martin Luther King, Julian Bond, Floyd McKissick, Richard Hatcher, and others, including some militants and black nationalists, committed or were preparing to commit themselves to RFK's Presidential candidacy because they saw in him the one man who would truly listen from the White House to their needs and their views instead of simply telling them what he thought they should hear. Rank-and-file Negroes responded partly to what he said and partly to who he was—a Kennedy. Although Gene McCarthy's stand on civil rights and on economic and social legislation was more generalized and soft-spoken than RFK's, it was not fundamentally different. His credentials and intentions on race relations were good. Nevertheless, the overwhelming majority of black voters felt that a rich, sophisticated Irish Catholic named Robert Kennedy was somehow the one who cared most.

A dramatic demonstration occurred on the night of Martin Luther King's assassination early in April 1968. Shaken by the brutal slaying of his friend, the Senator was urged by many of his advisers and local officials not to appear as scheduled before a waiting black audience in the heart of the Indianapolis ghetto. Violence had already begun to break out in other cities. Bob strode in, announced the terrible news, and spoke softly and quietly for a few minutes. He asked them to reject racial bitterness and hatred, to follow Dr. King's example of understanding and love, and to make a special effort as he had made when his brother was killed. He had never previously spoken of John Kennedy's assassination in public. The subject was too painful. Now, speaking with great emotion and pleading for understanding, he noted that his brother "was killed by a white man . . ."

What we need in the United States is not division; what we need in the United States is not hatred; what we need in the United States is not violence or lawlessness, but love and wisdom, and compassion toward one another, and a feeling of justice toward those who still suffer within our country, whether they be white or they be black.

So I shall ask you tonight to return home, to say a prayer for the family of Martin Luther King, that's true, but more importantly to say a prayer for our own country, which all of us love. . . .

Indianapolis, virtually alone among the major cities, witnessed no violence that week.

RFK did not condone Negro riots. They were an intolerable threat and detriment to everyone, he said, accomplishing nothing worthwhile and sowing the seeds of worse tragedies to come. But while he wanted lawbreakers brought to justice, he did not want legitimate grievances suppressed or legitimate causes of frustration ignored. It was remarkable, he said, that such violence was contained to a few and that the majority of blacks did retain faith in our system. He accepted a face-to-face, extremely personal denunciation from black militants in an Oakland campaign meeting because he recognized their need to explode in anger. The "naïveté" ascribed to him by James Baldwin after their uncomfortable meeting exactly five years earlier had disappeared, had it existed even then. He was careful not to confuse peaceful demonstrations or even noncoercive confrontations with riots and violence. In fact, the Poor People's Campaign of 1968, which culminated in a long encampment on the Washington, D.C., park land located between the Washington Monument and the Lincoln Memorial, grew largely out of an offhand suggestion that Robert Kennedy made to a civil-rights worker.

Before anyone expressed irritation that the Negro is not satisfied with the progress made in recent years, he said, let him declare "that he would willingly change the color of his skin and go to live in the Negro section of a large city." For it is now, he said, "when submission gives way to expectation, when despair is touched with the awareness of possibility, that the forces of human desire and the passion for justice are unloosed."

He spoke for civil rights in the South early in his Presidential campaign and received a tremendous reception—not only by blacks but also by young people, moderates, and intellectuals who had hopes for a new South. He spoke with equally biting candor in the North. Thousands of white Northerners, he reminded his audiences, had been willing to march at Selma, Alabama, but were not equally willing to help in their own cities. He sought to stir and change minds as his own had been stirred and changed. In the course of a few years his thinking had shifted from virtual unawareness of the problem to recognition of the need for voting rights and then to other rights and then to urging federal, local, and citizen action to end discrimination and deprivation more quickly and effectively than the mere granting of rights could accomplish.

The problems of Watts, Harlem, Bedford-Stuyvesant, south Chicago, and north Philadelphia, he knew, could not be solved solely by laws protecting legal rights. They required fundamental changes in conditions of housing, education, and employment. They will be solved, he had said two years earlier, "only when the people of the ghetto acquire and wisely exercise political power in the community—[and] establish meaningful communication with a society from which they have been excluded."

Not content with merely recommending that kind of solution, he set out to demonstrate that it could be done, and chose, after a February 4, 1966, walking tour, the Bedford-Stuyvesant community, a decaying slum-ridden ghetto of 450,000 people overcrowding some nine square miles in Brooklyn. It is the second largest ghetto in the nation, with a population greater than that of most American cities, a juvenile-delinquency rate twice the average for all New York City, and rates of unemployment, underemployment, school drop-outs, disease, crime, and infant mortality far above the national average. Much of its business enterprises had moved out. It had no real community institutions, community spirit, or community hope. Its affairs were governed to the extent they were governed at all by largely remote, impersonal, and uninterested white bureaucracies splintered among several different levels and jurisdictions. The city's education, hospital, and urban-renewal plans had largely passed it by.

RFK's response was to seek the revitalization of Bedford-Stuyvesant through the fullest possible application of the concept of local community action and control. This concept ultimately became a focal point of the Federal antipoverty programs but had first originated as a part of his efforts to combat juvenile delinquency as Attorney General. The impossibility of large cities adequately meeting the needs of local neighborhoods had been further impressed upon him during the landmark hearings on urban problems conducted by Senator Abraham Ribicoff in 1966–1967. "Democracy, in any active sense," Lewis Mumford had told that subcommittee, "begins and ends in communities small enough for their numbers to meet face to face."

By the time that testimony was over, Bob had already labored long and hard to organize such a community. He worked doggedly to establish a "Bedford-Stuyvesant Restoration Corporation," controlled and staffed by resident blacks to sponsor and direct all necessary planning and implementation for community and capital development, cultural and community centers, business and customer credit, and job training. Simultaneously, he obtained the cooperation of nationally known business leaders such as Benno Schmidt, Douglas Dillon, André Meyer, David Lilienthal, Tom Watson, and William Paley to establish a "Bedford-Stuyvesant Development and Services Corporation" to round up outside financial and technical assistance and to bring in new industry and business investment. He enlisted the support of Republicans Javits, Rockefeller, and Lindsay, the Federal, state, and city governments, various private foundations and enterprises, union leaders, and local universities.

The problems were enormous and the progress slow. But a start had been made even by mid-1968. Run-down streets were being converted into recreation areas. Decaying brownstones had been refurbished. Dozens of new small businesses were established. Hundreds of unemployed residents were trained and put to work in the neighborhood. Eighty lending institutions established a mortgage pool for new low-cost housing. IBM located a major plant in the area. A new spirit of hope infused many in the community who had never hoped before.

It was a bold experiment in community self-rejuvenation, a drive for community self-sufficiency on a comprehensive scale that had never previously been tried. Already, before its own success is assured, the Bedford-Stuyvesant experiment has spurred similar efforts in other poverty areas in the country. RFK hoped for the creation of hundreds more. Despite problems of personality conflicts within the community, despite the cries of black militants that this was only more white colonialism, and despite the complaints of traditional liberals that he was giving up on integration by "gilding the ghetto," he forged ahead. To achieve integration in a white-dominated society, he reasoned, the black man needs both economic and political power to buy his way in. In Frank Thomas and John Doar he obtained top talent to head both corporations and he spoke to me with more enthusiasm about this one effort than any other he had ever undertaken.

Two premises were basic to his approach. The first was the importance of the community, of obtaining a sense of community, of by-passing all the overlapping layers of state and local bureaucracy that crippled neighborhood initiative and improvement or drained off Federal funds. It was the local residents of Bedford-Stuyvesant and its future counterparts whose participation was most impor-

tant—through the purchase on credit of cooperative housing, through the elections of corporation board members,
through their employment on new buildings and other
projects, and through the acquisition (by purchase or profit-
sharing plan) of equity shares in the new business establishments located in their neighborhood.

His second basic premise was the need for a greater
effort in these areas by private enterprise, not instead of
but along with the efforts of the Federal, state, and local
governments. (The Federal government's contribution to
Bedford-Stuyvesant came through a measure he skillfully
steered through all the legislative shoals, disproving those
who alleged he could not get things done as Senator.)
He sponsored legislation more comprehensive than any
subsequent imitations offering tax incentives to private
business to use its vast resources in creating real jobs and
income in urban poverty areas, supplementing and to the
extent possible supplanting handouts from the government. The latter, he said, are humiliating, inadequate, and
self-defeating, creating "a screen of government agencies
keeping the poor apart from the rest of us." He also sponsored legislation offering tax and interest-rate advantages
to private firms willing to build and rehabilitate large
numbers of low-cost housing units in the ghetto. Again
the traditional liberals were suspicious of his catering to
private business and its profit motives instead of relying
on Federal bureaucrats. But RFK was not impressed by
either the arguments or the accomplishments of the traditional liberals regarding ghettos.

Similar concepts of concern underlay his efforts to improve the lot of not only blacks but all citizens—through
better schools, housing, health, social security, and above
all jobs. He sought ways of merging the growing needs
of the urban population for new facilities and personnel

of every kind with the growing needs of the poor, both black and white, for jobs and income of any kind. Medical care and education, he said, needed more local community orientation. The wars on poverty and pollution, he said, needed more private-enterprise participation.

He talked some of fiscal policy, favoring Federal revenue sharing to permit states and cities to decide on their own priorities within broad guidelines. He spoke out repeatedly against air pollution, a curse in New York City. He urged the Federal government to do more for education than blindly dole out small sums here and there. He talked some of auto safety and conservation, of labor and the aged, of business and trade. But his real passion was for the poor, the dispossessed, the unrepresented and isolated who were largely outside the political system. No politician in modern memory ever took such interest in the rights of the Indians and the Mexican-American farm workers. No member of Congress ever took such interest in the black children of the District of Columbia, visiting their schools without fanfare to urge them not to drop out, inviting their parents to his swimming pool, organizing a mammoth telethon to raise money for the homeless children of Junior Village. It is "unacceptable," he said over and over again in his campaign, that a child should go hungry in the Mississippi Delta, that affluent white Congressmen should cut off the welfare checks of parents for staying with their children, that so many young blacks should be out of work when so many public works are badly needed, that the richest nation in the world should lag behind others in preventing infant mortality and providing hospital care. "We can do better." Indeed, he warned, we must do better if the country is to avoid bitter division and disruption.

He rejected the old New Deal–Fair Deal solutions, many

of which the John Kennedy Administration had expanded and revamped without replacing. Public housing, he said, had perpetuated segregation and ultimately brought new slums. Payroll taxes were a regressive and inadequate way of financing Social Security. Welfare programs had perpetuated dependency and shattered family integrity. Farm price-support programs had kept food from the needy while doing little for the family farmer. FHA and Federal highway programs had financed the division between suburban affluence and urban despair. Liberal opposition to business profit had hamstrung private enterprise's entry into the ghetto. Labor-union power had hamstrung efforts to hire hard-core unemployed and accelerate low-cost housing construction.

None of this represented a repudiation of his brother's program. He was carrying forward the transition which JFK had begun. The focus on local planning and community action to help the nation's poor had begun in 1962 under the President's Committee on Juvenile Delinquency and was carried into the antipoverty program under preparation at JFK's direction at the time of his death. The entire thrust of John Kennedy's first legislative program in the White House had concentrated on getting people back to work, helping people out of work, caring for those too old to work, and ensuring a decent minimum wage for those who did work. From that base, the new President launched into all the other unsatisfied needs of American life. His proposals laid special stress on more and better education—of the poor, of adults, of more doctors and nurses, of farm workers' children, of more scientists and engineers and teachers, of college students as well as elementary and secondary school students.

Some of the Kennedy measures revitalized New Deal and

Fair Deal programs for social insurance, welfare, agriculture, and conservation. Some revived forgotten programs for youth, national parks and forests, and migrant workers. Some represented unfinished business, such as Medicare, aid to education, housing, college aid, and air and water pollution control measures. Some represented new approaches to the problems of job training, health, transportation, poverty, illiteracy, consumer protection, and, most dramatically, civil rights and space exploration. The civil-rights revolution and the space-age revolution came upon the American people almost simultaneously, competing for headlines and public funds. JFK did not see how a nation that prided itself on its greatness could afford to ignore either one.

Perhaps President Kennedy's most important domestic legacy outside the civil-rights area was one in which RFK took no real interest and which JFK himself learned from others. That was the so-called New Economics, which proposed a more active and daring role for the Federal government in the nation's economy, rejected the notion that Budget deficits were all bad, and recognized that fiscal policy was an important tool for the creation of jobs and growth and not merely a matter to be left to bookkeepers in the Bureau of the Budget. The answers to the problems of economic stagnation and growth were to be found, President Kennedy both learned and taught, not in ideological slogans or partisan complaints but in tailored technical solutions.

Without either price and wage controls or a reversal in the declining rate of unemployment, he kept inflation almost at a standstill. The unhappily cyclical pattern of the American economy, which had produced recessions and heavy unemployment every few years, was fundamentally altered. It was altered, first, by John Kennedy's willingness to ignore what his landmark Yale commencement address termed our traditional but dangerous "myths" regarding the national debt and budget deficits and, second, by his willingness to cut taxes massively, despite the resulting deficit, at a time of rising Federal expenditures and prosperity. He had campaigned committed to "getting this nation moving again," and, having fulfilled that commitment, he urged this unprecedented tax cut in order, as he put it, to prevent the continuing economic recovery "from running out of gas." Republican traditionalists were shocked by his seeming disregard of the deficit. Democratic traditionalists were shocked that he sought to boost job expansion by turning back money to private citizens and corporations to spend instead of channeling it through Federal programs and agencies.

Although profits increased, taxes decreased, the stock market rose, and business prospered mightily, the nation's business establishment remained basically hostile and suspicious toward the President who had helped make it all possible. Even deeper was the distrust with which the same business establishment would later regard Robert Kennedy, despite his offers of tax incentives. Those New York business leaders who worked directly with RFK regarded him as pro-business in the best sense. But the general business attitude toward him, as toward his brother, was negative in the extreme.

The cause in both cases was an unreasoning attitude on the part of those businessmen who did not know the Kennedys personally and who relied instead on mistaken but widespread assumptions in the business press and business community about all Northern liberal Democrats in general and the role of the Kennedys in the steel-price dispute in particular. There is nothing to be gained by documenting here in detail once again the facts on the steel crisis to which these business spokesmen will still not listen anyway

—the facts that the Kennedys did not launch a steel anti-trust investigation as a tactic of intimidation without any subsequent proof of conspiracy; that they did not direct FBI men to awaken reporters in the middle of the night to obtain information on this case; and that JFK did not refer directly or indirectly to all businessmen as SOBs. I do not minimize the anger and tenacity with which the Kennedys sought to roll back a price rise JFK regarded as ruinous to his Administration's hopes for the national economy. But United States Steel's swift breach of the understanding in which the President's good offices had been enlisted to hold down wage demands was an affront unlikely to be ignored by any self-respecting President. The instant increasing of prices in identical amounts by other companies was a co-incidence unlikely to be ignored by any antitrust division (and the FBI is simply the fact-gathering arm of all Justice Department divisions). And the refusal of a few smaller companies to join in that price increase presented an opportunity and obligation to save public money that quite naturally was taken up by the Department of Defense, much as General Motors resisted the steel price increase of 1969.

It was not the objective facts that widened the Kennedy–business gap but the pre-existing feeling on both sides that the other was the enemy. JFK had consulted with the business establishment in the course of selecting his Cabinet. He had appointed many businessmen to top jobs. He had renewed relations with the Business Advisory Council after its members had been offended by Secretary of Commerce Luther Hodges. But he had little respect for most of the negative and narrow legislative positions put forward by organized business, despite his regard for many individuals among them. And businessmen in turn felt that his aides and agencies were excluding and harassing them.

Both brothers went to some effort to ameliorate the division after the steel crisis. RFK pointed out that the Justice Department's antitrust efforts were over the long run in the best interests of a free competitive system. That got him nowhere. JFK went further in wooing, pleading, befriending, and encouraging businessmen to join in mutual efforts and understanding—and that got him nowhere. It was then that the President became discouraged and sometimes angry. A lack of business confidence in the White House, he felt, could be reflected in time in the press and polls, in the stock market, in business plans for expansion and new investment, and in the availability of executive talent for his Administration. Yet his efforts to win business friendship and respect had been largely met with increased hostility. While he had little regard for many individual union leaders, he felt that labor as a body—even when he was curbing its gains or restricting its privileges—at least responded more positively in the national interest.

John Kennedy's relations with labor had fluctuated over the years. His stress even as a young Congressman on union democracy, and his role as a Senator in labor reform, earned him the suspicions of many labor leaders. But these were offset, particularly among the rank and file, by his constant efforts for higher minimum wages, better working conditions, improved social insurance, and other liberal legislation. Robert Kennedy in time stood for all that and more; but most labor chieftains never outgrew the antagonisms toward him they had developed when he was counsel to the Senate committee investigating labor racketeering.

His indictment of management racketeers as well, his acquittal of honest labor leaders, and the clear evidence of guilt on the part of those who were punished were all ignored by his critics. They were instead preoccupied with the notion, particularly after his continued work along these lines as Attorney General, that he was obsessed by a desire to "get" Teamster boss Jimmy Hoffa. Some fifty-four union officials and thirty-one businessmen were prosecuted for violations of the labor-management racketeering laws by the Justice Department during RFK's tenure. It could hardly be said that he singled out Hoffa for "persecution." It is true that Bob Kennedy was disturbed that the nation's most notorious labor leader flaunted an apparent immunity from the law; and his peace of mind was not eased when a divided jury in Nashville—which the Justice Department discovered had been corrupted—enabled Hoffa once again to escape conviction for having accepted payoffs from an employer. But it was not because of any obsession that the department thereupon instituted two additional suits against Hoffa, both of which were successful: a prosecution for the jury-tampering charge in Nashville and a prosecution for the diversion of union trust funds in Chicago.

Hoffa's charge that RFK had ordered illegal evidence-gathering methods was heard and rejected by the courts. He was sentenced to Federal prison after a new Attorney General had taken over the department. Bob's only involvement at that stage was to ask privately—though in vain—that the customary practice of taking prisoners away in handcuffs be omitted in this instance.

He knew nothing of the Solicitor General's later statement that the Justice Department may have improperly overheard evidence affecting one of the Hoffa trials. But questions regarding electronic eavesdropping ("bugging") and telephone wiretapping were to trouble him both as Attorney General and as Presidential candidate. Under a long-standing FDR Executive Order, wiretapping by the FBI was authorized in cases involving national security. It was not otherwise authorized and was indeed illegal. Under Supreme Court opinions, bugging devices planted by trespass were also illegal. In RFK's first year as Attorney General he had endorsed—without White House clearance—a broader wiretap bill opposed by civil-liberties groups. Subsequently he proposed a bill which would on balance have reduced the illegal wiretapping then taking place, and many of the same civil-liberties groups endorsed his bill. Neither bill passed; and confusion in the public mind between wiretapping and bugging and between authorized and illegal uses added to his subsequent problems.

The facts, however, are clear: Robert Kennedy, during the entire period of his service as Attorney General of the United States, did not at any time direct or authorize the Federal Bureau of Investigation to tap telephone wires, except when requested by the FBI, in writing, in cases involving national security. Nor did he at any time knowingly give permission or even tacit consent to plant any electronic eavesdropping device illegally by trespass. He was at no time informed that the FBI was engaged in illegal bugging, with the exception of one case in Las Vegas which came to his attention through the press and which he then immediately halted. In one case in which a legal, nontrespass bugging was initiated with his consent, he obtained a court order as an additional safeguard. He was led to believe that the evidence produced by bugging to which he listened on two occasions had been legally obtained by local law-enforcement officers.

No doubt he was wrong to assume that, because he had received and approved no bugging requests from the Bureau, no bugging was being conducted by the FBI during that period, unless by chance it was done under specific authorizations from his predecessors. Perhaps he was misled into signing documents not fully explained to him; and perhaps the FBI mistakenly believed that RFK knew such practices were being initiated as well as continued, mistakenly believed that he had authorized or accepted such practices and thus operated under the authority given them by former Attorneys General without informing the then Attorney General. Certainly Bob Kennedy was zealous in his pursuit of organized crime and urged the use of all possible tools, but he did not favor or condone illegal techniques of surveillance.

Late in 1966 a series of public statements and "leaks" to the press from FBI Director J. Edgar Hoover suggested that RFK as Attorney General had increased such dubious practices. Then a United States Senator already hard hit by the Manchester publicity, RFK replied with the facts, to no avail. He asked me to look into the matter. While I could not prove his suspicion that the Johnson White House was responsible for these stories, it did appear that its own position on this issue was not consistent with the published version; also that the agent who had served as liaison between Hoover and RFK had apparently but with good intentions confused or misled both as to the other's position; and finally that full disclosure and debate on this subject would not harm RFK in the slightest but might considerably tarnish the reputations of other government officials.

Senator Edward Long of Missouri, whose reported connections with the Teamsters subsequently helped defeat him for renomination, was then talking of bringing RFK before a Senate committee hearing on the matter. I prepared a draft letter to Senator Long for RFK's signature calling for a complete hearing on the subject, including the cross-examination under oath of J. Edgar Hoover, all living present and past Attorneys General, all White House aides with FBI liaison, and others, including FBI agents accompanied by their directives, reports, and sample devices and a list of people, cases, and places such as foreign embassies that were covered. I took the draft to unofficial White House adviser Clark Clifford, pointing out that RFK had no choice but to demand this kind of airing if the Hoover stories continued but that such a hearing was not in anyone's interest. The stories stopped and the hearing was never held.

The attack was revived late in the 1968 primary campaign, however, by Drew Pearson, a long-time Kennedy critic. His column charged that RFK as Attorney General had tapped the wires of the late Martin Luther King and elicited scandalous personal information. In 1969 Hoover claimed that RFK had originally initiated this tap with the reluctant compliance of the FBI, a claim promptly refuted as "false" and "deceptive" by former Attorneys General Clark and Katzenbach. When the matter first broke into print in 1968, Bob regarded it as a shameful attempt to defame both him and Dr. King and wondered again why the FBI had given out only part of the story. The facts, he told me, were as follows: J. Edgar Hoover had claimed to him, on the basis of an FBI investigation predating the Kennedy Administration, that the Communists controlled King. RFK as Attorney General had three times warned King, who said he appreciated the warning, about Communist efforts to compromise the integrity of his movement through the persistent influence of an alleged secret agent in its midst. A tap had finally been installed on Dr. King's telephone in 1963 upon the FBI's written insistence that the national security required it; and, to RFK's knowledge, no personally scandalous information had ever been produced by any FBI wiretaps. He had never had any doubts about Dr. King's own loyalty or character; nor had the Bureau even requested permission from him to install a tap in King's home, as distinguished from his office. (In 1969 it was revealed that the FBI had tapped King's home.)

In 1964 RFK had publicly praised the civil-rights movement for its resistance to determined Communist efforts at penetration, acknowledged that his department was watching this threat continually, and stated that his practice was to bring such evidence to the attention of those in charge of the movement. Had he prevented the use in this case of an investigative device that would undoubtedly have been authorized if a less prominent figure had been involved, his double standard would surely have been publicly noted by those on Capitol Hill who knew the essential facts of this case.

No doubt Bob felt with hindsight that he had erred in not supervising more vigilantly all surveillance methods used by the FBI. But both of these episodes raised disturbing questions about the FBI and its Director, whose reappointment JFK had announced instantly after his election in 1960 as a demonstration of nonpartisanship. Whether or not Hoover believed he had authorization, he had knowingly engaged in surveillance practices of very dubious legality as well as morality in a wide variety of cases, subsequently resulting in the overturning of a number of convictions of those whose rights were violated. He had then released to the press without authorization classified documents from FBI files but had refused RFK's request that he release the full file. Without fear of being called to account by either the President or the Congress, he had used his venerated position as one of Washington's few untouchable bureaucrats to strike out both at a civil-rights leader he had once branded as a "notorious liar" and at a former Attorney General whom he had long disliked. He had disliked RFK for becoming the first Attorney General to assert authority over the Bureau and stand between him and the President (a practice that ended on the afternoon of November 22, 1963), and for pushing the FBI into civil-rights and organized-crime cases (thus ruining his much vaunted "batting average"). No doubt he was angered also by disclosures that the FBI had failed to coordinate with other authorities its information on President Kennedy's assassin before that November 22, 1963, trip to Dallas and was upset as well by the number of convictions then being reversed because of the Bureau's illegal bugging activities.

One court case in which the bugging question arose was that of former Johnson protégé Bobby Baker. It may be, as has been suggested, that Johnson as Vice President personally resented the Justice Department's investigation of Baker as an RFK attempt to embarrass him off the 1964 ticket. But in fact Attorney General Kennedy had not ordered or initiated the investigation, much less any bugging of Baker's friends; and he had relentlessly kept all political considerations out of his Criminal Division, which seemed almost to delight in prosecuting Democratic Congressmen, mayors, and contributors. In the 1968 Presidential battle, more than one key Democrat based his refusal to support RFK on the latter's role in convicting some powerful political figure in his community. One sought, in exchange for his help with delegates, RFK's intervention in getting a friend paroled or pardoned; another sought a friend's transfer to a more comfortable Federal prison. He did neither. While his compassion had deepened over the years, RFK had not grown soft on crime; and he lashed out both as Senator and candidate not only at organized crime and racketeering—which he had effectively reduced while Attorney General—but also at street crimes, looters, rioters, and other lawless elements. He criticized with equal vigor society's failure to provide the kind of police, judicial, penal, and other reforms that were needed to prevent and control crime.

For a "tough" Attorney General, he had demonstrated

a remarkable devotion to civil liberties. He insisted over J. Edgar Hoover's objections that ex-Communist Junius Scales be pardoned despite his refusal to inform on others. (As Senator, RFK would also protest the Army's refusal to permit Communist leader Robert Thompson to be buried in Arlington Cemetery, in accordance with his family's wishes.) He supported the removal of security restrictions on travel to Communist countries and on entry into our own. He drafted the law finally abolishing the national-origins quota system of immigration. He criticized the shallow, shrill thinking of the anti-Communist fanatics, following the lead of President Kennedy in this regard.

JFK's own evolution in this area was reflected not only by his role in the above changes but also throughout the government. He halted the Post Office's practice of intercepting Communist propaganda. He appointed to office or otherwise honored many of those who had been the most prominent targets, ten or twelve years earlier, of the McCarthy–McCarran probes. Awarding the Fermi prize to J. Robert Oppenheimer was an excellent example.

These were all personal decisions by JFK. Senator Eugene McCarthy in his 1968 campaign for the office criticized John Kennedy for having personalized the Presidency, and his premise was correct. Kennedy used his personal White House staff, his personal press conferences, his trips, television addresses, and telephone to spread his influence wide and deep. His personal identification with the office and its problems gave more Americans, particularly the young, a new and better grasp of what the Presidency could mean for our country. In the sense that he neither delegated major decisions nor submitted them to a Cabinet or National Security Council consensus, most of his decisions were personal.

The National Security Council had more appeal as a collective body for decision-making than the Cabinet, in the sense that its members, with the exception of the Director of Emergency Planning, were at least all officially concerned with foreign policy. But the rigidity, formality, paper work, and "protection of the President" inherent in NSC decision-making were unsuited to JFK's need to operate flexibly and to rely on personal conversations and staff. He convened the NSC infrequently after 1961, using it simply to keep everyone feeling informed and involved. He sensed that the NSC had been devised under Truman and used under Eisenhower to restore to the departments, to the military, and to the bureaucracy the control they had lost under FDR. Under JFK the White House was the dominant force in foreign policy. In the crucial early days of the Cuban missile crisis he did not convene meetings of either the NSC or the Cabinet but called together those advisers in whose judgment he had confidence regardless of title or rank, later labeling us the "Executive Committee" of the National Security Council.

I do not recommend his system for every President. John Kennedy had the necessary energy, talent, and confidence in his staff that made this system possible for him. It suited his nature and needs, his desire to involve himself at the ground level—particularly in the area of foreign affairs—and his determination to be master of the Executive Branch. It was his own combination of the Woodrow Wilson and Franklin Roosevelt approaches in which he had been steeped, an approach that grew as his own confidence and control of his subordinates grew.

Resistance from the Congress, however, was less easily overcome than resistance from within the Executive departments. JFK recognized that a majority in the Senate and particularly in the House consisted of Southern Democrats and Republicans unresponsive to either his ideas or his leadership. Until he could bring in a new Congress with his own re-election in 1964, he felt he could neither openly "declare war" on a Democratic Congress, as some urged, or abandon his most controversial legislative proposals, as others urged. His years as a young deferential Congressman and Senator, and his narrow margin of victory, caused him to move with considerable caution during his first two years. In 1963 even his Civil Rights Bill, his New Economics program, and his Nuclear Test Ban Treaty —all of which boldly challenged the bipartisan establishment on Capitol Hill—were the subjects of considerable Congressional consultation in advance as well as appeals for public pressure.

But as cautious as he was, the fact remains that most of the 1961 and 1962 Kennedy programs were enacted, including those measures that had been bottled up in the previous House of Representatives with its twenty-two additional Democrats. Nearly all of the 1963 Kennedy program passed, most of it, as mentioned, with the support of President Johnson in 1964 and 1965. The myth that Kennedy could get nothing controversial through the Congress is belied by the facts. The fact that he got anything controversial through the Congress at all is a tribute not only to the skills of Larry O'Brien and his staff but also to the President's own powers of persuasion and accommodation. He learned how to neutralize opponents as well as circumvent them—persuading obstreperous committee chairmen to hold a hearing or permit a vote, for example, even though they would cast their own votes against the Administration.

Even after fourteen years, John Kennedy had few intimate friends on Capitol Hill and no desire to spend his evenings socializing with them or their colleagues. Nevertheless, he made a special effort to gain the confidence of such powerful legislators as the late Robert Kerr in the Senate and Wilbur Mills in the House whose power could be used for either inertia or initiative. He understood the latter's unwillingness to be reversed by his committee or to have his committee reversed by the House, and he gradually nudged this highly responsible Arkansan into a position of leadership even on Kennedy's "Keynesian" fiscal policy. On the same trip in which he dedicated a dam in Mills' home district in Arkansas, he flew to Oklahoma with Bob Kerr for more dedications. (Although this was not one of them, there were always dams to dedicate in Oklahoma. In view of the staggering sums spent over the years of Kerr's service to make the Red River in Oklahoma navigable for commerce, JFK had earlier commented, it would have been cheaper to pave it over with beautiful boulevards.) Kerr had many of the hard-driving, power-manipulating instincts of Kennedy's father. Because JFK understood exactly what motivated the Oklahoma Senator and was frank with him about it, they developed a relationship of friendly banter.

In fact, JFK dealt with each Senator as an individual with different problems and pressures, treating no two alike, never regarding with uniform approval or disapproval the attitude of any one of them. He liked Senate Foreign Relations Committee Chairman J. William Fulbright, for example, but never regretted not naming him Secretary of State or not taking his recommendation *for* an invasion of Cuba at the time of the missile crisis. He did exceedingly regret not taking Fulbright's recommendation *against* an invasion of Cuba at the time of the Bay of Pigs. (Lyndon Johnson, then Vice President, later told me he wished he could emulate the time JFK effectively cut short a long, self-righteous sermon from Fulbright on our errors at the Bay of Pigs by quietly remarking, "You were right, Bill.")

Robert Kennedy as Attorney General had surprisingly successful Congressional relations—surprising not only because of his own more youthful impatience with Capitol Hill procrastination but also because his department's civil-rights and other activities greatly antagonized those Senators and Congressmen upon whose support the passage of his legislative program depended. Yet, as summed up by the *Washington Post* editorial on his retirement as Attorney General, he "guided more important legislation through Congress than did any of his predecessors in the past thirty years."

Frankly I doubt that he would have had similar success with the Congress as President. I believe he would have been barely nominated and narrowly elected President had he lived. But this would almost surely have been accompanied by bitter divisions within the party and within the country, in my opinion. His views and image would have continued to be the subject of deep controversy; and it seems unlikely that he could have taken into office with him in 1968 enough new and equally progressive Congressmen to offset the hostility he would face from the older, more entrenched members from the South and elsewhere. His hope was to build over the years a new Democratic Party that elected progressives from both suburban and working-class districts whose constituents, however diverse on certain sensitive issues, would respond to the strength of Presidential leadership.

While the foregoing is speculative, there is considerably less doubt that Bob Kennedy would have been a strong President. Having had more experience and preparation for executive command than JFK, confronted with more urgent domestic issues than JFK, and facing almost certainly a Congress even more hostile than that facing JFK, he would have moved with even less caution to exercise those unwritten powers that enable a President hamstrung by Congress nevertheless to lead the country. He would have enlisted private business and foundation resources, inspired community action, mobilized public opinion, energized political reform, increased academia's contribution to public policy, and drawn upon his prestige, experience, travels, and contacts to get things done when Congress or the bureaucracy balked. He would not have been content to leave the fate of the black, the poor, the migrant workers, the sharecroppers, and the Indians to a conservative Congress. Nor would he have left the decisions on war and peace to a vote of the National Security Council or the Joint Chiefs of Staff. He believed that the American people could be induced to do what was right, that our political system could be changed, led, and used accordingly.

JFK sought the Presidency in the belief that his values, standards, talents, and judgment would enable the country to move more vigorously toward a more certain peace around the world and a more equitable prosperity here at home. RFK sought the Presidency with more specific commitments—racial justice, an end to the war in Vietnam, and no more Vietnams; cleaning up our cities, providing jobs for all, strengthening progress in Latin America, and achieving a host of other reforms. JFK's final thirteen months had been his greatest thirteen months—resolving the Cuban missile crisis, building *détente* with the Soviets, championing civil rights, promoting the New Economics, triumphantly touring Europe, signing the Test Ban Treaty —and RFK wanted to start at that level, as far as it was possible, and build from there.

He would have been a more controversial President

than JFK, operating the Presidential office in much the same freewheeling way, being equally frank with the American people about their responsibilities and dangers, being equally adept at the political arrangements necessary to his program, but being less willing to bridge with soft words and adjustment the even wider gap that would have existed between his thinking and that of Congress. He would have walked in the ghettos and slums to cool tensions and hear complaints. He would have maintained open channels to the young and the disadvantaged. He would have traveled extensively to meet both the leaders and the citizens of other nations. (David Ben-Gurion told me early in 1966 that mankind's safety depended upon RFK's being elected President in 1968 and traveling secretly before his Inauguration to confer with Mao Tsetung. The subsequent upheavals in China diminished the merit of that proposal, but it is the kind of bold initiative that would have appealed to Robert Kennedy.) Like his older brother, he might well have been more appreciated as President by other peoples than by his own.

He would have, in short, exercised to the fullest in the White House the same sensitivity to the world's most pressing problems and most oppressed populations, the same determination to do whatever had to be done to ease those problems, and the same ability to work with political power, political techniques, and politicians that would have enabled him to reach the Presidency in the first place. He would, in one sense, have reunited the country—not by appealing to the lowest common denominator of opinion and not by obscuring issues or delaying disputes but by confronting the problems that divide us and working out specific solutions to them. Had he been able to demonstrate to the young, black, and poor that our system could work and that peaceful revolution was possible, to divert billions of dollars from military to domestic uses, and to bring to the Presidency the kind of leadership his older brother had offered, he might have united the country peacefully. There is no other way.

"The essence of . . . the Kennedy legacy," he once said in a speech referring to his brother, in words equally applicable to himself, "is a willingness to try and to dare and to change, to hope the uncertain and to risk the unknown." Both John and Bob Kennedy never stopped meeting that test until sudden death made it impossible for us to know how much greater their legacy might have been.

PART THREE

Retrospective

D URING THE 1968 PRESIDENTIAL CAM-
paign, one proud RFK staffer confided to the press that his
employer's campaign speeches were far better and bolder
than JFK's 1960 campaign speeches. Eugene McCarthy
implied that Robert Kennedy's positions required him to
disavow John Kennedy's. The cars of many anti-RFK Democrats sported bumper stickers reading BOB AIN'T JACK.

He wasn't, and he never pretended to be, despite some
conscious and some unconscious efforts to imitate his older
brother's platform style and a strong desire to identify himself with his brother's causes. Indeed, the loss of Robert
Kennedy is all the more grievous because we did lose something other than a carbon copy of John Kennedy. We lost
a unique individual with his own ideas and ideals and
potential for the future. It is not possible to measure fully
the changes he wrought, much less those he would have
wrought, in American policy and life.

If one compares RFK in his race for the Presidency in
1968 with JFK at the same age in his Presidential race in
1960, the differences between them prove many and im-

portant—not because they were basically different in character, nature, or motivation but because Bob in 1968 reflected far different kinds of pressure, public issues, and experience than did Jack in 1960. The questions of race, religion, and the cold war cast a far different shadow in 1968 than they had in 1960. While at times their greatness was manifested in different ways, both brothers were exceptionally great men and neither suffers in comparison with the other.

Bob Kennedy in 1968 differed from John Kennedy in 1960 in all the personal ways described in Part One. In addition, his greater experience and exposure gave him by 1968 more certainty and more ferocity about what he felt to be morally right. To achieve what he thought was right, he was even more willing than JFK had been in 1960—and JFK was not easily deterred then—to fight or give or sacrifice whatever was necessary.

Bob by 1968 had won the intense devotion of a far wider circle of close friends than Jack had ever sought, as well as the intense hostility of a far larger number of bitter enemies. Bob's most intimate friends were likely to be less concentrated than Jack's in their social, intellectual, economic, and ethnic backgrounds, although neither made new friendships easily. He had somewhat more rapport with blacks and somewhat less with workingmen than his older brother had. Blacks were in fact among his personal friends to an extent not true of JFK in 1960.

In that 1960 campaign John Kennedy sought to awaken American voters to the urgent needs of our time. In the 1968 campaign Robert Kennedy sought to remold American institutions to become more responsive to those needs his brother had succeeded in awakening. In 1960 JFK laid stress on updating the outmoded New Deal–Fair Deal programs. In 1968, those old programs having been updated without proving adequate, RFK laid stress on wholly new departures from the programs of a previous generation. In 1960 JFK warned that our position in the world was endangered if we did not spend more on missiles and on space exploration. In 1968, with our arms sufficient and our space posture secure, RFK warned that our position in the world was endangered if we did not seek bilateral curbs on missiles and put domestic priorities ahead of the burgeoning space program.

The typical public impression of John Kennedy was generally that of a forceful, graceful man, determined in his goals but soft-spoken in his ways. In private he was in fact very much that kind of man. The typical public impression of Robert Kennedy, particularly before the 1968 campaign, was generally that of a hard, relentless, and ruthless man, lacking consideration and compassion. In private he was in fact very different from that kind of man. If religion had not been a factor, John Kennedy as a Presidential *candidate* would not have incurred either the fervent devotion or fervent resentment he would later receive as President. Bob Kennedy, even *before* he became a Presidential candidate, was one of the most widely admired and widely detested men in American life.

JFK spent fourteen years as a member of both houses of Congress. Despite his conviction that real power lay elsewhere, he enjoyed his service and his associates. RFK spent three and a half years as a conscientious and surprisingly active member of the Senate but was frequently bored and impatient with its wrangling and prima donnas. Bob Kennedy involved himself far more deeply (if not more successfully) than Jack in the internal political struggles of the state which sent him to the Senate. In both the Legislative and Executive Branches he took more interest in problems of administration and implementation than Jack, whose penchant was policy-making. They reacted differently to such diverse persons and institutions as the military and diplomatic establishments, Lyndon Johnson, old-time Irish Catholic politicians, and *The New York Times.*

Considering the passage of time, some of these differences between JFK in 1960 and RFK in 1968 were inevitable. Events in general—and the Vietnam war and civil-rights revolution in particular—had combined to make the issues far sharper, feelings among the electorate far more heated, and divisions on the basis of age, wealth, race, and sometimes intellect far deeper in 1968. Representing New York in the United States Senate, moreover, required a perspective different from that of representing Massachusetts. Bob had learned from Jack and from his service with him, and he benefited in 1968 from Jack's reputation. Bob inherited some of his positions and policy advisers from Jack, who had been required to build his from scratch. Bob also inherited a few of Jack's political enemies.

Parts One and Two make clear other reasons for their differences. Their approaches to life differed in part because Bob had married far earlier than Jack, and his life and outlook had been shaped by these family ties longer (to say nothing of having produced more children); and in part because, since childhood, he had been more physically rugged than his brother, though he was shorter. Politically their appeal differed in part because Bob had run for elective office far less than Jack, and the sharp edges of his public personality were not yet as rounded off. Campaigning for the Presidency not only as a Senator but as a former Attorney General and National Security Council member whose brother was a martyred President made possible in 1968 a very different stature from that which was attached in 1960 to a seemingly untried Senator from

Massachusetts of the same age. According to Bob's own statement to me, all his own special talents and drive would never have been enough to make him a Presidential contender had it not been for his brother, his brother's election, Administration, and position in public memory, and his brother's mantle and legacy.

After the election, and particularly after the assassination of John Kennedy, it was widely assumed that Robert Kennedy would seek the Presidency. John Kennedy, even after he declared his candidacy in 1960, was widely assumed (as a young Catholic) to be seeking the Vice Presidency. Bob had past images to overcome in his Presidential campaign—as a prosecutor, as a carpetbagger, and as a Joe McCarthy supporter—more severe than those facing Jack in 1960. He lacked Jack's advantage of having been a well-publicized war hero.

Bob's position on deeply controversial issues was more sharply defined than his brother's had been in 1960. He had been to Indian reservations, migrant labor camps, and Mississippi Delta sharecropper shacks never visited by Jack. Yet the latter's Presidential race had to overcome the suspicion of the Kennedy father, the family wealth, and above all the barriers of religion and age which would otherwise have severely handicapped Bob's Presidential race eight years later. Bob in his Presidential campaign at forty-three felt compelled to prove his credentials to suspicious liberals, intellectuals, students, and doves; Jack had to prove in his campaign that a forty-three-year-old Catholic Senator with no executive experience could be reliable and trustworthy.

Finally, their contributions to the legacy differ because Bob Kennedy articulated his views primarily as a Senator and campaigner, limited only by his own good judgment and discretion. John Kennedy's most important policy pro-

nouncements came as President, when his freedom to in-
dulge in long-range, high-principled innovations was
severely limited by the burdens of nearly monthly crises,
by the restricting influences of limited resources, by the
caution-inducing cares of ultimate responsibility, and by
the desire not to flood Congress with bills having no prospect of passage. Many of his greatest contributions came
during his last year, after he had gained greater mastery
over both the job and his own political instincts. His freer
approach to the office during that period suggests what an
RFK Presidency would have been like under comparable
conditions.

Because of these contrasts between the two brothers,
some have said there is not one Kennedy legacy but two.
Yet the differences between them were far less numerous
and far less important than the similarities, excluding even
the usual number of common ties and traits two closely
allied members of the same family are certain to possess.
Perhaps it is not too surprising that two brothers both
attended Harvard, both served in the Navy, both maintained a lifelong interest in sports, and both spent virtually
all of their adult careers in public service in Washington.
It is not remarkable that both maintained, usually without
question or passion, the political and religious affiliations
they inherited from their parents, or that both were sometimes careless about the money they inherited as well.
Most of us know of other examples of brothers possessing
the same strong sense of family loyalty and unity (and in
some ways superiority), the same deep affection for each
other, for their own wives and children and parents, and
the same keen instincts for competition, for public service,
and for a sense of decency and compassion and humanity
in public affairs.

But the parallels in the careers of the two Kennedy

brothers went beyond those derived from a common family background. Their chosen associates were usually more intellectual and liberal than most of their father's associates, with a large seasoning of journalists and academics. They were both natural, spontaneous human beings, with highly developed senses of humor that were at their best when poking fun at themselves. Yet both were sensitive to criticism of themselves and each other, unlikely to forget past slights or to forgive incompetence.

Both advanced in the world of politics and government through a special capacity to lead and inspire, to attract talented assistants and devoted aides, and to generate enthusiasm, excitement, and hope among even the cynical, the skeptical, and the troubled. They were natural leaders in whatever they did, demanding and giving unswerving loyalty. Both demonstrated sweeping and creative initiative on the one hand and a persistence for following up detail on the other. Both gave bores even shorter shrift than hypocrites and not only avoided clichés but practiced a painfully honest candor in public as well as private utterances to an extent unprecedented in modern American politics—and indeed risky for their careers. Both demonstrated enough integrity and courage to get away (usually) with the kind of political arrangements or even compromises that were necessary to achieve what they deemed right.

Many men reach Washington and stop growing, stop learning, and, above all, stop listening. Yesterday's liberals have become today's conservatives, not because they changed but because they failed to change. The world passed them by in their self-importance. But not the Kennedys. Each one became through the years a deeper, wiser, warmer human being. Each one retained an open mind, remained alert to new ideas, and was continually willing to hear and to try new proposals and postulates. Both outgrew youthful weaknesses in judgment—a tendency toward hasty, snap judgments on the part of RFK prior to 1960, a tendency toward shallow, politically motivated judgments on the part of JFK prior to 1952. As the world changed, as the folly of war and the persistence of racism and the failure of traditional liberal answers all became more apparent, they changed their own outlook and answers.

Both men traveled extensively, around their own country and around the world, not sight-seeing but experience-seeking, gaining insight into different cultures and appreciation of coming crises. Both men read extensively, books and periodicals of all kinds and tastes, and both remembered and applied what they had read. Both men sought out the wise men of their times, consulting experts and specialists of many fields, and had the ability to sort the good advice from the bad and the practical from the impractical. But they listened to ordinary men as well, to their troubles and needs. Both demanded high standards from their staffs and expected us to work as hard as they did. From all this they gained and grew—and that capacity for continuing growth is itself a part of the legacy.

The change in Bob Kennedy during the last years of his life was not so great as it seemed to outsiders unaware of his growing compassion and liberalism as Attorney General. But both men over the years became more progressive in their outlook, partly from their growth and experience and new learning, partly from an increased willingness to listen to free-speaking advisers, and partly from their interaction with each other, particularly in civil rights and civil liberties. It is fair to say, in addition, that some of their attempts to master new subjects never fully succeeded. JFK would later show real aptitude as an economist, but both men ran for the Presidency with only a bare understanding of fiscal policy, even less of monetary problems, and none whatsoever of the agricultural programs they espoused.

As both were driven by enormous ambition and both had been endowed with extraordinary vitality and energy, they both became skilled politicians without being ashamed of that profession. Both knew more before they died about the political pitfalls, personalities, and profiles in all fifty states than any other professional politician. Yet both disliked small talk with small politicians and were shy with large crowds. Both were uncomfortable with the artificial gloss which political protocol imposes.

Both defeated popular moderate Republican incumbents to win their seats in the Senate. Both mistakenly but anxiously sought the Vice Presidential nomination before they were forty, and both refused to settle for anything less than the Presidency in the subsequent national elections. Both began their Presidential campaigns suspected by liberal intellectuals of being unprincipled political opportunists, opposed by the party professionals and old-line labor leaders as being too independent, and denounced by the business and professional establishment as being too liberal.

Both of their Presidential campaigns called upon a reluctant electorate to face up to the necessity for change, Bob Kennedy at a time when the voters were tired of change and Jack Kennedy at a time when they were unaccustomed to it. Both campaigned on the issues of the day, including moral, international, and economic issues; but both relied as well on personal charisma, on natural eloquence, and on an unusual ability to reach not only the well educated but also the young, the disadvantaged, the children who could not vote, and the women who apparently found some kind of gratification in screaming, jumping, and running up to touch them.

Both knowingly but fearlessly took risks—political,

personal, and physical risks—in their brief but very full lives. Both were the victims of assassination by gunfire from young, slight, faceless men acting out of senseless motives. Both were the subjects of moving funeral ceremonies as well as world-wide grief. They lie buried near each other in Arlington National Cemetery. That is enough parallel for any two men.

Yet the Kennedy legacy is based not on the parallel history of the two brothers but on their common philosophy, on the policies they developed and the guidelines they left for the future. How is that philosophy to be classified? It is not enough to say that it was rooted in the traditions of Woodrow Wilson and Franklin Roosevelt, for most of the questions had changed and so had their answers. It is not enough to say that they were both liberals, now that that term—in the process of being condemned by some, claimed by others, and stretched by still others—has lost much of its original meaning. Both strongly resisted being categorized as liberals; and the essence of the Kennedy legacy is its capacity to carry this country and its political thought beyond traditional liberalism.

If the Kennedy brothers were in fact liberals, it was not because they subscribed to some doctrinaire collection of dogma hallowed by the repeated embrace of various famous figures on the left but because they believed in innovation, in reform, in experimentation, and in peaceful revolution against the *status quo* and the establishment. Unlike some self-styled revolutionaries in our campuses and cities today, they abhorred and abjured violence. Theirs was not a simple destructive philosophy that sought to tear down structures or systems for which no superior substitute was offered. The Kennedys were not merely negative, they did not confine themselves to finding fault and seeing only the dark side of whatever institution or policy they were examining. Yet a theme reiterated over and over again in both 1960 and 1968 was "I am not satisfied . . . That is not acceptable . . . We can do better."

Neither Kennedy turned his back on the Old Politics and its practitioners while embracing the New. Their campaigns blended realism with idealism and practical politics with lofty aspirations. The traditional Democratic coalition—the big-city political organizations, the labor unions, the liberals and intellectuals, the racial and nationality groups, even the South and the farm vote—could not be ignored or destroyed, in their opinion; for the New Politics of the young, the disadvantaged, the reformer, the academic, the religious, and the amateur had not yet gained the political muscle necessary to take its place. Instead they wanted the remnants of the old and the new combined in a new coalition, rebuilt at the grass-roots level. It would principally depend not on a handful of leaders and supposed spokesmen but on rank-and-file Democrats—citizens who would respond not merely to the promise of patronage or the threat of punishment but to ideas, to leadership, and to the prospects of peaceful change through political action. This was exactly the kind of "coalition" the Kennedys had forged in the 1952 Massachusetts Senate compaign against Henry Cabot Lodge—giving authority on the local level to campaign "secretaries" who were new to politics, going outside the regular organization without trying to defeat it.

The Kennedy brothers applied their philosophy of politics to governmental affairs as well. They believed in the politics of persuasion, not the politics of violent confrontation or chaos, in international, interracial, and other disputes. They were opposed to the use of force of any kind whenever it could be avoided—by the police or by a mob, by the military or by revolutionaries, by minority groups or by vigilantes. They believed in letting reason rule and dissent flourish, without yielding to the easy answers of the extremists or providing simplistic answers of their own. Possessing an abundance of common sense and good conscience, as well as confidence in the capacity of those attributes to choose the right course, they were unwilling to leave war to the professional generals, peace to the professional diplomats, or politics to the professional politicians.

The policies of RFK in his last year went beyond what JFK sought in his last year. Building a new constituency of his own, speaking out for the dispossessed of the earth in a way JFK never had, he might well have carved out—had he lived to become President—a wholly new and different legacy of his own. But to a large extent even those policies of his last year had grown out of and built upon the principles and spirit of JFK and his Administration, an Administration in which RFK played a major role. On June 6, 1968, their legacies were still one, and Robert Kennedy would not be less proud to have his legacy merged in history with that of his brother Jack.

They shared a common attitude about citizen involvement. From the beginning of his full-scale Presidential campaigning in 1959 until his assassination in 1963, John Kennedy sought to shake Americans out of their complacency, to involve the young, to awaken aspirations, to encourage participation in politics and the Peace Corps and the public service. Because JFK succeeded in those endeavors, Robert Kennedy, from 1965 until his own assassination in 1968, was able to utilize his energies to protect the rights of dissenters and demonstrators, to channel their energies, to reform our political and governmental institutions so that the desire to participate could be realized.

They shared a common attitude about American power. In 1960 and 1961 John Kennedy (some inconsistent Inaugural rhetoric notwithstanding) warned that America was not omnipotent or omniscient, that it could not be omnipresent or stretch its global commitments beyond the realistic limits of its capacity to influence events. In 1967 and 1968 Robert Kennedy warned that neither our populace nor our economy was able indefinitely to support our role as world policeman and that a reshuffling of our priorities to meet more relevant needs would be required for both domestic and international peace.

They shared a common attitude about human rights. In 1963 John Kennedy declared, as no President had ever previously declared, that all forms of racial discrimination and segregation should be adjudged not only legally but morally wrong, thereby converting civil rights from a political football into a question of national honor. Robert Kennedy, having joined in that declaration and its implementation as Attorney General, strove later, as United States Senator and Presidential candidate, to achieve equality in practice as well as in theory for black-skinned, brown-skinned, red-skinned, and all other kinds of Americans.

They shared a common attitude about Executive power. From 1960 to 1963, after the torpor of the Eisenhower era, John Kennedy preached and practiced the doctrine of the strong Presidency, utilizing to the fullest all the written and unwritten powers of that office, unwilling to subordinate his own judgment to either the group decision-making of his Cabinet or to the insulated expertise of the permanent bureaucracy. In 1968 Robert Kennedy differed from many liberals (who had been antagonized by the Johnson Presidency) by continuing to stress the need for leadership in that office, the single most potent position from which the unrepresented and underprivileged could be championed effectively.

They shared a common attitude about escalation in Vietnam. In 1961 President Kennedy rejected the recommendation that he place American combat divisions (as distinct from more men to be used as advisers, instructors, and for logistics and supply) in Vietnam, convinced that such a move would only lead to Americanization of a largely civil war that the Vietnamese would have to settle themselves. From 1965 to 1968 Senator Robert Kennedy became one of the nation's most forceful voices against the government's policy of escalation in Vietnam.

They shared a common attitude about nuclear arms. In 1963 President Kennedy's proudest moment came with the final ratification of the Nuclear Test Ban Treaty, the first solid step toward disarmament in the nuclear world. In 1965 Robert Kennedy's first major speech in the United States Senate urged early conclusion of a Nuclear Nonproliferation Treaty. Both brothers spent the last three years of their lives warning against the spread of nuclear weapons and a resumption of the arms race.

They shared a common attitude about Latin America. In 1961 President Kennedy initiated the Alliance for Progress, a long-range effort to secure political and economic independence for Latin America through revolutionary but peaceful reform and development, stressing self-help as well as financial assistance from the United States. In 1965 Robert Kennedy traveled throughout Latin America, bringing back a message filled both with pessimistic reports on our neglect of the *Alianza* and optimistic reports on the potential of the continent.

There is more to this list—including common objectives on education, health, conservation, consumer protection, welfare, housing, and urban redevelopment—objectives that were sought by President Kennedy and then expanded and improved by Senator Kennedy. The ending of religious barriers to the White House is an important part of their contribution. But the above will surely suffice to show that there is indeed a Kennedy legacy, that it consists not of two legacies but of one, and that it is with us today regardless of Ted Kennedy's personal error or political future. It is broader and deeper than it was after the death of John Kennedy, more powerful, more precise, and more urgently needed. It is not simply a jumble of personal styles and surviving politicians; it is not simply history or memories or a list of statutes and proclamations. It is a composite and coherent body of concepts and principles which evolved from many people, not only the Kennedys, over many years. It is these concepts and principles—so long as they are dynamic and not dogmatic—which can continue for years and possibly decades to be relevant and effective in meeting rationally and humanely the challenges of the modern world.

The task of defining this legacy would be greatly simplified if the two brothers had relied upon a single unifying theme or guiding principle. But the Kennedys were not much given to talking in the language of "grand designs." Nor were they given to oversimplifying multiple, complex problems into slogans or picket-line placards. John Kennedy originally applied the New Frontier label to his public philosophy but subsequently interpreted that label in differing ways and most of the time ignored it altogether. Bob Kennedy rejected all the campaign slogans put forward by his advisers and advertising agencies in 1968 and never did settle on one phrase that could symbolize all he intended. Both concentrated on specific subjects rather than on an underlying philosophy, having had no well-defined political approach when they began public life.

Three over-all concepts can be said, however, at least to sum up much of their collective wisdom and work.

First is the Kennedy brothers' belief in peaceful revolution, in achieving radical change without violence at home and abroad. John Kennedy, though he often resented the term, was a pragmatist—not because he believed that government should become a largely administrative function requiring only expert bookkeepers and technocrats—but because he believed our system could be made to work, that it could be revised and reshaped and used as an instrument to influence human events and to bring hope to human lives. He avoided the rigid shoals of ideology but not the open seas of idealism; and these same ideals eventually carried Robert Kennedy far beyond the traditional waters of liberalism.

Both brothers sought basic changes in the nation's priorities and in the allocation of its resources, RFK accelerating what JFK had started. Both recognized that the accepted concepts of liberalism handed down from the thirties were not always enough for the sixties. Both sought, to the dismay of old-line New Dealers, to obtain through tax changes the enlistment of private industry's desire for profit in the drive for job expansion. Both sought, over the opposition of powerful labor leaders, to disregard entrenched union practices in efforts to hire hard-core unemployed and nonwhites. Neither was satisfied with merely updating the programs of Franklin Roosevelt and Harry Truman on housing, agriculture, welfare, and other problems that did not now respond to those solutions. Both wanted to depart from the typical Democratic doctrine that Federal money and omniscience were the answers to every problem. RFK's initiation of the Bedford-Stuyvesant experiment in community control and development illustrates as nothing else could his search for new institutions for the poor and the powerless who were largely outside the political system.

Injustice, in their view, did not justify violence because our system made it possible to persuade the majority to change. Having reconciled the diverse forces that struggled within themselves, they believed that other men—black and white, rich and poor, Communist and capitalist—could be reconciled as well, not by compelling one side to submit to another, not by obtaining consensus at the lowest common denominator, but through the rule of reason and the art of persuasion, by accepting differences and dissent without rancor. The Kennedys did not favor peace at any price, for that would only encourage one side of a dispute to force its will on the other. But any resort to violence represented to them a failure of policy and a foothold for hate.

Second, the Kennedy brothers believed in the fundamental concept of free choice for all who were willing and able to exercise it in a way not harmful to others. That raises difficult questions about our response and our responsibility in cases where other peoples are deprived of that choice by armed outsiders and then look to the U.S. for protection. But their own lives, in one instance after another, demonstrated man's ability to disregard fate, to challenge the odds, to hammer out his own contribution to his fellow men in his own way. All nations, they believed, should be free to choose their own form of government, their own leaders, and their own social and economic systems without the United States, the Soviet Union, China, their agents, or anyone else preventing them from making that choice. In our own country, blacks should be as free as whites to choose their schools or jobs or neighborhoods. Discrimination and involuntary segregation of any kind deny freedom of choice, and wars and depressions severely limit it. Until students have more voice in the conduct of their universities, until the poor have a real voice in the management of antipoverty programs, until local communities such as Bedford-Stuyvesant have a greater voice in determining their fate, until all the decision-making institutions that shape our future are opened up democratically—including churches and unions as well as governments and political parties—democracy, the Kennedys said in effect, will be imperfect in this country and our children will suffer limits on their future.

This introduces the *third* and most important theme of the Kennedy legacy—a pervasive sense of responsibility for the future of our children, for those already born and those yet to be born, for those who live in this country and those who live in other lands. As frank as they were about this generation's ills, the Kennedys had an underlying confidence in the next. Without rejecting the wisdom or the best traditions of the past, they wanted more innovation and experimentation in government to make their children's future brighter.

Their greatest concern when war seemed imminent over Soviet missiles in Cuba was its unfairness to the very young, to those who had never had a chance, never savored life, never cast a vote or made a move to bring on the hostilities and devastation that would fall most heavily upon them.

Their most often cited statistics on the issue of race related to children, to the Negro or Puerto Rican or Indian or Mexican-American child who would have far less chance than his white counterpart to attend a decent school and find a decent job and live in decent health and housing.

Their interest in preventing not only wars of mass destruction but the waste of our natural and material resources, their interest in preserving wetlands and wilderness areas and seashores and forests, in halting the radioactive and other pollution of our environment, in improving the quality of American life, reflected their concern for those future generations for whom, JFK once wrote, the occupant of the White House must act as President.

It was the children, they realized, who suffered most from our outmoded, humiliating welfare programs, from rising unemployment, from hunger and crime and slum living, and especially from inadequate schools. Because they both dearly loved their own children and had such high hopes for them, because they both—particularly RFK —had a natural rapport with almost all the children they met, because they both felt that children represented the future, the hope for better times, the means to a better world, the Kennedy brothers both consciously and unconsciously fashioned their public philosophy toward them.

Had John Kennedy lived, ours would be a different world today—because Vietnam and the cold war and black power and student idealism would be on a different course. Had Robert Kennedy lived, it would be a different world —because he would have, however narrowly, been elected President, living proof that the American system is responsive to change, living evidence of what one man who cared could accomplish, a living symbol of hope for all who now despair of ever ending racial discrimination and war. The impact of that double loss cannot be fully grasped. No one can assert that American history would have remained unchanged if both Jefferson and Paine had been killed during the first five years of the movement for independence or if either of the Roosevelts had been gunned down during his first Presidential term or campaign.

Yet the Kennedy legacy was not wholly dependent upon the Kennedys, wholly devised by them, or meant wholly for them. Their principles and policies had many fathers and many followers, including many who supported other Presidential candidates in 1968. The loss of the two Kennedys, and the present removal of Ted Kennedy as a Presidential candidate, need not mark the end of the Kennedy legacy. Others must now carry it forward. For those sufficiently free of inflexible dogma and traditional liturgies to believe that a peaceful, human revolution is possible, for those who seek to remodel rather than throw out or throw over with violence and hate our present political system, the spirit and method of the Kennedy legacy provide the guidelines and the motivation for the reconstruction of our society. If enough men of goodwill can undertake this task now in the spirit and philosophy of John and Robert Kennedy, it is not too late "to seek a newer world." But we may not be given a second chance.

PART FOUR

Prospective

T HE SHOCK OF ROBERT KENNEDY'S
assassination in June 1968 left the Democratic Party and
political life in this country depressed, dispirited, and dis-
united for months thereafter. This was devastatingly true
of the amorphous "Kennedy group," composed of those
men and women who had worked for Bob or both Kennedys in politics or government, at the local or national
level, in high positions or obscure. While still in the depths
of grief following his funeral, I was besieged with inquiries from strangers as well as co-workers seeking a new
outlet for their energies and idealism and asking the same
questions over and over: "What are we going to do now?"
"Where do we go from here?" The questions referred to
the long-range future of the Kennedy constituency and
legacy, as well as to the immediate problem of the then
upcoming Democratic National Convention. The latter
required an answer first, to whatever extent we could
give one.

Some members of the Kennedy team soon returned to
the campaign arena in aid of Senator McCarthy. Some

went to work for Vice President Humphrey; a few supported Governor Rockefeller; others worked for local candidates for public office. Still others waited hopefully for Ted Kennedy or some unpredictable new development. But many—key leaders and rank-and-file followers—felt unwilling and unable to rejoin the fray before the convention in any serious way. The memories of criticisms directed at Robert Kennedy from the other camps, the bitter hopelessness that had seized us upon experiencing this second Kennedy murder, the necessary absence of any cohesive leadership or even communication within the remaining Kennedy team, all inhibited any effective move to another candidate.

It might have seemed logical for the bulk of the Kennedy strength to move promptly into the McCarthy effort. The Minnesotan's willingness to be the first to challenge the party establishment in New Hampshire was admired by us all; his mobilization of student power had given a much needed lift to the peace movement; his credentials as a liberal Congressman and Senator were good; and with important exceptions—such as gun control, the powers of the Presidency, and empathy with ghetto dwellers—his approach not only to Vietnam but to many other issues of the campaign had been similar to, if less specific than, RFK's. An ultimate combination of the Kennedy and McCarthy forces had long been deemed by most of the leaders of both groups (each thinking their candidate would triumph) to be necessary, desirable, and likely.

Unfortunately, what is apparently logical does not always occur in politics. The Kennedy delegates were not a bloc, once their leader was gone. They had rallied to his candidacy for a variety of reasons, not all related to his stand on Vietnam or even to other issues. For many it was his strength of leadership, for many it was his personal charisma. At no time could RFK himself have taken all of them into the McCarthy column had he lived and so desired, just as Senator McCarthy could not have taken all his delegates into the Kennedy column had he so desired (and neither would have so desired). Old wounds from the Kennedy–McCarthy primary fights were still unhealed in August 1968; too many of us were still traumatized by the events of June to work for a former opponent; and no effort was made by the leaders of either camp to bridge these divisions and seek a common cause.

Convinced that Senator McCarthy could not obtain a majority of convention delegates to halt the pro-Administration juggernaut, Senator George McGovern of South Dakota offered himself late in the summer as an alternate attraction for those Kennedy workers who were contemplating support of Humphrey or dropping out altogether. A thoughtful and extremely conscientious member of the Senate, McGovern had been close to both John and Robert Kennedy. He was one of the first to speak out against America's deepening involvement in Vietnam. He had, as mentioned in Part One, been aproached in 1967, after Kennedy and before McCarthy, by those seeking a candidate to pit against President Johnson. Having quietly worked with Kennedy in the South Dakota primary, he felt—after RFK had been assassinated and McCarthy had still been unable to put together a potentially winning combination—that his own candidacy might make less inevitable a victory for the pro-Vietnam forces at the convention.

Contrary to press reports, I neither urged nor helped direct his brief campaign, although I finally cast a quiet vote for him at the convention partly because of our long friendship. I had in fact replied skeptically when he telephoned to tell me that he was converting his candidacy from favorite-son status to a serious national effort. In the absence of a first-ballot deadlock McGovern had no prospect of affecting the outcome. Nevertheless, he emerged from the convention with increased national stature and respect, despite understandable resentment from Senator McCarthy, and managed to shake off the ill effects of the Chicago Convention scene on South Dakota voters in time to win re-election to the Senate.

Hubert Humphrey's nomination became inevitable after Robert Kennedy's assassination, but his campaign sagged as a result of it. His "politics of joy" approach had become an embarrassment. Many of his biggest financial backers, the Vice President candidly told me in a mid-July meeting, had been motivated chiefly by their hostility toward Robert Kennedy, and the latter's death had ended their willingness to contribute. The Administration forces were excluding him from convention arrangements, he said, and the McCarthy forces were needlessly poisoning the already bitter atmosphere within the party. He would not flatly repudiate the Administration's previous decisions to escalate the war in Vietnam, he told me, because he still saw nothing wrong with them; but he vowed to propose an independent, dovelike position of his own on the war before the delegates deliberated in Chicago. Unfortunately, intransigence on the part of the Administration forces prevented both Humphrey's issuance of such a statement and a truly deliberative convention.

Party and Chicago leaders, symbolized by Mayor Richard Daley, were fearful that anti-Vietnam protests would turn the convention and the city into a shambles and equally fearful of the harsh confrontation that was both threatened and desired by a small minority of visiting revolutionaries. Yet the convention planners proceeded to produce exactly the same effects themselves through excessive, indiscriminate, and undisciplined security arrangements, both inside and outside of Convention Hall. Needlessly harassed delegates and newsmen on the inside became increasingly antagonistic; and youthful demonstrators on the outside, only a minority of whom were organized troubleseekers, found themselves driven from the parks and peaceful parade routes into confrontations with the police and National Guard.

Insufficiently prepared by training or leadership to withstand the obscene insults and obnoxious tactics of the ill-intentioned few, too many policemen and Guardsmen responded with night sticks, tear gas, Mace, and physical assault on the well-intentioned many. Bystanders were caught up in the violence, some cheering on the police and some being attacked by them. The result was a sick and ugly chapter in American political history.

The convention itself was too discordant behind barricades for the incumbent Democratic President even to appear before it, though it was ruled with skilled rigidity by those voicing their virtual last hurrahs as party leaders. It proved little more than the overdue need to overhaul that entire system of selecting candidates. A national primary might well destroy party cohesion. Without a runoff it could produce nominees unrepresentative of majority opinion within the party; and a runoff would only double for the exhausted survivors the exorbitant financial cost of entering such a primary. But all delegates to a national convention, if it is to fulfill its dual role of achieving a representative choice and a reconciled party, should be selected in a democratic fashion in the same year as the convention on a one-man, one-vote basis in which each delegate's position on the candidates and issues is known to all Democrats in his area. The Platform Committee, similarly apportioned, should be a quadrennial agent for innovation based on expert study and debate. A real dialogue on the real issues facing the party should replace parades and pomposity on the convention floor. These and other reforms are required now for a truly open convention.

At least the Democratic Convention of 1968, unlike the Republican Convention in Miami ("polite, white, and irrelevant," to use the words of Adlai Stevenson III), faced up to reality instead of turning its back on it. Despite—not because of—its attitude toward the street demonstrations, the convention surprised itself by adopting several limited but meaningful reforms. In abolishing the unit rule, in insuring genuine participation by blacks in the selection of Southern delegations, and in paving the way for other convention and party reforms in the future, the Chicago gathering did take several important steps forward—steps that will have a liberalizing effect on Democratic politics long after the tear-gas smoke that obscured them has figuratively as well as literally drifted away. Many members of the "Kennedy group," it might be noted, played prominent roles in the convention proceedings.

The convention's finest hour was reached in its full-scale debate over the platform plank on Vietnam. Those of us who participated as members of the Platform Committee in the drafting of the minority peace plank had to overcome some internal tensions of our own, related to personalities, pride of authorship, and primarily the old Kennedy–McCarthy divisions. But we managed to produce a statement on Vietnam which, without being either as perfect or as different from the majority plank as we said it was, offered the party an important symbolic opportunity: an opportunity to tell the country that the nomination of Humphrey did not mean a continuation of the

Johnson Vietnam policy, an opportunity to tell the young dissenters in the streets of Chicago and back home that their efforts to achieve change through orderly political processes had not been entirely in vain.

Considerably influenced by Ted Kennedy's nationally televised speech on Vietnam the previous week in Worcester, Massachusetts, our plank was deliberately mild. It contained no condemnation of American or South Vietnamese leaders or even past decisions. Its prospects already weakened by the Soviet invasion of Czechoslovakia (also the previous week), it avoided any hint of unilateral withdrawal or an imposed coalition government. It was in fact wholly consistent with the objectives, if not the tactics, of the Johnson Administration's policy as it would be developed later in the fall.

Vice President Humphrey had hoped for a compromise Vietnam plank moving vaguely and gingerly away from the old Administration position. He had authorized approaches to several doves on the Platform Committee, including myself. But nothing came of them. The Administration forces refused to compromise and the McCarthy–McGovern–Kennedy forces needed an open floor contest. Even though Humphrey would apparently take no action that might alienate his pro-Administration supporters, I still had a faint hope, as I spoke from the rostrum near the close of the debate, that the Vice President would at least quietly pass the word to his supporters to permit the "peace plank" to pass without his open endorsement. Had he done so, there might well have been celebrations instead of riots in the streets of Chicago that night. Then he could have endorsed the entire platform with the minority plank in it, and the disgruntlement of those Southern Governors and others who in November were able to deliver very few votes to him anyway would have been more than offset by a surge of workers and enthusiasm at the start of his campaign. But Humphrey, still unwilling to offend the Lyndon Johnson–George Meany–John Connally loyalists, who had been the most powerful sponsors of his nomination and could not accept this seeming repudiation of Administration policy, did not pass this word, and our plank was defeated. So, in November, was Humphrey.

Actually, by the time the platform was debated, the nomination was not then in doubt, Ted Kennedy having conclusively removed himself from the consideration of a convention still unenthusiastic over its choices. McCarthy's strength among delegates, particularly after a well-publicized statement that seemed to them to dismiss the Soviet invasion of Czechoslovakia, was less than his strength in the electorate as a whole; and his supporters were hard put to convince party leaders that, in addition to the Oregon votes, McCarthy's losing primary votes and Bob Kennedy's winning primary votes should be combined to form a mandate for McCarthy.

A large number of both Humphrey and McCarthy delegates told me they thought that RFK, had he lived, would have been the strongest candidate at the convention, avoiding most of the wrangling and violence. A prolonged spontaneous tribute to him—in the singing of repeated choruses of the "Battle Hymn of the Republic" following a convention film biography—symbolized for many of us the strength and affection he retained on that dispirited floor. During the summer the continuation of the Vietnam war and Humphrey's own failure to mount an independent and inspiring campaign had drained the momentum from the Vice President's drive for the nomination that was nevertheless his by default. A narrow RFK victory would most likely have emerged from Chicago had fate not removed him from the contest. No one doubts that he could then have run a better election campaign than Hubert Humphrey; and, though he had more enemies, doing only slightly better would have been enough to elect him President.

Humphrey's wisest decision at the convention was his selection of a running mate. His choice of Senator Edmund Muskie of Maine at first disappointed those hoping the new Presidential nominee would move to heal party wounds by nominating a younger, more dovish Vice Presidential candidate. But Ted Kennedy, Gene McCarthy, and George McGovern were not available, and Humphrey had sensed that the selection of Sargent Shriver might bring more disdain than enthusiasm from some Kennedy partisans. Talking with Ed Muskie backstage during the Vietnam debate (when he appeared for the majority plank and I for the minority), I told him that if the endorsement of a Kennedy associate such as myself would help him turn back the other names then being mentioned for the Vice Presidential slot, he had mine to use or convey to anyone he thought appropriate.

Muskie's natural, low-key warmth and candor were a refreshing highlight in the campaign that followed, and they contrasted sharply with much of his party's effort. For Richard Nixon did not win the 1968 election; the Democratic Party lost it. Its always tenuous unity, already coming apart over Vietnam, was shattered beyond repair at Chicago. Its always woeful national machinery was, except for the "fat-cat" President's Club, in rusty disrepair after four years of neglect.

During those four years the Democratic Administration had been required to deal with highly controversial problems of war and peace, black-white relations, and inflationary and recessionary dangers, problems for which the voters tend to blame any incumbent. Unfortunately, the

Johnson Administration failed to apply to national politics in the broad sense the same courage, effort, and skill it had shown in Congressional politics. Lyndon Johnson failed to build in the public mind over this four-year period a perspective or philosophical framework within which the average citizen could better grapple with these difficult problems. Thus the party had been losing direction, spirit, and enthusiasm even before it split open in 1968.

McCarthy and most of his supporters ultimately if belatedly endorsed Humphrey, but all overtures seeking to utilize their manpower and energies in the campaign came to naught. Ted Kennedy, George McGovern, and virtually all Robert Kennedy supporters (including myself) endorsed the party's nominee promptly, but the momentum and enthusiasm of most members of the "Kennedy group" had never recovered from the events of the previous June. The Administration managed to halt all bombing of North Vietnam just prior to the election; but otherwise its political influence with the electorate was considerably less than it had been with convention delegates. Disgruntled peace partisans frequently sought to deny free speech to Humphrey and other speakers by drowning them out through mass heckling. Some Democratic candidates avoided identification with Humphrey and, until the last week, even refused to support him.

Humphrey's own team was divided and disorganized. His powers and patronage as Vice President had been too limited to build a grass-roots organization. He was never noted for attracting a strong staff. He was burdened in some states by Old Guard politicians who had taken command of his fight for their delegates in order to stop Robert Kennedy. Jurisdictional and personnel overlapping, and sometimes undercutting, occasionally broke out within the jerry-built Humphrey chain of command in Washington, D.C., and several states. Many of the union organizations and big-city machines and, with lesser impact, the older farm and ethnic organizations surprised skeptics of the Old Politics by providing substantial money and manpower for the Humphrey campaign. The labor unions were particularly effective in exposing what lay behind George Wallace's appeal to blue-collar workers and their families. But most of these political, labor, and other leaders and power-brokers in the old coalition could no longer promise the votes of a preponderance of their members, much less the votes of those members' wives and voting-age children.

Humphrey himself had trouble getting started. Fearful that a bold stand against the Chicago police riots or the bombing of Vietnam would alienate Daley, Meany, and other powerful supporters, but unable to understand the antipathy of liberals for whose programs he had fought brilliantly over a period of some twenty years in Washington, the Vice President at first permitted himself to be rattled by the hecklers, to be swayed by the hawks, and to talk too long. But almost singlehandedly he pressed on, tireless and optimistic. In the closing weeks, following a Salt Lake City speech that came close to the minority plank, his masterful second effort—aided by the customary shrewdness of his new National Chairman, Larry O'Brien, as well as the belated bombing halt—made the final outcome far closer than any of the Vice President's critics had predicted.

It was not, however, an election campaign fulfilling the bright promise of the so-called New Politics. Both major party conventions had been run and won by skilled practitioners of the Old Politics. Except for the South's break from the Democratic column, the traditional coalitions of geographic, economic, and ethnic groups played familiar and important roles in both camps. The strongest advocates of mass participation under the New Politics—the black voters, young voters, and poor voters—still had, for a variety of reasons, a low turnout at the polls on Election Day. Both major candidates appealed primarily to the voter's pocketbook, to his new fear of crime in the streets, and to familiar schemes for enriching the quantity rather than the quality of American life.

There was no debate like the Kennedy–Nixon 1960 series on TV or even a real dialogue between the nominees. The winning candidate avoided altogether any hint of the specific approach he would take to the overriding issue, Vietnam; and because some voters identified Humphrey with the existing Vietnam policy and some identified him with a change potentially greater than Nixon, the outcome could not be called a mandate on this issue. That, it should be added, is a sad state of affairs in a nation that prides itself on being governed by the consent of the governed.

Equally sad for a democracy was the advantage gained by Nixon's ability to outspend the Humphrey forces by upwards of ten million dollars. This nation's political system will not truly be open to rich and poor alike until such disparities—and the necessary reliance on wealthy contributors and powerful pressure groups—are reduced. Millions of small donors, to whom no candidate would feel mortgaged, should be encouraged through a partial tax credit or deduction for reported contributions of no more than twenty-five to fifty dollars. Publicly financed voter-information pamphlets mailed to every voter's home, as now is done in a few states, would start every candidate on equal footing. A requirement for free radio and television time, accompanied by a suspension of the "equal time" rule and a limit on radio and television expenditures on behalf of any one candidate or party, would greatly enhance the very public interest that all broadcasters are licensed by the public to promote. No one can take pride in a Presidential election decided even in part by which candidate can obtain the most money for TV and other expenses.

Indeed, the 1968 Presidential election as a whole gave little cause for pride. The ability of former Governor George Wallace of Alabama to get on the Presidential ballot in every state was at least an indication that our system remained relatively open to outside challenges; and his absence from the race might only have made Nixon's electoral-vote total even higher. But the fact that some ten million Americans, roughly one out of every eight voting, cast their ballots for a candidate distinguished only by his backward views on race hardly proved, as some optimists claimed, America's rejection of extremism. In addition, an estimated fifteen million Americans, even though registered, remained on Election Day too uninterested, alienated, or busy to vote—including many of our brightest young people and idealists to whom no candidate offered sufficient motivation to exercise a choice. An estimated twenty-eight million other potentially eligible citizens of voting age also did not vote, many of whom could have with some extra effort. Surely we can do better.

The 1968 Presidential election was a reminder as well of the potential danger of our Electoral College system. With a slightly different distribution of the vote, Nixon could have been defeated by the voters yet elected President with a majority of the electoral vote. With a still different distribution, no one would have received an electoral majority, and the Wallace electors would then have bargained with their fellow members of the Electoral College—mostly faceless, some faithless—to choose a President. If they failed, the House of Representatives would have chosen on an undemocratic one-state, one-vote basis. Clearly it is time to disregard the Founding Fathers' fear that inadequate education, communication, and transportation rendered untrustworthy a direct vote by the American people 180 years ago.

The election of 1968 demonstrated that the American voting public today, as well as the leadership of both parties, is more pragmatic than ideological. The voters proved to be closely divided and, despite pressures from both extremes, largely close to the middle of the political spectrum. They paid less attention than ever to party lines, splitting their tickets constantly between national and state candidates of different parties.

The new President appears to fit this atmosphere. While he has over the past twenty years generally been found on the ideological right, exacerbating fears of domestic and foreign Communist conspiracies, he has never joined the extremists of his party and has tended to surround himself with able, pragmatic men. Having survived his defeat for the Presidency in 1960 and a subsequent California gubernatorial defeat in 1962, having escaped the necessity of running against another Kennedy in 1968, and having finally won the Presidency by the narrowest of pluralities and the smallest popular vote proportion of any winner since 1912, Mr. Nixon has already demonstrated both the luck and the tenacity he will need in his present post. But he will need more than that.

His silence in the campaign no doubt increased his freedom of action to move in any direction on Vietnam and race relations once he reached the White House. But it also increased the likelihood of his aggrieving even more members of the public once it became clear that he had no personal or universally popular solution to either problem.

The Democratic majorities in both houses of Congress, on the other hand, may not be as great a liability to President Nixon as first assumed. Not only does control of the Congress by the opposite party provide any President with a ready-made scapegoat to explain his failures during the next election, but this Democratic Congress may be largely attuned to this President's way of thinking. Some of its most vociferous liberal voices are gone. The formal Democratic leadership machinery in both houses has not in the past asserted forceful leadership for the party beyond Capitol Hill. Most of the leading liberal Democrats in Congress are sufficiently patriotic and pragmatic to support those proposals from the White House they regard as a step forward. And roughly six out of seven Southern Democratic Congressmen, joined by fewer than one out of ten Northern Democratic Congressmen, consistently vote with the Republicans to constitute a clear conservative majority.

If, however, the President permits these Southern Democrats to set the tone and tempo of his legislative program, he faces trouble even more serious than a legislative stalemate. Nixon in effect gave up on attracting black votes in the 1968 Presidential race, pursued instead a "Southern strategy" that only alienated them further, and as a result received an even smaller portion of this vote than he had in 1960. This was "smart politics"—his prospects for doing well in the ghetto were at best poor anyway and the potential gains of the "Southern strategy" proved greater. But as a result he made even more difficult the task of winning the confidence of black citizens without which he cannot possibly succeed in his efforts to reunite the country and move forward without violence.

The young, the poor, and, to a lesser extent, big-city dwellers and working men and women generally also face the new President with suspicion, if not outright hostility. These are the very groups who must be brought back into the mainstream of American life and thought if domestic peace is to prevail. (I recall Bob Kennedy's commenting wryly on a newspaper report that his courting of votes in the ghettos, slums, and colleges was "dangerously dividing the country." "Who do they think is alienated in this country," he said to me, "The Southern Governors and Wall Street bankers?") If President Nixon continues for very long to cut back on certain social programs to help finance an arms race, and to cut back on job growth as one way to restrain inflation, those hardest hit will be the dispossessed groups already most resentful of the American system in general and the new Administration in particular. The result will be more bitter divisions and dissensions and both the fear and the threat of more disorderly demonstrations and violence.

There will be danger, then, in many senses of the word and in many facets of American life. The political danger may well be a country-wide wave of repression and reaction that will stifle dissent and liberal thinking for years to come. In 1968–1969 this nation was already moving slightly to the right; and more violence and disorder could push it very far to the right and President Nixon along with it. Even without such a development, existing Republican advantages among publishers and contributors, combined with the natural advantages of publicity, prestige, and power afforded any incumbent President, will make the task of dislodging Nixon in 1972 a difficult one for the next Democratic nominee, whoever that might be.

A few dark-horse names, including those of George McGovern and the new National Chairman, Fred Harris, will be mentioned between now and then—a few new names could possibly emerge from the 1970 elections—but it is lamentable that a party once so rich in talent and so lately in power has seemingly narrowed at this early date its list of likely Presidential prospects for 1972 to a few familiar names.

The 1968 nominee, Hubert Humphrey, is certain to stay active as titular leader of the party, raising funds, rousing the faithful, and reckoning his chances for another assault on the summit. As a private citizen out of Washington, he is unlikely to maintain the same access to press and public opinion that he once enjoyed, and his return to the Senate in 1970 seems more likely as of this writing than his return as Presidential nominee in 1972. But Ted Kennedy's accident has altered the picture for 1972, and, in or out of the Senate, Humphrey's experience, leadership, and integrity will be felt throughout the country in party affairs.

The future of Eugene McCarthy is more difficult to predict, partly because of his own public pronouncement that he will not again run for the Senate. Whatever outlet he chooses in the future for his intellectual energies, the disappointment of his followers with his vote for Russell Long for Senate Whip, with his abdication of his Senate Foreign Relations Committee post to a hawk, and his statement that he never thought he could be nominated in 1968, leave little likelihood of his being the Democratic nominee for President in 1972.

Ed Muskie, thrust suddenly in 1968 into the critical eye of the national spotlight at a time of turbulence, showed qualities of character and judgment that stood up well under pressure. Both liked and respected by his colleagues in the Senate, he has compiled a record of sufficient liberalism and sufficient regularity to please both groups within the party. His supporters justifiably feel that his well-received efforts in 1968 entitle him to seek the top spot in 1972; that he should no longer be confined to the Senate; that he could not again take second place on the ticket; and that his loyalty as Hubert Humphrey's running mate marks him as a comer.

Until July 1969, when Ted Kennedy's car overturned in a pond on an island off the Massachusetts coast, killing its other occupant and leading to a plea of guilty for leaving the scene of an accident, the young Senator from Massachusetts was almost a shoo-in. He was the symbol of that "Kennedy group" to whom the Kennedy legacy seemed particularly to have been bequeathed as well as the last surviving Kennedy son. He was the natural leader among those Kennedy men now holding state-wide elective office. His name neither imposed upon him an obligation to seek the Presidency in 1972 (or any other year) nor imposed upon JFK and RFK supporters an obligation to back him. He wanted to be his own man and stand or fall on his own merits. But it would have been foolish to deny the advantages of the name, the smile, the voice, the accent, the mannerisms, and, above all, the experience.

Having coordinated Western states in JFK's 1960 campaign while still a greenhorn nationally (he was Massachusetts campaign manager in 1958), Ted headed RFK's campaign effort in 1968 with considerable skill and energy. Long regarded by his older brothers as "the best natural politician in the family," he traveled widely in that campaign (as he had earlier on behalf of other candidates) and was even more widely in demand. Not having earned the antagonisms that Bob had earned, being more at ease with politicians than Jack, lacking his brothers' shyness, and possessing his own kind of humor, Ted was a popular and relatively noncontroversial speaker. His recorded endorse-ments on radio and television were eagerly sought by Democratic candidates in the autumn election campaign.

Ted Kennedy had been elected to the Senate from Massachusetts in 1962 amidst considerable skepticism about whether he was sufficiently experienced to deserve that high office on grounds other than his name and connections. (President Kennedy found amusing irony in the charge of "nepotism" leveled by newspapers which had long operated on that very principle.) But Ted surprised the skeptics, particularly the members of the Cambridge intellectual community, by settling down to become a first-rate Senator. He was effective on behalf of his own state and imaginative on a growing number of national issues. Senate elders were pleased that he did not use his fame to overstep the traditionally deferential role of freshman. Senate liberals were pleased with his leadership in civil rights, immigration, refugee relief, health and other areas. More of a "Senate man" than his two older brothers, who were less patient with the pace of that chamber, he did not take on as many outside constituencies as his brother Bob, nor did he take on as many enemies.

Above all, Ted Kennedy demonstrated one quality that had characterized his older brothers at the same age—the quality of continuing growth. Observing him in Jack Kennedy's campaigns of 1958 and 1960, in his own campaign in 1962 (in which he overcame strong opposition in both the primary and the election, rather than being handed the seat as an heirloom, as critics have charged), in the Senate, and in the national campaigns that followed, I noted ever deepening interests and public self-confidence in the young football player to whom JFK had first introduced me in Cape Cod in 1953. Barely surviving a plane crash in June 1964, Ted had devoted his long, virtually immobile hospital confinement to study and to sessions with local scholars (as well as compiling a private book of tributes to his father and trying his hand at painting watercolors). Like JFK's brush with death in a hospital in 1954, the experience seemed to accelerate the pace of Ted's growth; but this development was largely overshadowed by RFK's role in the Senate spotlight. The murder of his two brothers accelerated his growth even more.

It was not surprising that, following Bob Kennedy's death in June 1968, many Democrats wanted Ted Kennedy for President, whether he was ready or not. He had not yet regained his full stride after the assassination and funeral, at which he delivered a stirring eulogy; and he had new responsibilities to the family to consider. Yet grief had not shattered his native ambition or dulled his political instincts. Having decided that neither the fears of his family nor his obligations to it should cause his withdrawal from public service, he could hardly be uninterested in the growing talk of his Presidential prospects. But 1968 had demanded too much of him already. He decided during the summer not to endorse any of the contenders for the Democratic nomination, not to meet or bargain with any of them, not to be present as a delegate when the balloting was held, not to be available for the Vice Presidency in any circumstances, and not to seek the Presidency.

His Worcester speech on Vietnam on August 21, the Wednesday before the Democratic National Convention, was, to be sure, deliberately timed to assert his interest and influence regarding the most controversial platform issue on which he was willing to succeed to his brother's leadership. But the reference in that speech to the fact that he would not be a candidate for office that year was a genuine statement of intent. He did not regard the McGovern candidacy as a stalking-horse for his own, and he neither encouraged nor discouraged the South Dakota Senator about entering the race.

Two days later, arriving in Chicago for the convention, which opened Monday, August 26, Steve Smith was asked by Chicago Mayor Daley whether Ted was available for the Presidency. With almost absolute control of the Illinois delegation, Daley had maintained his customary public silence, despite a general assumption that anyone so close to LBJ would endorse Humphrey. The Mayor had earlier expressed concern to Ted that his statement taking himself out of the Vice Presidential race was unnecessarily taking him out of the Presidential race as well. Daley wanted an answer before the Illinois caucus met the following Sunday afternoon, and Steve not only reported the conversation to his brother-in-law but also alerted old Kennedy campaign friends and contacts among the delegates to explore potential strength.

Ted gave no positive answer, and Daley postponed his Sunday caucus without an endorsement. Jesse Unruh followed suit with the California delegation, and the ensuing wave of rumors built rapidly into a "Draft EMK" movement. Uncommitted delegates, McGovern delegates, many McCarthy delegates, and a surprising number of Southern favorite-son and lukewarm Humphrey delegates prepared to follow Illinois and California to another Kennedy. Our private vote estimate climbed to within a hundred of the necessary convention majority. McCarthy himself indicated to Steve Smith that, once his own name had been placed in nomination, he might make a speech withdrawing it and suggesting that his delegates support EMK. (This conversation in fact occurred after Ted had conclusively ended the boom in a talk with Daley.) For a few days, for a young man still mourning his brother and attempting to decide his future over a thousand miles away by telephone, the fervent pleas to stop Nixon, to carry on his brothers' ideals, and to make the most of a Presidential opportunity that might never recur posed a most difficult dilemma.

Very likely he could have been nominated. But before the Daleys and Unruhs would go out on that limb for him they needed some positive assurance from him that he was willing. Any such move on his part might well have compromised his position as a man who could be trusted and supported by all factions because he was above the battle, as a man from whom every ambition had been temporarily purged by grief. That kind of compromise might have hurt Ted's prospects in the 1968 election, possibly in future elections, and even his prospects for the nomination in the 1968 convention itself. Earlier there had been a small but unavoidable suspicion, moreover, that Mayor Daley's real motive might have been to lure Ted out of his posture of noninvolvement in order to draft him for the Vice Presidency.

In my conversations by phone with the Senator I counseled him not to place himself in a position where the convention would offer him the Presidential nomination, for that no man could turn down. Despite my own desire to resume the effort twice tragically interrupted, and despite the heady excitement over the Ted Kennedy boom which was by then seizing many of my close friends among the delegates, I had several questions. Once the frenzy of convention week died down, how vulnerable would he be in a more conservative electorate to suspicions (and Nixon charges) about his experience and maturity, to the kindly-sounding suggestion (not without merit) that it would be better to let this family alone for this year, and to a feeling that he was seeking to capitalize on tragedy, on public emotion, and on a famous name? If elected, would he have had time to gain sufficient standing with the Congress, with the disaffected groups in this country, and with other nations to provide the kind of leadership he could be capable of providing at a later date? Should he, at this stage of his life, and in that year of years, be required to give up his remaining privacy to expose himself, in an emotion-charged atmosphere, to every suggestible psychopath seized with the notion of shooting another Kennedy?

Whatever his reasons, including his still sorrowful feelings from that sorrowful summer, Ted Kennedy refused to make any positive move, asked that his name not be placed in nomination, and ended the boom. Having already made clear his unavailability for second spot, he quickly and repeatedly endorsed the Humphrey–Muskie ticket in public and in television commercials in order to allay any talk that its defeat was desirable to clear the way for him in 1972.

Two months after Nixon's victory EMK was elected by his Senate Democratic colleagues to be Assistant Majority Leader, providing him with a new stature and platform from which to speak his mind on the full range of national issues. Muskie had already decided that the incumbent Whip, Russell Long, could not be unseated. Long himself scoffed when Ted announced, for it takes more than a magic name to be elevated to an unglamourous leadership position in the Senate. But despite the opposition of Long's fellow Southerners and hawks (plus Gene McCarthy), Ted Kennedy launched a whirlwind campaign and won.

Despite Ted's own doubts about whether he wanted the Presidential nomination in 1972, it was widely assumed in the first six months of 1969 to be his. Then in July tragedy once again struck the Kennedy family. Leaving a party on Chappaquiddick Island for 1968 Kennedy campaign workers, accompanied by one of the finest of the girls with whom

I worked in RFK's national headquarters, the Senator drove off an unlit, unusually narrow bridge that angled sharply and unexpectedly to the left. The car, upside down on the bottom of a pond, immediately filled with water, and his companion, Mary Jo Kopechne, drowned. Despite a concussion suffered in the accident and a sudden sense of actually drowning, Ted somehow escaped, but his efforts to save Mary Jo were in vain. Then, overcome, as he said, "by a jumble of emotions—grief, fear, doubt, panic, confusion, exhaustion and shock," he conducted himself in what he called an "inexplicable" and "indefensible" way. Instead of reporting the accident immediately to the police by means of telephone from one of the nearby cottages, he walked back to the party, summoned two of his friends to return to the pond, directed their equally unsuccessful efforts to dive for Mary Jo, and then swam the channel from Chappaquiddick Island to Martha's Vineyard and collapsed in his hotel room. Contrary to one report, neither he nor anyone on his behalf talked to me (or, to the best of my knowledge, anyone else) by telephone that night. The failure of his two companions to make certain that the accident was properly reported was equally indefensible.

Because Ted had failed to report the accident to the police until the following morning, he pleaded guilty to the charge of leaving the scene of an accident and received a suspended sentence of two months in jail. Because the presence of a girl in his car and liquor at the party fanned the flames of ugly suspicion and wild speculation about his motivations for not going to the police immediately, he followed his appearance in court with a contrite televised address to the people of Massachusetts. Having been called to Hyannis Port several days after the accident to help analyze his legal position, I can vouch for the fact that he was grief-stricken over Mary Jo's death, unable to comprehend his own actions that nightmarish night, wondering "whether some awful curse did actually hang over all the Kennedys," and genuinely in doubt about whether he should remain in politics and public life. Critics and skeptics continued to hurl challenges to his TV statement, but I know of no facts inconsistent with it and know also that Ted was more desirous than some of his advisers to state the essential facts as soon as the courtroom proceedings were over.

The people of Massachusetts responded to his request for advice with an overwhelming plea that he remain as their Senator. But recognizing that his judgment under pressure would understandably be questioned for at least the next several years, the Senator was wisely adamant about removing himself from all consideration for the national ticket in 1972. As of this writing, a new inquest was scheduled, and new rumors, distortions and exaggerations appear every week. No one can be certain how this tragedy will unfold; and thus speculation at this time about his Presidential prospects in 1976 and thereafter would be presumptuous and premature.

Nor can I predict the role of the "Kennedy group" in the 1972 Presidential contest. Not all the political, intellectual, and other figures who carried the banner for JFK and RFK had felt bound to rally to EMK's standard. But his candidacy more than that of any other potential contender had offered most of them the prospect of working enthusiastically as a group once again. His candidacy offered the youthful activists the best possible outlet for their energies and commitments and offered the country and party their best hope for avoiding the kind of dangerous confrontation between mossbacks and redhots that was so destructive last year. To rally our "group" and the young and the best of our party in 1972, to avoid the mistakes of 1968, more than a Presidential candidate of quality will be required. He must be committed to a program of peaceful revolution and political reform that goes beyond traditional liberalism and breathes new life and meaning into the presently ailing Democratic Party.

The closeness of the popular vote for President in 1968 obscured for some the adverse trends which had since 1966 beset the Democratic Party nationally. Today, with the single exception of New Jersey (where a gubernatorial election is held this year, 1969), the Democrats no longer hold the Governor's chair in any of the Northern industrial states that previously formed their chief electoral base. Their Presidential candidate can no longer win more than a fraction of the once "solid" South. They lost in 1968 not only the White House but the seats of such distinguished Senators as Joseph Clark of Pennsylvania, Wayne Morse of Oregon, and Mike Monroney of Oklahoma. Robert Kennedy's New York seat was filled by the appointment of a conservative Republican Congressman who had consistently voted against the policies of both Kennedys. Bright new Democratic prospects for the Senate such as John Gilligan of Ohio, Leroy Collins of Florida, and William Clark of Illinois were defeated, in contrast with the host of bright new Republicans coming up fast in recent years. Democratic majorities in both the House and the Senate, largely meaningful only on paper and at organization time anyway, further declined in 1968, even though 1966 had already reduced their numbers drastically. Among the new and relatively new members of the House and Senate, Republicans already have a two-to-one majority.

In truth, the Democratic Party nationally has grown old beyond its time in recent years, not only in leadership and candidate material but also in organization and ideas.

It should be understood that there is very little by way of a national party structure in American politics. Every four years the fifty state Democratic parties draw together in convention to nominate a ticket and the Republicans do likewise. But in the interim the national committee structure amounts to very little, superseded if its party is in the White House and powerless if it is not. Unlike the British parliamentary system, the legislative leaders of the opposition do not thereby command their party. The use of Capitol Hill as a platform from which the loyal opposition can mount an alternative program and strategy is invariably hampered by a lack of common policy and purpose. Today most Democratic Congressional committee chairmen and even some legislative leaders are unwilling to be guided by the Democratic platform, much less the Democratic National Committee or the defeated Democratic Presidential nominee. In both parties each new Presidential nominee discovers that he must hastily build his own campaign team onto what little national organization is in existence.

He discovers as well a wide divergence of views within his own party. The age-old dream of a political realignment that divides all liberals into one party and all conservatives into another becomes less and less of a possibility as issues multiply and overlap. (Would Democrats such as Senator Fulbright, Mayor Daley, and Senator Dodd be placed in a conservative party, disagreeing with one another and with their fellow party members on the basic issues of civil rights and foreign policy? What is the "liberal" position on foreign aid, gun control, TV regulation, and arms to Israel, and how many "pure" liberals and "pure" conservatives agree on these and other issues?) Under the two-party system—which has well served the cause of majority rule and political coherence in a nation so large and diverse as the United States—each party, however reshuffled, is certain to end up as a coalition of differing individuals and interests.

Nevertheless there exists, in each state, the same two major party labels providing some form of continuity and organization to the political process; and the Democratic Party has consistently since Franklin Roosevelt's day held an edge over the Republican Party in voter identification on a nation-wide basis. This developed in the 1930s through an awkward combination of big-city voters with farmers, organized labor with intellectuals, Southerners with blacks, and Catholics with Jews. But the dwindling number of farmers increasingly turned Republican (except for 1948) once they were rescued from the Great Depression; many of the big-city voters, including union members, have become more conservative middle-class suburbanites; and the long-overdue insistence on a truly integrated party in the South has driven enough segregationists into other arms to make the national Democratic Party a weak second or even third in most of that region.

The South is not a one-issue region. It is no longer governed by men elected solely on their promises to block the black man's progress. As it became more urbanized and industrialized, Democratic Presidential nominees won some support in that area, not by soft-pedaling the race question but by reminding Southerners of their historic stake in the economic and social programs of the Democratic Party. But the growth of union and nonunion labor in the South has not had the liberalizing effect once anticipated. Whatever George Wallace decides to do nationally in 1972, the growing number of registered black voters, white moderates, Northern transplants, and enlightened publishers, businessmen, and intellectuals now organizing the Deep South for the Democrats have a long rebuilding task ahead before any Northern liberal can count on much help in a Presidential election.

Of more importance to the future of the Democratic Party has been the growing inability of other coalition leaders to "deliver" their votes. The average voter today, compared with his father, is better educated, better informed, and better able to judge the candidates and issues for himself by watching television. He is more affluent, less likely to be interested in what little low-paying political patronage remains, less likely to be influenced by political favors or handouts, and—regardless of affluence—less likely to be subsidized or assisted in the old personal and political ways that preceded the flowering of the New Deal. As a result, he is less likely to look to his ward chairman, union leader, or fraternal-association president for guidance in choosing his candidates. As the old ethnic, economic, occupational, and other distinctions fade in an ever larger, more homogeneous society dominated by the uniculture of the television tube, he is less likely to think and vote in terms of his membership in some bloc but to do so as an individual with his own concepts and concerns.

The old brokers of political power—such as the ward captain, union president, or ethnic-group leader—are no longer needed to represent their voters' views, now that periodically published polls relay them directly to the candidate. Nor are they needed in the campaigns to the extent they were before television increased the candidate's ability to appeal directly to individual voters. The modern political, union, and ethnic-group leaders are the first to acknowledge that they can no longer impose political unity or discipline within their own jurisdictions. Many of the younger union members, for example, are less and less interested in the old political struggles and programs. Affluence has made them conservative on taxation, inflation, and the racial integration of their neighborhoods. Even many of their leaders have little or no sympathy for the blacks and youngsters who picket and protest against the *status quo* and the establishment much as these leaders themselves did a generation or more ago. An increasing number of workers are Federal, state, and local civil servants who do not relate their security to the party in power.

Other elements in the old Democratic coalition face a similar erosion. The big-city organizations have less patronage because of civil service, less power because of television, and fewer voters because of the movement to the suburbs. The poor and the nonwhites left behind in those cities have been consistently less likely to register and vote. The Irish, Polish, Italian, and other ethnic groups who fought their way up the political ladder find their nationality clubs of interest primarily to the old and feel challenged by the blacks, who in turn feel competitive with the Puerto Ricans. New-style black leaders, no longer hand-picked by whites, are less willing to engage in the old bargains and less able to deliver many votes.

Meanwhile, the younger intellectuals and activists in the Democratic Party, both more affluent and potentially more numerous than before, have less interest in the familiar pocketbook issues of importance to their elders. They want more stress on the very issues the party had previously avoided to maintain unity—foreign policy, black power, civil liberties, political reform, community control, birth control, and support for the arts, to name but a few. Their efforts are viewed with resentment by the older leaders, whom they in turn resent for blocking the way to innovation.

Rent by these internal clashes between young and old, intellectuals and trade unions, reformers and regulars, black nationalists and white nationality groups, big-city and suburban leaders, the Democrats are unlikely to reverse their present political decline by relying on the ever less powerful power-brokers of the old Democratic coalition. The latter clung to majority control in the 1968 Democratic Convention thanks to the power and patronage of an incumbent Administration and the accident of two Kennedy assassinations; and they worked well in the election campaign on behalf of Hubert Humphrey, who was probably the last nominee of the Old Democratic Politics. But within the Democratic coalition, political power is undergoing a painful process of redistribution. The unions and city organizations must share their power with newly potent forces among the minorities, the suburbanites, the academics, the young, and—more and more—rank-and-file citizens who identify with no special group or bloc whatever. A new coalition—if an array of individual voters rather than blocs can even be called a "coalition"—is rising which can be won only from the bottom up by a new kind of politics.

The transition to the New Politics was stepped up by John Kennedy's successful campaign at the grass roots to overtake the old Democratic establishment in 1960. It was greatly accelerated by Robert Kennedy's campaign of 1968, which appealed not only to the young, well-educated, and reform-minded whom McCarthy also led but also to union members over the heads of their leaders, to black and white ethnic neighborhoods alike, to Southern moderates and city dwellers. Both the Johnson Administration's Vietnam war policy and the attacks leveled against him by the dissenters took their toll on the party's power. But it is foolish to blame Johnson, Humphrey, McCarthy, or any other proposed scapegoat. The old Democratic power politics, the old rules of mediation and accommodation—

like the old slogans and solutions of the New Deal—are simply no longer enough to assure party victory.

I am concerned about the future of the Democratic Party because I am concerned about the future of the Kennedy legacy, and because I am concerned lest the finest of our youth see no future in working within this country's political system. The Democratic Party must, both nationally and at all local levels, shake off any identification as the party of the *status quo* and cut its ties with racism, bossism, and corruption. Its campaigns and candidates must appeal to the young and independent-minded, and must be oriented not to the programs of the past but to the real issues of today and tomorrow—not only the old liberalism of economic security but world peace, human rights, institutional reform, and greater quality in our culture and environment. Unless those campaigns can offer something more than a rehash of the New Deal, the Fair Deal, the New Frontier, and the Great Society, unless they can appeal to the consciences of the unorganized, uncommitted middle-class majority and not merely their pocketbooks, the Republicans will build up their own plurality of the indifferent affluent.

Candidate styles must be suited not to the usual partisan exaggerations, but to the candid detachment and understatement that JFK and McCarthy showed to work so well on television. The party must—through direct primaries, party-sponsored polls, thoroughly open organizations, and more frequent communications and public conferences—enable every interested Democrat to participate in key decisions on the selection of party leaders and candidates as well as issues. Students and housewives, as well as precinct committeemen, must provide much of the manpower in campaigns operated more out of storefronts than hotel rooms. But politics still means legwork year in and year out, not sloganeering for a few months every two or four years; and the New Democratic Politics must build on, not cast out, those precinct workers, small-town and county chairmen, women's club members, and others who have long rung doorbells, registered the voters, and manned the polls simply because they believed in the Democratic Party. In between campaigns the party must involve its less active members in such activities as political education, social action, legislative pressures, crime prevention, and the organization of antipoverty units, consumer and marketing associations, and recreational groups.

Nor can the party permit any one group in the coalition to have its own way at the expense of the others—to become exclusively the party of the poor, or the well-educated, or the big cities, or to demand a litmus test of such ideological purity that a majority of voters will never qualify. In short, the Democratic Party to succeed nationwide in the 1970s—and to deserve success—must be a more democratic party. It must be liberal in the original sense of the word, with a mind open to new ideas and a membership open to all, both representative and responsive, combining the idealism and realism of John and Robert Kennedy, while reconciling, as they sought to reconcile, the fortunate and less fortunate in our society. Power up, not down, must be the guiding principle.

Evolution in this direction will vary from state to state. It will be slowed by traditional rivalries and existing suspicions within the liberal wing of the party and by the temptation on the part of some to form or follow a third or fourth party. It will be slow in those areas where a handful of party officials and contributors—mostly white, male, affluent, and over fifty—are more concerned about concentrating control in their own hands than they are about the crisis facing their party.

Evolution within the party—and, indeed, implementation of the entire Kennedy legacy—will also depend, possibly disproportionately, on the extent to which the youth of America are inclined and invited to involve themselves in this effort. To the extent that they organize their potential number effectively on behalf of political reform and progressive candidates—not necessarily through the Young Democratic organizations which are often too sterile and isolated from real political action to be meaningful—and to the extent that they learn to live with disappointments, defeats, and different points of view, the students and other young activists who mobilized in 1968 behind Kennedy and McCarthy can become indispensable to the party machinery, influential in the party councils, and instrumental in moving their party in the right direction. To the extent that they pursue within the party those tactics of violent protest and polarization which generate more adverse than positive reactions, or which limit the rights or exclude the participation of others, they will at best be wasting the influence which their numbers, energy, and education could give them and at worst entrenching the very establishment leaders they oppose. To the extent that they decide they cannot work through the present system at all, and tune out, drop out, set out to destroy it, or set up splinter efforts, they will enable the practitioners of the Old Politics to remain in power at least a little longer.

Young high-school graduates should not be excluded from this process. The distinction in our voting laws between those who have attained the age of eighteen and those who have attained the age of twenty-one has become outmoded. This country has in the past extended the franchise when it recognized that for *voting purposes* there was no longer any valid reason to distinguish between the electoral rights of landowners and the landless, whites and Negroes, men and women. No one claimed that these new voter groups were identical to the old, merely that they could no longer be fairly or logically excluded. Today the statutes relating to the dividing line between adults and children concerning their responsibility for property, crime, financial affairs, and family relations frequently breach the traditional floor of age twenty-one; and the statistics relating to employment, taxation, marriage, and education all reflect the increasing responsibilities and capabilities of this age group compared with twenty-one-year-olds of a generation ago. It is true that many eighteen-year-olds—like many twenty-one-year-olds and even twenty-four-year-olds—will be more experienced, more independent, and bear more responsibilities later in life. But there is no study indicating that their *voting judgment* will be any more informed, intelligent, or mature than it is between eighteen and twenty-one and no reason to classify them with children, much less with aliens, felons, lunatics, and others judged unable by definition to cast a responsible ballot.

John Kennedy once opposed amending the Federal Constitution to lower the voting age, although favoring it in his own state, on the grounds that more national demand should precede any amendment to the Constitution. But that was before the two latest states admitted to the Union had broken the custom of twenty-one, before his own Presidential Commission on Registration and Voting Participation had urged it, before the polls showed a majority of the population favoring it, and, above all, before he and his brother helped spark young men and women aged eighteen to twenty to demonstrate their capability in political, public, and social service.

But regardless of their eligibility to vote, we should

not ignore the message of our discontented youth, even when they use unruly or distasteful tactics to gain attention to that message. It is basically a message of concern that the Kennedys helped to ignite and that many of us share: a deep moral concern about not only the abominations of Vietnam and the ghetto but also the whole lack of meaning in American life, the lack of relevance in our institutions, and the inequities, inadequacies, anachronisms, and, above all, hypocrisy which still prevail despite —and in part because of—this nation's unprecedented affluence, freedom, and leisure.

We have the time, the money and the freedom, the young say, to do what? They feel powerless in the face of war, poverty, and injustice and certain that those who do have the power will not use it to cure these ills. Like the proverbial man too heavy to do any light work and too light to do any heavy work, they feel trapped between the petty insignificance of daily living and the massive immutability of gigantic institutions. The killing and burning in Vietnam against an enemy they could not hate, on behalf of a regime they could not respect, turned them away from their own government. The arbitrary Selective Service System's requirement that they participate in this killing in order to fulfill what they feel to be phony rationales rapidly deepened their disgust. They have asked why young men opposed to an unjust and disastrous war were in jail while its perpetrators were in office. They have questioned the morality of military might both sooner and more sharply than most of their elders. For a time the McCarthy and Kennedy campaigns drew their energies but ended up frustrating their hopes.

Very few of these restless and rebellious young people are Communists, anarchists, or even socialists in any strict definition of that term, despite a lot of romantic talk

about Che Guevara and Mao Tse-tung. Most are not
hippies or Yippies. Their goals and complaints, often in-
articulate, sound—when articulated at all—not only radical
but revolutionary. But the heart of the Kennedy legacy
also recognizes the need to *revolutionize peacefully* by
altering radically and swiftly both our present public
policies and our public decision-making apparatus. It
recognizes that this is the only way our present system
can cope with modern man, modern technology, and
modern economic problems—indeed it is probably the
only way it can survive. Inasmuch as most (and the best)
of the young protesters are willing to see those same goals
accomplished peacefully if possible, their objective might
more accurately be termed our system's salvation rather
than its destruction.

To be sure, their announced objectives and objections
are not always constant or consistent. Some students, striking out blindly in their frustration with society, are found
demonstrating first for integrated universities and then for
segregated universities, for academic freedom one year
and for curbs on it the next, against intemperate police
behavior but for intemperate student behavior, in favor
of admitting thousands of more students but against expanding the university physically, for alternatives to the
draft but against ROTC in any form. Not all these positions are wrong or even inconsistent; but many young
demonstrators neither think through their complaints nor
effectively persist in them. The grievances vary from
campus to campus and from student to student; and it
makes no more sense to generalize about all colleges than
it does about all students. Most campuses, but not all those
under attack, are in need of reform but not always the
reform sought by the attackers. Most students, but not all
those in demonstrations, have legitimate grievances, but

they are not always those for which the demonstrations are undertaken.

A small number of students—having been raised in an atmosphere of direct and indirect violence, which is usually condoned if done in the name of national foreign policy or state police powers—have themselves resorted to disruptive tactics, coercion, and violence. The fact that it is usually, but not always, violence against property (such as windows, furniture, and files) rather than violence against person (which they have more often suffered themselves) does not make it any less intolerable. Any use of violence or vandalism is self-defeating and inconsistent with their professed ideals, no matter how much they were provoked or frustrated, no matter how many times stolen files helped expose their university's ties with the military-industrial complex. Little is accomplished, however, by calling these militants inconsistent. That fact is obvious even to them. Asserting the need for more democracy, they are as impatient with democratic procedures as are, in their own way, the establishment types they attack. Insisting on the recognition of student rights, they often ignore the rights of the majority of students by preventing classes from meeting. Citing the campaign failure of Senator Eugene McCarthy, they either imitate or invite the heavy-handed tactics of Senator Joseph McCarthy. Asserting identification with the far left, their tactics increase the power of the far right. In short, most of this violent minority have no coherent, consistent objectives other than confrontation for its own sake and have no constructive role to play on the campus.

The small self-promoting extremist organizations, such as the Students for a Democratic Society (SDS), which publicly proclaim their leadership of the student revolution, have comparatively little grass-roots strength on most

campuses in the absence of a re-escalation of the Vietnam
war, even less strength in the black ghettos and white
slums, and almost no rapport with the workers with whom
they assert identification. On the campuses they have more
imitators than followers. But small nihilist groups have
frequently succeeded in arousing large portions of their
fellow students and many faculty members behind them,
not because they are part of a highly organized national
conspiracy with a network of trained *provocateurs* but because those less militant students also feel frustrated by the
existing system or outraged by the unfair or unnecessarily
rough measures undertaken to repress the extremists.

The real causes of the student revolution are not youthful conspirators—much less overpermissive parents, radical
professors, or too much coddling by the authorities. The
real causes are the basic ills and deformations of our system and society which students perceive more clearly than
most. To assume that their unrest is only a collegiate fad
that will disappear like goldfish swallowing, or recur every
spring like panty raids, is to underestimate its seriousness.
To dismiss it with the observation that boys will be boys
and soon will be brokers and lawyers is to underestimate
their seriousness. To treat only the symptoms and not the
causes can purchase only a temporary respite. To try
curbing it with Federal or state legislation, which lumps
all student misbehavior under one repressive label, which
cannot distinguish between violent demonstrators committing outrages against the university to achieve unjust
demands and peaceful demonstrators protesting outrages committed by the university against their just requests, is not only futile but foolish. Even if it could
succeed, it would only turn the next generation of students
back into the deadly conformity and complacency that
Jack Kennedy campaigned to shatter on the college cam-

puses from 1956 to 1960. That kind of indifference and inertia still afflicts too many students attending the less activist colleges. It is a tragic error for either college officials or public officials to take any satisfaction from this "silent" majority.

Our task, instead, as Professor Kenneth Keniston of Yale has put it, is to turn the private alienation of the well-motivated mass of student protesters into public aspirations; to mobilize their energetic discontent into constructive channels of reform instead of confrontation; to obtain their help in reinvigorating our society. That will not be easy. There is no point in preaching gradualism to black students after a century of discrimination. There is no point in telling white activists to be patient about the war when their draft boards are impatient, or to await the next Presidential election when they gave their all to the last one and regarded its results as a tragic farce. There is no point in telling them to use reason and persuasion with establishment figures who will not listen to reason or persuasion. There is no point in telling them to accept war, racism, and human selfishness as immutable facts for their generation merely because they are still a part of ours.

Instead it is the nation's liberal leadership who will have to be patient and not panic, to rely on reason and not repression. We are the ones who should be challenging and changing the old system, beginning with the university and not stopping until government and society itself are rid of inequity. If we can do that, I am certain that the great majority of concerned youth will have the good sense to realize that this nation's violence against the Vietnamese does not excuse violence on the campus; that a resort to force instead of law ultimately gives the upper hand to those who are most powerful in our society, not those who are most moral; that disruptive, lawless tactics on the far left can only increase the influence of the far right; and that political campaigns, lobbying, litigation, collective bargaining, cooperatives, community service, and public advocacy, to name but a few channels, offer more hope of their making some headway against the evils of our society than taking the law into their own hands.

John Kennedy stirred young people to involvement in the Peace Corps, the civil-rights movement, Washington summer internships, politics in general, and domestic social concerns as well. Robert Kennedy encouraged their work in VISTA, in community service, and—with Gene McCarthy —in political campaigns on a scale never before undertaken. Now, instead of excluding them from political decision-making, or denying them the channels of communication by which they can tell us how to alter or end the injustices they see in our system, we must give them increased opportunities for public and quasi-public service, especially on behalf of peace, racial democracy, and national reconciliation.

One area in need of a creative revolution is that occupied by our colleges and universities, once revolutionary influences themselves. Some of those institutions are still centers of free thought that combat hypocrisy and irrationality wherever found and some still implant in their students a philosophy with horizons wider than mere materialism. But in more than one modern American university, trustees are remote, self-perpetuating, unrepresentative bodies; administrations are preoccupied with the fund-raising needed to keep pace with expanding demand; faculties are preoccupied with research, writing, and outside consultancies; student bodies are too large to avoid mass computerized treatment; and big-city campuses are increasingly surrounded by impoverished black or Puero Rican neighbors who are resentful of the universities' largely white affluence and expansion. Such universities have too little time or inclination to challenge the policies of the government-business complex which finances them and too little time even to identify the causes of student discontent. They have studied and urged the reform of other institutions without studying or reforming their own. On the dozens of campuses I have visited, students note that our nation is increasingly in need of new ideas and solutions, that our cities are increasingly in need of leadership on local social problems, and that university communities, students included, are ideally equipped to respond, but that the universities are not responding.

It is not surprising, therefore, that students have demanded a larger voice in the conduct of university affairs, signed petitions, picketed meetings, and held protest demonstrations. Particularly when recalcitrant administrators refuse to negotiate or even listen, they have staged sit-ins, sometimes disruptive, always noisy, and in some cases increased their numbers tenfold when excessive force was used to rout them. They gain sympathy from other students and help from other campuses. They gain spontaneous leaders from each crisis. Faculty members, some of whom are more concerned about their own popularity than the university's integrity, join them.

While I cannot condone the violence that has no place in any university in any circumstances, this trend should be viewed in the perspective of the sit-in strikes of the 1930s. Then it was the more militant workers who wanted a larger voice and more rights. Then it was their movement which spread, not primarily through the handful of Communists seeking to exploit it but through the sympathy of fellow workers who felt their demands were just and the police too brutal. They, too, were told that they should go elsewhere if they did not like their own facilities; that there could be no redistribution of power into their hands under our tried and traditional system; and that all such radical and un-American demonstrations and disorders were simply a matter for the local police. But in time the owners and entrepreneurs changed their views, collective-bargaining and grievance machinery was established in every major industry, worker power was recognized as a permanent force, and both state and Federal laws generally reflected these changes.

Without weakening educational standards or services, an equally responsive restructuring of our colleges and universities would seem in order today—to make them less authoritarian, to give students a real voice, to restore meaningful communication and participation in university government.

The Reverend William Sloane Coffin has written: "I am not suggesting that students should have their way but that they should have their say in both curricular and extracurricular matters." Hopefully this would not require Federal legislation. These institutions are as essential to our national life now as private industry was in the 1930s; and Congress, having asserted the Constitutional authority to extend and deny them financial aid, might well assert the authority to legislate on student rights and grievance procedures. But principally it is the task of the trustees, administration, faculty, and students of each institution to make certain that it is an open institution—open to the maximum number of qualified students regardless of race or income, open to changes in curriculum, personnel, and approach.

When university power and admissions are largely restricted to those who are white and affluent, or when the disruptions and obstructions of a student minority shut down some or all classes for the majority, that is not an open institution. When a professor feels intimidated because of his views or a black student feels intimidated because of his color, when a curriculum or appropriate course of study ignores a whole segment of American culture and Negro history, when a college dean prohibits all protests or when protesters prohibit that dean from teaching, when trustees bar recruiting on campus by a far-out political organization or students bar recruiting on campus by a manufacturer of napalm, when left-wing speakers are kept out by the university or right-wing speakers are drowned out by demonstrators, that is not an open institution. Administrators not open to reason or negotiation are no more entitled to support than unreasoning students presenting nonnegotiable demands. Classes in ROTC that are controlled by the Pentagon have no more right to be given college credit in an open institution than classes in black studies that are controlled by outside independent groups; and neither secret armaments research nor secret student armaments can be permitted in an open community of peaceful scholars who must remain free to criticize the established and the powerful, free to seek unsafe and unpleasant truths.

When a truly modern and open institution has assured student rights to the satisfaction of the great majority of activists, then disruptive tactics by the violent few are likely to fade in the face of firmness and patience. If this can be handled by the college without submitting to student force or resorting to outside police, who often use unnecessary roughness on the abusive and innocent alike, the institution is better served by maintaining, through faculty and student bodies, the control of all discipline on the campus. But an open institution of reason and learning is wholly vulnerable to mindless aggression from those who

would substitute force for reason, who would prefer destroying the university to improving it; and in those circumstances each campus is entitled to take whatever steps
are necessary to continue academic freedom.

In part, student dissatisfaction in America merely re-
flects a global phenomenon, as distinguished from a global
conspiracy. As the postwar baby boom and increased
standards of living have swollen the number of full-time
college students the world over, as television and a more
intensive education increase their perception of society's
shortcomings, and as the trends toward earlier puberty
and longer academic training extend the period of "youth,"
militant student demonstrations of dissatisfaction have become a common world-wide occurrence, shaking governments in France, Spain, Japan, Czechoslovakia, Greece,
Mexico, Britain, and most other parts of the college-edu-
cated world.

Student unrest in turn is but one part of an increasing
human tendency to challenge nearly all forms of authority.
Youngsters question the wisdom not only of their teachers
but of their parents as well. Laymen and clergymen
resist the orthodoxy of their ecclesiastic superiors. Union
members reject settlements negotiated by their leaders.
The citizens of small nations resent control by the large.
Even some Soviet citizens and poets sign petitions of dissent against Kremlin policy. Presidents, popes, police, the
rulers of one-party nations, all find their positions challenged from below as never before. Television—an agent
of change that keeps recurring in these pages, indicating
that Marshall McLuhan is not totally pulling our leg—has
helped make every man king, a more informed and vocal
critic of his world. Participatory democracy is not solely
an American political movement, or even a movement, but
a healthy, irreversible trend of our times. Institutions of

every kind that are insufficiently responsive and representative are losing their claims to legitimacy and their hold on people's loyalty. This nation's political and governmental institutions must be peacefully but quickly reshaped to guarantee equal access by all to the democratic process.

It is within this kind of political framework that the substance of the Kennedy legacy as a forward-moving philosophy of peaceful revolution becomes so important. Although it evolved in almost haphazard and sometimes inconsistent fashion through the lives, words, and actions of two unique men and their associates, it has emerged in my view as a coherent body of principles. It draws upon the best of our national and Judaeo-Christian heritage to bridge the currently growing gaps between the generations, between the poor and the middle class, between black and white, between ghetto and suburb, between technocrats and laymen. The channeling of youthful energies into constructive outlets, the fulfillment of participatory politics, the reform of the Democratic Party and its procedures, even the election of a Kennedy Democrat as President—all of which would be consistent with the *political* thrust of the Kennedy legacy—will all mean very little unless as a result this nation's policies and principles are changed in accordance with the *substantive* thrust of that legacy. Political success will matter little unless the precedents and principles proclaimed through the lives of John and Robert Kennedy—their reliance on reason, reconciliation, and peaceful revolution, their emphasis on the future of our children, their faith in peace and freedom—can all be applied to today's needs.

Where else but to this legacy can we turn to meet the problems of a nation in transition—a nation moving uncertainly from a production-centered economy to a more urbanized and automated service-centered economy, from a predominantly middle-aged, middle-class society to a two-class, media-oriented society of the young, from a more predictable citizenry concerned with questions of quantity to an impatient citizenry concerned with questions of quality, equality, and individuality?

Traditional liberalism still clings to such precedents as the New Deal, farm parity, and public housing; it is still committed to a defense of big government, high taxes, centralized bureaucracy, and the notion that all wisdom and assistance must stem from Washington—without re-examining the adequacy or even the relevance of these postures for today's world of accelerated growth and technological change.

The rigid and arrogant extremists who claim with no authority to represent the *New Left,* their rhetoric more inflammatory than meaningful and their attitude toward blacks sometimes more patronizing than understanding, would substitute hate and violence for human rights in order to import forms of revolution unsuited to our society.

Modern pragmatism—not as John Kennedy practiced it but as Richard Nixon apparently intends to practice it— will not still the savage frustrations of those youths, blacks, and others who want some compassion and imagination in governmental decisions, even if it means the decision-makers make some mistakes.

Traditional conservatism, which has long preached the doctrines of decentralization, community control, citizen power, and participatory democracy, shies away from actually renovating and innovating the necessary institutions when confronted with this opportunity.

The *irresponsibility* of hippies, yippies, crazies, and po-litical or social drop-outs solves nothing, and undermines the structure of family life which is still, as the Kennedys demonstrated, the one commitment that can best reinforce all others.

Only the approach which I have called the Kennedy legacy—not because the two deceased brothers alone developed it but because their lives and philosophy best crystallized it—sets forth the priorities and principles needed to achieve a peaceful human revolution in our time. A nation that spends most of its enormous Federal income on stockpiling massive weapons and fighting Vietcong guerrillas, while its cities decay and its schools deteriorate and its least advantaged citizens despair, is bound to face revolution of one kind or another. To make that revolution our servant and not our master, to turn it away from violence on the left and repression on the right, we need the Kennedy legacy.

To repeat here all the unfulfilled but urgently needed proposals of John and Robert Kennedy is not necessary. To suggest all the detailed solutions which are consistent with their convictions but which move with new developments beyond their proposals is not possible. Even a listing of all the national problem areas in need of their approach would be too long for this volume. I want instead to pay attention, as the Kennedys paid attention, to top priorities and to realistic possibilities.

Even the few changes sketched broadly and briefly below will be fiercely resisted by those who have a vested interest in the present way of doing things. More than twenty years of cold-war pressures, more than thirty years of New Deal precedents, more than one hundred years of white-supremacy practices, will not be easily set aside. Even after such changes are undertaken, some will be subject to delay and evasion. Some will soon lose the passionate interest of those who prefer manning the barricades to making real progress. I do not claim that my views on these questions are those which would be expressed by John and Robert Kennedy were they living today. I state only that they are the views of one whose whole outlook has been infused with the principles and practices of the Kennedy legacy.

The opportunity and obligation to carry on the Kennedy legacy ultimately devolves most strongly upon the office in which JFK most fully developed his philosophy and in pursuit of which RFK most fully developed his philosophy. Regardless of who fills the position and what views he may hold on key controversies, the American Presidency remains the potentially greatest champion of the unrepresented and unborn, the potentially most important source of national reconciliation and education, the potentially most powerful force for change.

Any man who occupies that office in the latter third of the twentieth century has responsibilities that go far beyond the success of his party or even the defense of his nation. Balancing blocs and sectional interests, effecting a national consensus or international confrontation, allocating resources and arranging alliances, these are the political tasks in the broadest sense that every President undertakes and every Presidential candidate understands. But in addition he inherits with the oath a larger historical task— the task of preserving America's long-range role in the affairs of mankind. If to advance its short-term interests he brings upon it the condemnation of future historians, or dishonors it in the eyes of other nations, or alters its unique balance between majority rule and minority rights, between harmony and diversity, between the rule of law and the role of change, he will have sadly failed his duty, no matter how much approval he receives from Congress and the country. We could, if any President so induced us, become a nation of concentration camps or underground bomb shelters or indolent pleasure palaces. We could become an island without allies or a house divided along racial, economic, regional, or intellectual lines. We could become wedded to the *status quo* or fearful of dissent or unwilling to dare or even care. No President should permit that. Every President must be the custodian of our national character, the chief trustee of the great American experiment to which all mankind still looks. To fulfill that obligation he needs not only extraordinary judgment but also the freest possible discretion to apply it.

Thus I do not share Senator Eugene McCarthy's regrets that John Kennedy personalized the powers of the Presidency or his view that "the New Politics requires a different conception of the office of the President." With the members of the Legislative Branch more inclined almost by definition to take the more provincial and popular route on most sensitive problems, it is strong leadership from the White House—whether it is centralized as it was under Johnson, personalized as it was under Kennedy, or institutionalized as it was under Eisenhower and apparently is under Nixon—that offers more hope for progressive action than any dispersal of Presidential power through the Executive bureaucracy or through all branches and levels of government.

Those of us who worked in the Robert Kennedy campaign encountered firsthand the political power an incumbent President can exercise through his control of a wide variety of public-project funds, patronage, and such intangible prestige or pressure items as White House invitations and telephone calls. We did not like it. But those of us who worked in John Kennedy's White House encountered firsthand the existing limitations already hamstringing the Presidency.

Most Cabinet members—to say nothing of the Joint Chiefs of Staff and the heads of the CIA, FBI, Federal Reserve Board, and Selective Service—usually have a semi-independent power base of their own as well as important friends in the Congress and press. At times negotiations must be conducted by a President with his own subordinates before he can open negotiations with Congress or another nation. A President can make choices, select options, and exercise judgment on the matters presented to him by past events, by other nations, by political pressures, and by the policies of his predecessors; but rarely is he able to make a "decision," particularly in foreign affairs, in the sense of writing a whole new formula on a clean slate. He is able to conceal less security information from the public than he would like to conceal. He is in danger of receiving less candid information from official sources than he would like to receive. He cannot ever be certain of converting his publicity into popularity or his popularity into power. The proportion of Federal jobs outside the merit system has fallen from eighty-eight per cent to less than one per cent; and to fill even this one per cent of "patronage" he has a hard time finding men with the necessary qualifications who are willing to accept Federal pay scales.

The only institutional changes needed with respect to the Presidency are in the direction of strengthening its occupant's hand—giving him the right to veto single undeserving items in an appropriation bill without vetoing the entire bill, emergency power to increase or decrease taxes or expenditures temporarily within limits while awaiting Congressional action, more flexibility to reorganize the Executive Branch, less interference with his own prerogatives, better pay for his top administrators, and better means of keeping them independent from powerful Congressional chairmen and special-interest constituencies.

In the absence of these changes—most if not all of which seem unlikely to be enacted at any early date, if JFK's experience is any indication—it is preferable simply to leave each President free to reform the office to meet his own needs, as JFK did, using his unwritten powers more than an enlargement of his written powers. It is better to risk an abuse of discretion than to risk a return to the pre-Civil War impotence of the nation's one unifying office.

The principal restraints on the White House, JFK found, came indirectly from public opinion and directly from Congress. It is true that the growth of the President's office and authority has altered the original balance between Executive and Legislative power. But rather than react to this imbalance by placing harmful curbs on Presidential power—even in foreign relations—the answer lies in improving the role of the Congress, enabling it to exercise the same kind of creative initiative, cohesive approach, and national leadership as the White House, and giving it the same resources for expert advice. Sharpening its effectiveness will better enable it to spotlight excesses and abuses of Executive power; and making it more representative and responsive can only help a meritorious President get his legislative program through.

Congress, however, has done more in the way of approving Executive reorganization and enacting social reform than reorganizing and reforming itself. There have, over the years, been shifts in power within Congress from one group to another—from the party caucuses to the Rules Committee to the leadership to the committee chairmen and back again. Minor steps forward which passed the Senate in 1968 will be considered again. But not since passage of the Legislative Reorganization Act of 1946 has Congress taken major steps forward to produce a net, long-term increase in that body's positive policy-making contributions—to streamline its procedures, elevate its debates, permit its majorities to be felt, make it more representative of grass-roots change, safeguard its ethics and honor, and restore its ability to analyze, to articulate, and to govern affirmatively and creatively, instead of serving merely as a filter for detail and delay.

Congress does the bulk of its important work in committees. Indeed, one Congressman has perceptively described the House as "a collection of committees that come together in a chamber periodically to approve one another's actions." Yet most of those committees still do not have adequate staff assistance for both majority and minority members or expert advice on such complexities as economics and weaponry beyond that provided with some bias by the Executive Branch or private pressure groups. They still do not have consistent jurisdictions and procedures or an obligation even to consider major issues or proposals. There is still no Committee on Urban Affairs, for example. Nor does the typical committee have any assurance that a majority of its members could convene, conduct, or conclude a meeting without the presence or consent of its chairman, who reached that powerful post without regard to his ability, his health, his interest in the subject matter, or his attitudes on vital issues. To be sure, replacing the seniority system with the election of each chairman by his committee might well invite the worst kind of Executive Branch lobbying; but surely some form of merit selection can be devised that preserves the independence of the Legislative Branch.

A bill endorsed by a House committee today, and strongly desired by both houses tomorrow, can still be bottled up in the House Committee on Rules indefinitely. A bill actually passed by both houses but in different forms can still die in a conference committee composed of members opposed to the bill. In recent years the precious time wasted on such matters as constituent errands and local projects, private bills and petty feuds, needless delays and irrelevant debates, duplicate hearings and functions of the District of Columbia, has grown greater and greater. Appropriations have been enacted later and later. Congressional sessions have lasted longer and longer (with intolerable congestion in the closing weeks). The lack of effective rules of cloture in the Senate and germaneness in the House have frequently tried the patience of the public. At the heart of the Kennedy legacy is institutional reform, and Congressional reformers should begin in their own bailiwick.

Below the Washington level, the problems of institutional reform in our governmental structure are intimately associated with the most pressing domestic problems raised by Robert Kennedy. They range from the tax reforms sought by both Kennedys to court reform and the modernization of state and local government structures, from an end to gerrymandering to an end to slum-spawning building codes and zoning ordinances. All over the nation aspirations have raced ahead of institutions, ahead of their ability to deliver, ahead of their available resources, even their relevance to current needs. The individual citizen, as RFK stressed, feels powerless, almost anonymous, in the face of massive and impersonal governmental, corporate, and educational structures.

State governments are hamstrung by out-of-date constitutions, unrealistic fiscal limitations, unrepresentative legislative bodies, underpaid and understaffed public servants, and inefficient, underfinanced programs. Power-brokers and pressure groups have greater leeway in our state capitols, and the Federal government overpowers all in the competition for talented administrators and, most important, tax resources.

Failures at the state-government level are magnified at the city-government level. In many of our older and larger cities in particular early seventeenth-century institutions of local government are confronted with late-twentieth-century developments in urbanization, technology, population, and expectations. An indifferent and ill-equipped state government, with a regressive and inadequate tax system, cannot meet the rising needs of these cities. Their tax bases, their white populations, and their political power seep out to the suburbs while the least trained and least prosperous of rural America move onto already overburdened city-welfare and public-school rolls. Fragmented Federal grants, as Robert Kennedy pointed out, sometimes make matters worse.

Within many of our larger cities, power is chaotically splintered among multiple competing or overlapping local authorities of a special or general nature (1113 in Greater Chicago alone). Entrenched and largely white bureaucracies are too often remote both ideologically and geographically from the desperate needs of the ghetto. The high hopes and good intentions of once enthusiastic mayors have been sapped by a growing feeling of pessimism, a sense that the big city is ungovernable, a loss of morale, an inability to attract and keep top talent, and a tendency to blame all ills on Washington. This same sense of helpess isolation and futility about "the system," this feeling that all the problems are too big and all the governments too distant, has gripped many private citizens as well. Big-city dwellers moving to the suburbs have found new satisfaction in their greater ability to exert power over their social environment.

Inspired in part by RFK's efforts as Attorney General and particularly by his precedent-setting initiative in Bedford-Stuyvesant, a new formulation of the old concept of decentralization with community control has arisen from this atmosphere of malaise. Many neighborhoods in our larger cities have populations greater than that of a large-size town. Lost in one huge unit of government or arbitrarily divided (or deliberately gerrymandered) into many, the residents of such a neighborhood have no community council because it would be powerless, almost no communication with the centralized bureaucracies that run their affairs, and thus little or no sense of responsibility or sometimes even hope. To them the concept of community control offers a way out.

So long as it is confined to appealing Jeffersonian slogans that sound like conservative Republican doctrine—giving government back into the hands of the people, encouraging an old-fashioned sense of community spirit, enabling people to feel responsible for their own destinies—the new philosophy of community control has few opponents. Its implementation enables private business corporations and foundations who are unable or unwilling to be enveloped in massive Federal programs to find an outlet for their public energies by joining in these community efforts. It increases the opportunity for individual citizens to assume meaningful responsibility. It runs counter to cherished liberal notions about Federal patrimony, racial integration, and corporate greed, as Senator Kennedy discovered in Bedford-Stuyvesant, but that is only another indication of the limitations of traditional liberalism.

Nevertheless, widespread application of this concept to city school systems, health programs, and other services will require some hard choices for both the local residents and those who have heretofore exercised authority in their locales. It will require the dispersal of effective political power in specified decision-making areas to new neighborhood councils; the evolution of both the machinery and the motivations for widespread participatory politics within each community; and the assurance to these newly created community councils that they will have a meaningful voice in planning the future of their communities, operating their facilities, and finding the resources needed to implement those plans. Federal, state, and city governments will be required to provide services and assistance even to those community councils which assail them. It is not surprising that this movement has been opposed by those politicians who prefer the security of the *status quo,* as illustrated by Congress's elimination of neighborhood control in neighborhood poverty programs.

All opposition to decentralization is not selfishly motivated, however, for the dangers inherent in the movement are real. Community control is workable only if both "community" and "control" are carefully defined in advance. There is a danger in extending the new movement too far, splintering those municipal services that cannot logically be splintered, proliferating the already excessive number of overlapping governmental subdivisions, and adding more confusion and chaos instead of creative government. Decentralization was not intended by RFK and other sponsors to encourage a polarization of the races; and there is danger that the movement, improperly conducted, will reverse the process of reconciliation, splitting the population along ethnic lines, reducing teachers and other municipal employees to the status of community "hired hands," and fragmenting the single city into a host of antagonistic neighborhoods and groups unwilling to pull together as one people. Nothing is accomplished by a decentralization so complete that it casts adrift a series of communities unable to provide their own expert personnel and technological or economic resources. That only reverses the true meaning of community.

Nor can community control mean total control. No one

has or should have total control in the United States. If decentralization to the community level is to succeed, the plan must not only assure all those in charge that they have sufficient decision-making authority but also assure all those affected that they have sufficient safeguards against the abuse of authority. If angry ideological fanatics take over a decentralized institution for their own ruthless purposes by terrorizing the people and wrecking reform, then the state or city government must have carefully defined and limited authority to protect the public's interest in peaceful, democratic processes in much the same way the Federal government can intervene in Mississippi or some other state. The surest answer to extremist control is the broadest possible participation by the people of the community and their willingness to insist upon a representative board, on limitations on the exercise of power, and on guarantees of personal liberty. Decentralization cannot otherwise succeed.

On the other hand, there is also a danger that community control will be confined in most cities to little more than slogans and a few cosmetic changes, thus further embittering those whose hopes have been raised. There is a danger finally that the movement will be confined to the nonwhite ghettos where it may understandably be viewed solely as a means to end white exploitation and neglect—when it is in reality a means by which all communities can regain power and initiative in local affairs.

Decentralization was intended, to be sure, to offer one avenue of escape from racial inequality. Ghetto schools that have long been the stepchild of predominantly white school systems, for example, hope to reverse their decline through community control. But there are other and more turbulent avenues of escape which our nonwhite citizens will seek in coming years. The mood of desperation that filled many black Americans in the spring of 1968, after the killings of King and Kennedy, was a measure of the void that these two assassinations left behind. To whom in the power structure could blacks turn then for help and understanding? Who after RFK could bridge the widening communication and credibility gap separating white and black Americans?

Some whites suggest that it is time for a pause, that the white majority is becoming tired of continued civil-rights agitation, demonstrations, and legislation. But consider how the black minority feels about continued discrimination, segregation, and subjugation. The gains in Negro income, employment, education, political participation, and opportunity since the election of JFK have been substantial; but it has all been too little and too late to enable the black man to catch up with the white. Liberals dismayed by black moves to obtain their own college dormitories or communities forget that comparatively little integration has occurred in this country despite historic court decisions and statutes. The basic injustices of unequal housing, schools, and jobs remain; and no government in history ever maintained for very long both domestic tranquillity and injustice.

The black revolution, which spread from the Deep South to the Northern ghettos of Harlem, Watts, and Hough to the college campuses, is not as philosophical as the white student revolution. Black college students seek black-studies programs because they are the spokesmen for a whole race in search of its identity, a race whose history and culture in Africa and to a large extent in this country have been excluded from the usual texts. Many of them resent being spotlighted in a hostile environment that is geared to the white man's world. But basically their effort is a part of the

over-all black revolution against inequality and injustice
of which John F. Kennedy spoke in 1963. That revolution,
unlike the student rebellion, is concerned not with the
stultifying effects of affluence but the lack of it, not with
irrelevant institutions but inequitable and inadequate institutions, not with empty days and dreams but empty
larders and bellies. Unlike the gap that divides the white
students and white working men, the black student has a
bond of mutual support with his brothers on the street that
makes joint action possible. The black revolution and
the white student revolution do have one characteristic in
common: both are here to stay, not because of their extremist leaders on whom the mass media focus their
cameras, not because of conspiratorial fringe groups who
claim to speak for the whole, but because in both cases
great masses of moderate but angry, law-abiding but bitter,
rank-and-file members see revolution as the only means by
which their frustrations and deprivations can be heard and
remedied.

Thus neither of these revolutions will end until their
root causes have been removed; and the longer any revolution continues, history shows, the greater the danger that
both sides will become more deeply embittered and more
prone to extremist leadership. "Those who do nothing," as
President Kennedy said back in 1963 in his historic civil-
rights message, "are inviting shame as well as violence.
Those who act boldly are recognizing right as well as
reality."

It is now recognized that the kind of equal-rights legislation pioneered by Kennedy in 1963 is inadequate.
Brought here a chattel in the chains of slavery, eman-
cipated only in theory a hundred years ago, denied for all
that time the opportunity to live and work and hope like
other Americans, the black man now needs more than the

assurance of equal opportunity and equal rights—he needs
the assurance of equal results. For one generation after another the white man destroyed the black man's family life
and then called him inherently immoral, destroyed his
economic prospects and incentive and then called him inherently lazy, destroyed his educational standards and opportunities and then called him inherently less intelligent.

Comparisons to European immigrants who "pulled
themselves up by their boot straps" mean very little to
those whose grandfathers did not come to these shores
voluntarily, whose fathers were excluded by virtue of un-
concealable color from a fair chance, and whose children
have no boots—with or without straps. Sermons about hard
work mean very little to the average black college student
who will earn less than the average white who dropped out
of school at the end of the eighth grade. Examples of illus-
trious Negroes in baseball or the United Nations or statistics on recent gains mean very little to those unjustly
imprisoned in American ghettos both real and figurative.
For they are understandably unable to be satisfied by im-
provements in prison treatment when what they really want
is to be out of prison entirely. White liberals have promised
this for decades; but the bonds of injustice have never been
shattered, only polished, adjusted, and occasionally made a
little more comfortable. The gaps between white affluence
and black poverty, and between white education in the suburbs and black education in the ghettos, have in fact
increased over the last enlightened generation.

Now it is not surprising that the new black leadership
will no longer docilely accept policy decisions from the
white community or even the leadership of white liberals
regarding what is best for black men. Like everyone else,
they want "a piece of the action," they want experience and
responsibility for their own leaders who will never other-

wise be developed, and they rightly regard community control and participatory democracy as conceptual steps to obtaining these gains. They feel entitled to try their own way—black power, black studies, black capitalism, black culture, sit-ins, shutdowns, reparations, and demonstrations. Nor is it surprising that a variety of vociferous spokesmen has come onto the scene, each trying to outdo the other, sometimes in outrageous statements and exaggerations that are designed to attract attention and thus followers in the black community and to irritate or frighten their tormenters in the white community.

They are much like the proverbial mule driver who believed in sweet-talking his beast into action but first clubbed her over the head "in order to get her attention." While the various leaders and groups jockey for position with a wide variety of tactics, their goals (excepting those of the ultramilitants who seek an overthrow) are not very dissimilar, radical, or even different from what John Kennedy urged years ago: decent schools, decent homes, decent jobs, a fair chance for their children to develop and apply their talents to the utmost of their capacity, the respect that is due them as human beings by the police and all others, and a chance to participate fully in all phases of American life as first-class citizens, including control of the institutions and enterprises that principally serve their own neighborhoods. Legal and economic gains alone will not suffice. The black family today needs both bread and hope, both security and pride, both a fair share of the pie and a voice in deciding how it is sliced. Integration into white society, it should be noted, is no longer regarded by many black leaders as an end in itself, and they are increasingly doubtful that it is a practical means to achieve the ends they do seek.

The black militants rarely have large followings, and

the extent to which those followings are increasing is due
to the white community's inaction rather than their own
rash actions. But the militance of an entire race is rising.
Despite President Nixon's plea for us all to lower our
voices, the black-white dialogue is fast becoming one between deaf men shouting at each other ever louder in vain.
Already we are past the point where we can be certain that
the reasonable and the predictable will prevail in relations
between the races.

In a nation of two hundred million people, the number
of black citizens is too small, their leadership is too divided,
and their community resources are too limited for them
to obtain these goals entirely on their own if they are to
obtain them peacefully. The task of ending all forms of inequality between the races is the one great task facing all
concerned members of this generation of Americans. What
the Kennedys helped begin we all must finish if the militant radicals of both colors who preach separatism and retaliation are not to gain more influence and turn America
into a nightmare of violence, repression, and ultimately
guerrilla warfare and concentration camps.

The Report of the Kerner Commission outlined what
needs to be done, and no one should be surprised if the
nation's refusal to do it is labeled white racism. Merely
making economic and political rights available will never
be enough. Basic changes in the concepts and even the
structure of our economic and political systems will be
necessary. Above all, it will require an enormous shift of
resources as well as opinion; but as Edward Kennedy has
pointed out, we have been spending three billion dollars a
month on behalf of the freedom of fourteen million South
Vietnamese, and we can surely afford at least as great an
effort on behalf of the freedom of twenty-two million black
Americans.

In the long run, the cost of poverty and inequality—in crime, welfare, violence, and dry rot within our society— far exceeds the cost of their elimination. Poverty is not simply a Negro ghetto problem. It afflicts other minorities —the Puerto Rican, the Indian, the Mexican-American. It afflicts more whites than all others combined. It afflicts more rural than city dwellers. Twenty-two million Americans live below the poverty line, hungry, sick, bitter, and largely idle. No one before or after Robert Kennedy has so clearly articulated their despair. Many are too old or too young to work. Some cannot work. For those who are physically able, even if untrained, there is no substitute for earning hard cash through meaningful, lasting, adequately, paying jobs. Full employment is both an economic possibility and a civil-rights necessity.

The lion's share of such employment should come from a Federally stimulated economic expansion, from the upgrading of existing but inadequately funded and coordinated Federal job-training, job-placement, and antipoverty efforts. Existing youth work programs must be expanded, not curtailed. Tax incentives can help private industry create extra jobs. Tougher enforcement can help more unions open up their membership and apprenticeship programs. But to complete the task a final comprehensive guarantee is required. The job-training and job-creating programs of President John Kennedy, followed by the emergency employment and business-development proposals of Senator Robert Kennedy, must now be followed by establishing the Federal government as the "employer of last resort." This means providing permanent, dignified work with on-job training and incentive wages for every American able and willing to work, not through direct Federal employment but through Federal financing by grant and contract of enough job-creating activities by state and

local governments, private business, and nonprofit institutions. Surely we have the ingenuity to match the need for
new employment and better wages for the poor with the
need for an estimated 5,200,000 more men and women in
our parks, hospitals, slums, schools, and fire and police
auxiliaries.

Such a program is preferable to a new, vastly expanded
program of welfare under any other label that isolates the
poor behind a curtain of paperwork and bureaucracy
rather than bringing them into the mainstream of our
society. For those mothers, children, aged, handicapped,
and others who clearly cannot work or be trained to work
—and their proportion on the present welfare rolls is large
but in dispute—there must be adequate protection under
an automatic Federally financed income-maintenance system with national minimum standards which permits no
arbitrary exclusion, discrimination, humiliation, invasion
of privacy, or disincentive to work. As RFK told the Senate, it is outrageous to force a slum mother to choose between caring for her children and feeding them, or to
force a slum father to choose between seeing his children
hungry and not seeing them at all. It is unfair to permit
some states in the competition for new business to undercut
others by reducing welfare standards and expenses, and
equally unfair for more conscientious states to bear the
financial burden of caring for poor families attracted to
their borders by the comparative generosity of their statutes. Mr. Nixon's plan is headed in the right direction.

An end to all poverty and discrimination will not mean
an end to all crime. But ending those conditions that make
young men desperate for money and despairing of earning
it, angry at the society which has ill-treated them and indifferent to its code, lacking in self-discipline and lacking

in self-respect, would do more to prevent crime than curbing the rights of accused persons. Both as Attorney General and as Senator, Robert Kennedy demonstrated that there is nothing illiberal about warring on crime. The disturbing increase in muggings, assaults, robberies, and other street crimes in our major cities—which make many of their public avenues and parks unsafe for man or woman late at night—is not due to an increasing failure to obtain convictions as the result of the Supreme Court's application of the Constitution's protection to the lowliest among us. On the contrary, at least four out of five such crimes are committed by individuals who have previously been convicted. Unfortunately, they have too often been sent to courts too congested in their caseloads and too antiquated in their machinery to handle each individual case fairly, sensibly, and quickly; to probation, rehabilitation, and parole officers too overworked and underpaid to give them real help; and to aging penal or correctional institutions where all too often degradation suppresses any remaining decency, and the impressionable and the incorrigible ultimately emerge indistinguishable.

All work involved in the administration of justice, from patrolmen to parole officers, should be given the funds and effort necessary to achieve true professional standards—with professional training, salaries, promotion practices, life insurance, pensions, and leadership. This will help make it possible to attract and retain college graduates from all ethnic backgrounds who can, in the case of police officers, build rapport with local communities, exercise discretion in their choice and use of weapons, withstand verbal abuse, avoid temptations inconsistent with their duties, and distinguish between those situations requiring maximum force and those in which the public interest would only be endangered by it.

True law and order, Robert Kennedy reminded us, is not of interest only to the prosperous white community. Most crimes occur in poor areas against poor people. The ghetto dweller is three-and-a-half times more likely to be robbed than the non-ghetto person. His sister is three-and-a-half times more likely to be raped. Too much of his community's meager income is likely to be taken outside the ghetto through numbers, vice, narcotics, and other rackets controlled by organized crime. He may want less police abuse but he clearly wants more police protection. He, too, will gain from more massive research and enforcement programs aimed at narcotics offenders and juvenile delinquency. Only the most unthinking black militant can believe that gun-control laws are intended to deny protection to the black minority.

Long, sad experience has taught that possession of a gun is more often provocation than protection. Black and white alike would be better protected by effective controls requiring the registration of firearms and the licensing of owners. Hecklers told RFK in the Oregon primary that this would not cause criminals to turn in their guns, and it would require some effort to keep the inconvenience to hunters and hobbyists down to a minimum. But such legislation would check the frightening number of guns owned by irresponsible people in this country, increase police capability to trace weapons used in crimes, and reduce the number of murders committed in family arguments, in resisting arrest, in riot and sniper cases, and in other assaults and robberies. Hand guns in particular—and there are an estimated twenty-four million of them loose in this country—are widely used in homicides but never in hunting. Those of us who worked with John and Robert Kennedy cannot have a detached view of this subject. But it is hard to assail our bloodthirsty entertainment media for merely presenting portrayals of violence to adolescents, addicts, and others of diminished responsibility when the actual tools of violence remain so available to them.

Crime, riots, and civil-rights problems generally came to mind when the Kennedys spoke of the urban crisis. But in truth they were talking about a whole series of urban crises afflicting that seventy-three per cent of our population that lives on one per cent of our land. So long as our elected white officials regard these urban problems as affecting principally the black minority, they are unlikely as a matter of practical politics to undertake the actions or find the funds needed to end them. But these are not ghetto problems only.

The crisis in urban housing, with over four million substandard homes of one kind or another, is most acute in the ghetto; but rat infestation, congestion, lack of modern plumbing, dilapidated structures, and a lack of facilities at the price desired are not problems confined to the ghetto. The crisis in urban health takes its worst toll among the children of the ghetto; but infant and maternal mortality, unsanitary conditions, overcrowded hospital waiting rooms, insufficient public-health clinics, skyrocketing costs, and even hunger are not confined to the ghetto.

The crisis in urban schools destroys what little chance most ghetto children have for a better future; but increasing drop-out rates, shabby fire-trap school buildings, untrained teachers, and inadequate materials and curricula are harming other children as well. Affluent whites in the big cities who complain of the cost and difficulty inherent in sending their children to private schools are paying a special price for having permitted the deterioration of public education.

The crisis in urban transportation particularly handicaps the employment efforts of inner-city dwellers; but congested streets, antiquated public transit systems, and uncoordinated planning and research help push transportation costs in time, money, discomfort, air pollution, and noise beyond reasonable levels for everyone.

To the urban crises in welfare, law enforcement, and employment already mentioned could be added the urban crises in air and water pollution, in consumer protection, in garbage collection and waste disposal, in noise and vermin abatement, and in environmental planning and beauty. Underlying them all is the crisis in urban revenues, as municipal governments continue to rely largely on inadequate, inelastic, and regressive tax systems. Such taxes have already been raised to the breaking point, for recent years have witnessed a rapid escalation of costs and indebtedness, insufficient help from state and Federal programs, and an adverse shift within city limits in the ratio of major taxpayers to tax users.

These problems, as RFK sought to illustrate in Bedford-Stuyvesant, can be attacked only as an entity. In the past many piecemeal programs, traditional New Deal solutions, and Federal matching grants have hurt as much as they helped. We accomplish nothing by the enactment of housing programs that enable only the comfortable to increase their comfort at the expense of the poor, facilitate the flight to the suburbs, concentrate less affluent citizens in already overcrowded areas, add to urban blight and suburban sprawl, arouse exaggerated expectations for which funds are never made available, and build new public housing that poverty soon converts to new slums. We accomplish nothing by training ghetto dwellers for jobs that do not exist, or providing jobs where there is no public transportation to reach them. We accomplish nothing by improving the standard of education available to children too sick or too hungry to benefit from it, or too likely to be forced out into the labor market before they can complete it.

What is the net gain in bulldozing ghettos to build new business districts if black families are effectively excluded, law or no law, from suburban and other white neighborhoods? Or in employing a previously hard-core unemployable if his new earnings are quickly taken from him by the slumlord, the credit fleecers, and the rackets? Or in hiring more social workers to tell more slum dwellers that they should move to a home in a better environment for their children that will take less of their welfare checks if they cannot also be told where such housing is available?

Nevertheless, the basic ills of urban life can be alleviated. Much of it must be done at the local level, improving and enforcing fair-housing laws and building codes, amending tax and criminal codes that discourage landlords from making repairs, and designing community projects of the Bedford-Stuyvesant type. Private enterprise and private citizens can do the most, including tenants' unions. In terms of governmental aid, the Kennedys focused their attention primarily on what could be done on the Federal level; and the Federal government can help in all these problem areas if it adopts the aforementioned objectives for its own—if it lives up to its own 1968 targets for the financing of more attractive low-income and moderate-income housing and less restricted rent supplements, if it can promulgate standards that break through outmoded municipal, industrial, and trade-union restrictions on building practices, if it can provide credit and tax incentives for a greater effort by private enterprise, if it can encourage the growth of new towns, if it can spend as much on housing research and development as it does in other "R and D" areas, if it can enforce the termination of all racial housing barriers, if it can reduce the fragmentation of its grants and programs to the cities, if it can increase the flow directly to the cities through a less clogged and leaky pipeline, if it can cut down on excessive red tape and bureaucratic centralization, and if it can simultaneously improve living standards and job opportunities in rural America to prevent its poor from swarming into the cities. Above all, the Federal government must make additional tax sources and resources available to local governments to supplement but not to supplant their present efforts. As John Kenneth Galbraith has pointed out, our recent rapid national growth has given most of the money to the Federal government and most of the problems to the local governments. It is time that both revenues and problems were shared more equitably and directly. Mr. Nixon's tax-sharing plan is a start.

Domestic demands on the Federal budget are not limited to urban needs. For rural and suburban as well as urban Americans, for white as well as black, for middle class as well as poor, the unavailability of low-cost medical care—from birth-control programs to pharmaceuticals to old-age "extended care" facilities—is a national travesty requiring national legislation. If we share the Kennedys' concern for our children, we can only be shocked by the widespread lack of prenatal, pediatric, and psychiatric care they receive. It is unacceptable, as Bob Kennedy would say, that the United States ranks behind so many other nations in the prevention of infant mortality, maternal mortality, malnutrition, and mental retardation; incredible that we could be so short of physicians, dentists, nurses, hospital beds, and mental-health clinics and unable to prevent these and other health-care shortages from growing worse. Robert Kennedy did not, as some suggest, "discover" the issue of hunger on his trips to Appalachia and the Mississippi Delta. He merely articulated with passion, as his brother had in West Virginia years earlier, the immorality of a nation so rich and abundant paying some farmers not to grow while an estimated fourteen million rural and urban families lack sufficient food.

Both Kennedys, had they lived, would have devoted even more attention to the preservation of our natural as well as human resources. Both were offended by smokestacks polluting the air, strip mines scarring the land, chemicals and sewage fouling the water, and billboards, highways, high-rise apartment towers, and junk heaps gradually encroaching on what greenery we have left for our children. The technological "progress" that gave us radioactivity, pesticides, fertilizers, the internal-combustion engine, and tons of mining, chemical, nuclear, and residential wastes had to be curbed, they believed, before man—with the aid of overpopulation and undisciplined self-interest—progressed himself right out of existence. We do not even know how far we are today from the danger point where the consumption of oxygen by this nation's booming population will exceed the supply of oxygen produced by the greenery we pave over at the rate of one billion acres a year. Today's filthy lakes and waterways are the forerunners of a dangerous water shortage. Someone should be worrying about these questions now on behalf of future generations—not merely a few scientists and conservationists but governments whose tax, urban, agricultural, and other policies are encouraging this depletion of our heritage.

At the root of the Kennedy legacy—in its concern for the succeeding generations, in its reliance on the qualities of the mind, in its preparation for continual change and renewal—is education. Only an educated people can find rational solutions to the problems we face. Without education there is no escape from the ghetto, no end to unemployment, no reversal of crime rates, no ability to master the technology of our times. It has rightly been said that there is no place on earth where the truly well-educated are truly poor. A wise investment in education brings a return in tax savings, tax income, and economic growth that no other investment can match.

Yet the enormous increase that has happily occurred in Federal aid to education over these past several years has still not come close to assuring quality education for every American child, much less quality institutions of learning beyond the high-school level at a cost within the reach of every young man who seeks admission. We have too few teachers, many underpaid, and too few classrooms, many inadequate, at all levels of education—and the trends are adverse. Surely it was a peculiar ordering of priorities that caused Federal elementary and secondary school assistance per child to decline while Federal funds expended per Vietcong killed were rising. Moreover, in the absence of proper testing and standards, as Robert Kennedy told the Senate, we do not know how much of this Federal aid is wasted on schools still employing untrained or uninterested teachers and administrators to teach outdated material through outdated methods in obsolete classrooms to children too handicapped by conditions in the home to absorb any new skills and too uncertain about their future to stay the full course.

Children with poor motivation, children with poor environments and vocabularies, children with health and nutrition problems—none is getting all the compensating help needed at the earliest age practicable. One out of four children entering the fifth grade today will never graduate from high school. Ghetto and rural students frequently start out behind suburban students and then fall further behind. Most inner-city schools are more segregated now than in 1954. Many are largely custodial institutions. Adult-education programs still help only a tenth of those grownups lacking an eighth-grade education. Only a thorough revamping of the present system can end the present costly loss of brain power this nation suffers.

We cannot do the job that must be done in education if we cling to all the old traditions that keep school buildings idle after hours and in the summer, impose useless information on our children, increase the turnover rate among young teachers, and stimulate racial, religious, and other fragmentation within the school and community. American education is cluttered with divisions, requirements, forms, and procedures that are unnecessary or even unrelated to human learning. We need special incentive and training programs to bring young men completing their military service into our elementary schools as teachers and principals. We need more bold experimentation with television to aid the student, computers to aid the teacher, and teaching machines to aid both. We need to restructure both our high schools and our universities—increasing the voice of students, faculty, and local community spokesmen, decreasing the importance of grades and social conformity, and weeding out the less useful courses in favor of those that will concretely prepare today's student to face today's problems outside his own home and profession. We need more and better vocational education and subsidized apprenticeship programs conducted in factories and stores during off hours by employers and unions. Considering the changes in our economy and technology since this nation first assured every child of the right to a free public education through high school, the time has come to extend that guarantee to include professional, vocational, or college training for everyone for at least two to four years beyond high school.

All this will take more money; and because local real-estate property taxes can bear no more of this burden, more funds must be found from other sources. But none of these domestic problems can be solved by money alone. Pouring more money into outmoded programs and machinery will do very little good. We must somehow come to grips with the fact that we are already living in the twenty-first century technologically—that the changes in means of communication, transportation, production, and calculation have rendered obsolete most of the basic twentieth-century institutions on which we depend—including our governmental structure, our cities, our defense and diplomatic establishments, our political parties and methods, our educational system, our courts and prisons and civil service and all the rest of the baggage we drag with us as time and events pull us rapidly along. If we do not give these changes the direction, the attention, and the money they will require—if we cannot apply the Kennedy formula of humanizing these pressures and processes in a manner that is consistent with our deepest values as well as our needs—then the prospects for peaceful change and harmonious innovations in this country's basic system are very slim indeed.

No one wants to pay more taxes. Yet virtually no one wants this nation to fail this historic test. That means we have to do more than reshuffle our domestic priorities and reallocate our domestic resources. It means that we must undertake what JFK planned for 1964 and what RFK sought for 1969: a net transfer of funds and energy now devoted to meeting problems around the world to the task of meeting problems here at home. So long as the Federal Budget is dominated by the Defense budget, so long as the Pentagon, not the Department of Health, Education, and Welfare, is the major institution in Washington, so long as military procurement takes one hundred times as many of our tax dollars as food for the hungry, the problems sketched above cannot be met. Even with the revenues expected from the continued growth of the economy, even with the savings expected from ending the fighting in Vietnam, even with the enactment of all the tax reforms and tax-loophole closings advocated by John and Robert Kennedy to spread more fairly the cost of saving our society, even with stricter controls on postal, agricultural, maritime, highway, and other subsidies, even with less bureaucratic inefficiency and pork-barrel and space-race waste, even with the termination of domestic programs no longer needed, the present high level of military-related expenditures will leave too little room for the kinds of increases in Federal funding required for a peaceful revolution in this country.

For this reason in particular I share RFK's doubts about candidate Nixon's call for an all-volunteer armed services. Even if and when our foreign policy or the world situation is sufficiently changed to lower drastically our need for a readily available manpower pool, enough men would volunteer only if military pay and benefit scales were so attractive and thus so costly that our domestic budgetary needs would suffer. Even then the burden of living a military life and dying a military death would still fall most heavily on those denied by race, poverty, or otherwise the education and skills required to find jobs in the civilian labor market; and a largely black army would be a large black eye for America in world affairs. Finally, a professional army—sure to be termed mercenaries—would, for the very reason that its burdens and risks would be of less concern to the general populace and thus the Congress, pose the threat of

becoming a highly independent military force, unlike anything we have known in this country. The very existence
of Selective Service today acts as a check on American involvement in wars which the public and Congress are
unwilling to support.

Nevertheless, drastic changes in our Selective Service
system are required. To place the heaviest burden of military service on those young men whose families are unable
by reason of poverty, color, or other circumstances to send
them to college is manifestly unfair. To dangle for years
the threat of military service over the head of the young
college man, who is thereby unable to plan with any assurance the timing of his graduate studies, marriage, or career,
is equally unfair. To defer some types of students while
drafting others makes matters worse. These broad defects
in the system are worsened by administrative rulings or
practices which have accelerated the drafting or retracted
the exemptions of those protesting against the present
Selective Service System, the war, or other policies; which
have refused conscientious-objector status to those who
were genuinely opposed on the grounds of conscience, not
policy or politics, to the particular war in which they were
asked to participate; which have insisted on narrow religious tests in defining true conscientious objection; and
which have excluded from most local draft boards any
representation of the black, the poor, and the young who
bear the brunt of those draft boards' decisions. Without
discussing trials appealed by my law firm, I should add
that nothing should inhibit the freedom of anyone to
counsel a perplexed or angry young man, privately or publicly, on the full range of choices open to him as he con-
fronts the complex Selective Service machinery—including
the path of civil disobedience if he is prepared to accept
the legal consequences.

It was one of the brightest and most thoughtful members of the "Kennedy group," Burke Marshall, whose Presidentially appointed commission recommended that each year's quota, as determined by military needs, be filled by a fair and impartial random selection of all young men at a given age, regardless of educational, occupational, or other status. Once that year of a man's life had passed, whether or not he was called to serve during that period and whether or not quotas were later increased, he would be free of all obligation and liability under the draft and permitted to pursue his studies or other plans without interruption. That proposed system is sponsored in the Senate at present by Edward Kennedy; and, if accompanied by a change in the aforementioned administrative practices, this would be far fairer than the halfway measures proposed by President Nixon.

It is popular to talk in some campus quarters about the concept of universal national service under which every young man and woman upon graduation from high school would be required to give one to two years in the service area of his choice—including not only military service but also work in the Peace Corps, VISTA, conservation, antipoverty, mental-health, and other programs. I am sympathetic to the spirit that motivates this concept and hope that some noncompulsory version of it can be devised as a means of earning an otherwise free post-high-school education or obtaining temporary credit against the draft to those who are needed, qualified, and accepted for nonmilitary service. But we should be careful not to remove the act of will which underlies the dedication and enthusiasm of such workers. Because a Peace Corps volunteer is a volunteer, his work may be both more effective and more satisfying. The opportunities for nonmilitary service must be increased, but the element of universal compulsion should be cautiously approached if we are not to have protests against these civilian programs similar to present protests against the draft.

The draft has been a part of the process by which the Defense Department has greatly extended its own domestic empire. Its support of research and education, health and hospitalization, science and technology, employment and job training makes it an omnipresent factor in American life that is in danger of becoming omnipotent. I admired Robert McNamara's use of this power and influence to help break down racial discrimination in housing. I admired its use to help salvage military-service rejectees from poverty backgrounds for a useful, productive life through modern educational techniques. But that same domestic power can also be used to create public demands for new weapons systems and public fears of disarmament.

The military-industrial complex cited in President Eisenhower's farewell message is not an insidious secret conspiracy of power-hungry generals and profit-hungry munitions makers. It is the growing stake in Defense Department contracts, grants, and other items shared by a growing number of corporations, employers, unions, universities, scientists, engineers, and whole communities as well as the various associations, lobbyists, and Congressmen who represent them all. The political power of that vast complex overshadows the coming crucial decisions on a new arms race and new arms control to an even greater extent than it did during the Kennedy Presidency.

On this question our nation stands today at a crossroads. The Soviet Union stands there as well. Perhaps by the time this book is published we shall each have made our choice, traveling together down the road of arms control or traveling together down the road of arms increases.

Either or both nations may delay a final commitment to either road until more certain of the other's intentions; or both may attempt to travel halfheartedly down both roads at the same time. But it is unlikely that either will ever be willing to travel down either road by itself. History demonstrates that, whatever the cost, each is determined and able to match the other stride for stride.

Seen in that perspective, the choice for both nations seems ridiculously easy. Why, I remember Kennedy writing to Khrushchev in effect, should either superpower spend on new and necessarily dangerous weapons systems billions of dollars better invested in hard-pressed domestic sectors when whatever marginal gain in security hoped to be obtained thereby will surely be offset by the expenditures of the other superpower? The United States alone has spent over a trillion dollars on arms since the beginning days of the cold war. The mind boggles in attempting to calculate how many homes could have been built and hungry children fed and old people nursed back to health with that staggering sum that was devoted instead to piling high an arsenal of weapons and delivery systems that dwarf by comparison the bomb that destroyed Hiroshima. The world spends three times as much on armaments today as it does on public health, more than the total income of Latin America, South Asia, and the Middle East combined. Yet who can say with assurance that we are any more "secure" now than we were before this spending orgy started?

Surely, as Robert McNamara has written, we have reached that point where we cannot effectively increase our security by acquiring still more military hardware. The same is true of the Soviets. Khrushchev before the Cuban missile crisis occasionally made crude references to the power of his rockets to destroy West European culture, and John Foster Dulles talked of massive (meaning nuclear) retaliation against any Soviet threat; but neither found either safety or satisfaction in the ability to use that kind of language. If anything, the dangers of an accidental or miscalculated war are far greater now than ever. While it is easy for the United States to place the blame for the start of this race on Stalin's aggressive behavior and his rejection of the Baruch Plan for Atomic Controls, it is not so easy to see why we should prefer *now* to resume an exorbitantly expensive and risky race when the alternative is so much safer and cheaper.

Both powers may fear an ultimate Chinese nuclear attack. But if this is because we assume Chinese war-makers are irrational, then a greater nuclear retaliatory capacity on our part can neither deter such an attack nor measurably lessen its consequences. If we assume they are rationally bent on destroying us, then a new Soviet-American arms spiral is likely to do nothing other than increase the time and cost of their building the nuclear capacity required. A solution to the Chinese puzzle, as I will discuss later, cannot rest on arms alone.

Nor can either the United States or the Soviet Union possibly wish to see the kind of proliferation of nuclear weapons to other nations that is certain in time to resume, despite the new treaty, if the superpowers resume their own unlimited nuclear development. We can hardly imagine the nightmarish world that would evolve if seven and then a dozen and then forty countries should acquire even a minuscule nuclear capability. It would be a world in which many a small nation, without even possessing a modern missile or bomber system, would be able to threaten its neighbor in some minor boundary dispute with the extinction of its capital city—in which an explosion could destroy West Berlin or Boston or Buenos Aires without any certainty as to its origin—in which nuclear devices would be sold like machine guns in the international arms market—in which a lunatic or junta could seize power in a small country to gain only a few days' control of its nuclear trigger—in which the prospect of a nuclear exchange, possibly sucking in all the superpowers, could exist in every local Middle East or Southeast Asia territorial war. Such a world would be in no one's interest. But like our involvement in Vietnam, it will grow step by step unless we stop it now.

In 1963 John Kennedy and Nikita Khrushchev started to stop it—with the Test Ban Treaty, the ban on outer-space weapons of mass destruction, and other steps. But those two leaders are gone. Robert Kennedy, who hoped to follow through on these steps, is gone. As I write, the United States is embarking on the deployment of antiballistic missiles (ABMs) and the development of MIRVs (multiple individually targeted re-entry vehicles); the Soviet Union is developing FOBS (fractional orbit bombardment systems); both sides are renewing the accelerated development of new missiles. Ahead lies talk of a spectrum bomb and a neutron bomb; and we are already headed pell-mell once again down the same dangerous path that historians tell us has previously led only to war. This next war, unfortunately—the equivalent of five hundred World War IIs in a matter of hours—may not have survivors to write its history.

In advocating the ABM program in a secret 1968 Senate debate, one distinguished Southern Senator told his colleagues, "If we have to start over again with another Adam and Eve, I want them to be Americans and not Russians." (I wonder whether he would have made the same choice if Adam and Eve were to be black Americans instead of white Russians, or a black Adam and a white Eve.) For myself, if all that mankind has built and learned and meant in these thousands of years of civilization is to be wiped out by FOBS and MIRVs, I have very little interest in the race, religion, nationality, or political belief of those unfortunate enough to survive.

Survival is not enough in this world. Even coexistence is not enough. With the billions of dollars to be spent on an American ABM system—a system that is likely to succeed only in accelerating Soviet missile development to enable the penetration of that defense if war breaks out —we could begin instead to build the kind of decent, united American society on which our real security ultimately rests. It is tragic that Nixon's first major decision as President was to yield to the military-industrial pressures to deploy ABMs around the country. For once deployment has started, no one who has worked with military budgets in the past can believe that the Pentagon will ever be satisfied with a modified or "thin" ABM system.

Military logic cannot confine protection (if it is protection) to only a dozen missile sites as though the others (as well as our people) are expendable, or retain the present version of the ABM once the means of offense again exceed the means of defense as they inevitably have in the past (the latter was cited by JFK in rejecting ABM deployment during his Presidency). Even if the Soviets develop multiple missile warheads of sufficient accuracy to hit our hardened missile bases with the necessary precision, no ABM system can add much protection to those bases against a saturation attack conducted with decoys and penetration devices. Nor is such protection needed to assure this country—or any potential aggressor—that we would still retain enough retaliatory power underwater, underground, and in the air even after suffering such an attack to inflict unacceptable losses on the attacker.

Protection of our missile sites by means of an ABM will not increase either the bargaining position or the sense of security of any future President facing a threat to destroy our cities and population. No ABM command system can be devised that will assure its being fired only by a deliberate Presidential or even civilian (or even human!) decision; nor will it assure those allies who have no such systems that we will be as responsive as they to a global attack. The prospects of an ABM's accidentally exploding the base or city it is intended to defend is no more remote than the prospects of a rational Chinese or even Soviet attack—and no system can wholly defend against, much less deter, an irrational attack.

It is highly doubtful, to say the least, that we will ever fire either our ABMs or our MIRVs—any more than we have fired the other missile and nuclear systems acquired over the past twenty years at such a tremendous outlay of dollars. They could not be used in Korea, Vietnam, Laos, Lebanon, the Dominican Republic, or guerrilla wars. They may well have been useful in deterring a nuclear attack upon us, if such had ever been contemplated, by Soviet weapons acquired in their race against us. Now, however, both sides know—and JFK took pains to make certain that both knew—that each currently possesses the power to inflict unacceptable losses on the other even if the other struck first, and neither can rationally initiate such an exchange at present levels of strength. It is at least partly for this reason that both sides now move with great caution, as they did in Cuba in 1962 and in the Middle East in 1967. Nuclear bluffs and threats have virtually disappeared.

Why then increase the present levels of weaponry in a hopeless search for "superiority"—for an ability to destroy the Soviet Union more times over than it can destroy us, as though once were not quite enough—a search which can only postpone disarmament agreements, since no nation will bargain when the other is superior? Why substitute, for the present balance of mutual deterrents, new elements of uncertainty and unpredictability regarding offensive and defensive strength that may in turn lead to dangerous feelings of either overconfidence or insecurity?

Undoubtedly the United States will travel that road if the Russians travel it, in order to make certain that within the minds of Kremlin military leaders no temptation to gamble arises on the basis of their recent increases in missile power. Undoubtedly the Russians will feel they must travel it if we do, in order to prevent what they might regard as a new imperialist offensive by the United States, linking to this theory not only our intervention in Vietnam and the Dominican Republic but also the Israeli attack on Egypt, the establishment of new anti-Communist regimes in such nations as Indonesia and Brazil, and our development of an increased capacity to send large numbers of American troops quickly to any spot on the globe. The accuracy or inaccuracy of either side's fears is not so important in this context as the existence of such fears. On both sides fear makes risks untenable and new arms inevitable. Somehow we must achieve a major breakthrough in this wall of mutual suspicion and distrust, a wall that has unfortunately grown since the death of President Kennedy despite genuine efforts by his successors to bridge it with additional bilateral agreements.

That major breakthrough must soon produce a halt to the potentially suicidal arms race. It must produce a series of effective arms-control measures that both sides will continue to observe simply because it is in their self-interest to keep the other side observing them and because modern detection and intelligence methods would enable either to know of any default by the other. The new Nuclear Nonproliferation Treaty, understandably regarded by the nuclear have-not nations as curbing only their own development, should be followed by a ban on all nuclear tests, including those conducted underground. Even more important, mutual restrictions on the development and deployment of both offensive strategic missile systems (including FOBS and MIRVs) and antimissile-missile systems (ABMs) should be developed in time to stop this madness before it spreads out of control. Experience indicates that what is once done in modern armaments is unlikely to be undone.

Other major steps might then follow, once both governments become convinced that the other is genuinely interested. Many of these steps were suggested by JFK in his 1963 address to the United Nations. The concept of nuclear-free zones—today applicable in Antarctica and outer space—could be applied to more populous areas such as Latin America and Africa, as well as the ocean floor. The old notions of both sides contributing some of their fissionable-material stockpiles to an international pool for peaceful uses, and of both sides contributing weapons systems to an internationally supervised scrap heap, could be revived. Curbs should be imposed on the disturbing traffic in conventional arms to Middle Eastern, Latin American, and other countries whose budgets have more important priorities. Safeguards should be provided in Europe and elsewhere against surprise attack and accidental war.

There is no shortage of important, largely self-enforcing proposals. Once both sides genuinely start down the road to disarmament and peace, or the road to armaments and war, they can go all the way and bring all the nations of the world down either road with them. The abolition of all national armaments becomes, when compared realistically with the alternatives, not an idle dream of the Kennedys and other idealists but a human necessity.

That will require, among other things, going beyond President Kennedy's sincere but sporadic support of the United Nations and converting it into a more meaningful international security organization. The latter need not be (and is wholly unlikely in our time to be) a world government, as that ultimate goal is generally conceived. But it must be a more effective universal body. It must possess sufficient independence and prestige to function in every kind of conflict. It must write universally acceptable concepts of international law to govern future disputes over such problems as a *Pueblo* type of spy ship, West Berlin access routes, the coming mare's nest of weather modification, and even the status of such territories as Taiwan.

In time that will require at least a voluntary yielding of some sovereignty by all nations; but by then national boundaries will have begun to look rather insignificant anyway, when viewed from the moon. We could start this long process of UN-building now by establishing under the UN a permanent Peace Force of specially trained and earmarked forces from nonpower nations and a permanent Peace Observation Corps ready to report on all threats to world peace. Revisions of the charter could improve its decision-making capacity, restrict the use of the veto, make more assured the representativeness of the inflated Security Council, and add more significance to the decisions of the bloc-ridden, palaver-prone General Assembly.

Thus far—in the area of peace-keeping, as distinguished from its work in economic and political development in the former colonial territories—the UN has proved to be a weak and disappointing instrumentality, primarily because the nations of the world have been unwilling to give it strength. The United States has not even verbally taken most of its foreign-policy positions within the context of the UN charter. Nor have we ratified the proposed conventions on human rights or subscribed without reservations to the jurisdiction of the World Court. The UN is still an infant, whom we do not help by overpraising, much less by trying to stuff it with solid foods it cannot digest. But it is unlikely to grow to maturity unless this nation joins now in efforts to strengthen its peace-keeping functions. The more our own government can help make multilateral remedies available for international disputes affecting our security, the less we will be forced to seek the kind of unilateral solutions that can only increase our burdens and risks. The UN provides a means by which the U.S. and Soviets can act together without charges of imperialism and can back away from their own conflicts without loss of face.

All this is not to suggest that the millennium in Soviet-American relations is at hand. Our conflicting interests and ideologies, our competition for the allegiance of other states, and the accidents of history that have made us both global powers simultaneously, all point to a continuation of the differences and difficulties between us. Neither a formal alliance nor an ideological rapprochement is feasible at any early date. On the contrary, there is reason to believe that the present collective leadership in the Kremlin, trained to survive under Stalin, is more conservative on both war and peace initiatives than Khrushchev, is more representative of Soviet military and bureaucratic anti-Western antagonisms than he was in his last year with Kennedy, and is more anxious than he was in that post-Cuban-crisis year to prove to the world's more militant

Communist governments and parties the Soviet Union's zeal in combating American interests.

A speculative form of illustrating this change is the guess that the new leadership would not have risked placing Soviet missiles in Cuba, fifty-five hundred miles from Moscow, but that, having once done so, they would have been less willing to pull them out, particularly now that Soviet striking power is approaching U.S. levels. Soviet interests—as illustrated by their role in Czechoslovakia, in the Mediterranean, in Vietnam, and in the Middle East —will not permit the cold war to end through a unilateral "cease-fire" from their side, no matter how devoutly American pacifists wish that to happen and no matter how strongly American militarists think our "superiority" will cause it to happen.

We should not, however, return to our old cold war posture of imitating the Kremlin's practice of interpreting every adverse move as preparation for world domination. That was a basic principle of John Kennedy's American University speech in June 1963. The Soviets have acted with some caution in following up in Czechoslovakia and in discouraging a wider war in Asia or a renewal of war in the Middle East. Indeed, our bombing of a Communist capital allied with Moscow would appear to be a more daring risk than any that the Soviets have taken recently. Their new missile buildup may well be nothing more than a logical response to—and an effort to catch up with—our own missile buildup in the early 1960s. While it will never be known to what extent our buildup helped bring JFK through the Cuban missile crisis, he recognized that at least part of our lead may have been a needless response to the "missile gap" myth of 1958–1960. Having contributed my share of campaign prose to that myth, I want clearer proof this time before launching a new arms-spending spree that the Soviets are actually achieving, or even aiming for, a superiority so vast that they will be free to attack us.

The strength of the Soviet Union and the United States not only pits them unavoidably as opposing world leaders. It also gives them a special responsibility to keep the peace, a special fear of losing all they have created, a special interest in preventing the spread of nuclear weapons, a special concern about possible Chinese ambitions, and a special need to divert funds from the armaments race to more constructive needs at home and in the developing countries. As JFK pointed out at American University, both nations have an abhorrence of war, neither has ever been at war with the other, and even a generation of cold war propaganda has had surprisingly little effect on "people-to-people" relations.

"Both of our countries," I told a Moscow audience (carefully screened) in August 1967, "revolutionary in their origins, and concerned with more than our own proud material progress, have a common obligation to work—both jointly and separately—for a just and enduring peace . . . not for a world condominium ruled by two superpowers, not for a temporary *détente* used to stockpile arms, and not through meaningless pacts and fruitless meetings undertaken for the sake of appearances . . . but realistic, effective, enforceable actions" (which I then listed, most of which are discussed in this book).

In short, while we cannot expect that either nation will give up the competition, or its repugnance for the other's system, or the covert as well as overt means of maintaining that competition and keeping watch on one another, that need not mean war or even a total absence of cooperation. If the United States, while maintaining its vigilance, can prove at home and abroad that its system is more capable of meeting human needs and aspirations than any other, then it can have confidence in the outcome of that competition without arming to the hilt.

The Kennedys helped make us face the fact that Communism is here to stay, whether we like it or not; that it will not be forcibly rolled back, militarily destroyed, politically suppressed, or wholly eroded from within; that it is not a centrally controlled and monolithic bloc seeking our destruction but a loose collection of diverse, sometimes disputatious nations and even different systems; and that much of its old missionary zeal and appeal to the world's dispossessed has disappeared. As a result, a more sophisticated and discriminating American attitude toward different Communist countries should now be possible.

A similar increase in the Soviet Union's sophistication about Western nations and world affairs could in time remove some of its misapprehensions about America. This could arise from the long strides in education and de-isolation that necessarily accompany its rush toward industrialization, scientific achievement, and first-class power status, strides that appear likely to increase both the number and the influence of its reform-minded intellectuals, pragmatic technocrats, and impatient consumers. This may not mellow the attitude of Soviet leaders; they may be only more tense and insecure if their people are restless. A new generation of leaders may in fact be more militant and less patient if they are less hungry or preoccupied at home. But the evolutionary process seems likely at least to make them better informed, more worldly, and more open to reason instead of blind passion.

We cannot count on, much less become involved in, any internal Soviet evolution which will at best be a long time in coming. But United States policy, in keeping with JFK's American University doctrine, can at least take care not to confirm the fears and charges of Kremlin hawks, not to live up to their worst descriptions of us. It can instead help convince the Soviet Union that a strategy of armed conflict is both self-defeating and unnecessary, that the western borders of her "Socialist Commonwealth" are not in danger of armed attack, and that more of her resources can be diverted to domestic needs.

Moreover, once we in the United States realize that we have to live with Communism if we are to live at all, then —regardless of those facets of the competition that flare up from time to time—all measures to increase contact, understanding, and experience in dealing with Communist nations would seem eminently sensible. This could include extensive two-way trade in nonstrategic goods, far more tourism in both directions, cultural, scientific, professional, and other citizen exchanges and cooperation on such other mutual interests as agronomy, oceanography, and Antarctica. It could include periodic, informal meetings (rather than crisis meetings where the summit offers dangerously close quarters) between the heads of our respective governments. Both nations can stretch their foreign-aid outlays further in a nation such as India by joint action under a World Bank-sponsored consortium. Both nations can use the United Nations as a framework for joint positions or actions not otherwise easily taken, as Kennedy and Khrushchev demonstrated in 1963 in banning mass weapons from space. Both nations, now that the race to the moon has been settled, can pool their efforts to explore the planets, as JFK sought from the start. A whole series of treaties, trade arrangements, and joint efforts can bind our two nations together in a chain of practical self-interest.

Every time the Soviets boast that they are overtaking us in the number of engineers or the production of electric power, we should publicly express concern that our superiority is being challenged and privately express relief that they are devoting resources to these goals. Every time American right-wingers charge that elimination of our excessively restrictive curbs on Russian imports and on American exports and export credits to the U.S.S.R. would strengthen the Soviet civilian economy as well as our own, and give Soviet technicians more information about our production and marketing methods, we should reply that these are excellent reasons to do so. Trade, like our 1963 sale of surplus grains to Moscow, gives us an opportunity to demonstrate that our aim is not the eradication of all Communist states, that nonmilitary avenues can lead to progress, and that two competing powers can work together on common objectives. Inasmuch as our trade restrictions on nonstrategic goods today deny them nothing they need and cannot get elsewhere anyway, we are punishing only our own economy by continuing those restrictions.

The approach to this kind of *détente,* an effort wholly consistent with John Kennedy's deeds and dreams during the last years of his life, should not be bilateral between ourselves and the Russians. Both West and East Europeans would rightfully resent that. "When the two great powers collide," a Russian diplomat told me, "the other nations of the world are frightened; but when we collaborate, they are terrified." With our Western allies, we should seek similar areas of cooperation with the smaller nations of Eastern Europe, not—as once thought—to wean any of those states away from Moscow but to woo those states and Moscow together into an ultimately reunited Europe.

As the ties of both alliances weaken in the absence of a clear military danger, and as East Europeans seek economic advancement through Western buyers, sellers, technology, and techniques without regard to the old dogmas (which their youth as well as ours regard as irrelevant), a burgeoning web of new diplomatic, economic, and other joint efforts is beginning to link the nations of Western and Eastern Europe. It is unfortunate that U.S. trade and other barriers have diminished our participation in this process and thus diminished our ability to assist or influence the growing economic reforms in Eastern European states. Economics can be a more irresistible force than political ideology or military might. The Soviet Union having learned in the case of Czechoslovakia both that these economic reforms can lead to political reforms and that they are not wholly reversible even by brute force, there is reason to hope that she eventually will "lead" her followers into economic and then other forms of a united Europe rather than be left behind.

The West is not faced, as some old-time cold warriors still maintain, with a choice between greater Western unity and East-West cooperation. These two goals, as JFK made clear in his 1963 trip to Western Europe, are not inconsistent. It is a united Western European market that attracts the Eastern European technocrats. It is only a politically united Western Europe too strong to be dominated by the West Germans that will reassure the East European governments and their Soviet guarantor. And it is only within the context of a reconstructed Europe, East and West, that Germany can be reunited without frightening her neighbors and without any need for walls, watchtowers, and barbed wire.

The United States must be part of this long evolutionary process, if only because both East and West Europeans will secretly feel safer if both their big brothers join the game. But JFK first learned the hard way and then taught that this country cannot dictate the process of Western unity or dominate Western European nations as once we did. Their postwar political and economic progress toward integration has been remarkable, and American attempts to do the job for them, including Kennedy's MLF, have only interfered with that progress. We support the political and economic integration of Western Europe, including the important addition of Great Britain to the Common Market, for unselfish reasons of world peace—not because it serves our narrow interests to see this large competitor arise across the Atlantic but because a united Europe can perform functions we cannot undertake and a divided Europe can only produce another belligerent Germany and another round of explosive rivalries. Thus we err in pushing unity so hard that not only Gaullists but other Europeans begin to feel that it must somehow be a move to further the American economic and cultural domination described by Jacques Servan-Schreiber in *The American Challenge.*

Unfortunately, before, during, and since the Kennedy Administration, American policy toward Europe has been largely sterile and static. Except in time of crisis, our policy-makers have largely ignored the slow disintegration of the alliance; and the *status quo* of a divided Germany and Europe has been dangerously left to bilateral negotiations, drift, and growing discontent. For ten years there has been no real conference of the Four Powers on Germany, no summit meeting of NATO governments, and no new movement toward an easing of this single most important East-West confrontation.

Re-examination of American policy is required, Robert Kennedy pointed out, if for no other reason than the fact that most Americans today are too young to remember *when* NATO was founded, *how* the cold war started, or *why,* after nearly twenty-four years, there still has been no final peace settlement of the Second World War. Without waiting for a new Berlin or Czechoslovak crisis, or for the Vietnam war to end, Western policy should recognize now that a Soviet invasion of the West is no longer a clear and present danger, that Eastern Europe is not going to be weaned away from the Soviet Union, and that European security cannot depend comfortably on an arms race between the two superpowers.

This is no call for dismantling NATO. I served as chairman of a special U.S.–United Nations Association commission which recommended early in 1969 ways to strengthen NATO, its consultative practices, the West European role therein, and U.S.–Western Europe relationships. But our report also stressed that these relationships should become the foundation for an all-European security system, a means of preparing a final European peace with the same success NATO had in preventing a final European war. We recommended creation by the four postwar powers—the U.S., the U.S.S.R., France, and Great Britain—of a ten-government European Security Commission, including both superpowers and both German governments, to prepare a final settlement, to create machinery for crisis management, and to negotiate a series of arms-control measures in Central Europe. The latter would include mutual reductions in troops and nuclear warheads as well as inspection and observation systems. All this would be undertaken under the supervision of the Four Powers, with full consultation on our side with NATO and with appropriate ties to the United Nations. Surely that would be far preferable to policies that either appease post-Gaullist nationalism or encourage a frustrated, restless West German government to go it alone both militarily and diplomatically.

The heart of our proposal looked to East and West German negotiations for a step-by-step eventual reunification of Germany in one form or another. Some form of peaceful if not final accommodation between the two Germanys must be the heart of any proposal for achieving stability in Europe. As important as reunification remains, I reminded the Germans in a 1966 lecture to the Free University of Berlin, citing JFK's own address there some three years earlier, this goal "will not come quickly, or as the result of Western pressure or threats on the East . . . or be helped by pretending there are not two Germanys at present, by thinking in grandiose terms instead of small steps, or . . . by creating demands in order to trade them away later." I urged the West Germans to recognize frankly that they were genuinely feared in Eastern Europe, that reunification could come only after the reconciliation of all Europe, and that both their safety and their prestige were secure without their possessing nuclear weapons or recovering the disputed Eastern territories. I suggested what our government must not command: that they should make a virtue out of reality by voluntarily renouncing on their own for all time the acquisition of any degree of ownership or control of either nuclear weapons or the lands east of the Oder-Neisse.

In West Germany in 1966 I found the voice of youth rising, and it is far louder today. Although realistic on reunification, it disdains the political cant that impedes progress toward political and even humanitarian contacts between divided friends and families. Promises that cannot be fulfilled, formal protests that have no prospects, wishful thinking, cold-war rhetoric and all the illusions and guilt feelings of the past twenty years—these are rejected today by young Germans and other Europeans, East and West, just as they are rejected by young Americans. The old shibboleths about the cold war, the iron curtain, the balance of power, even nationalism, are of little interest to young Americans and young Europeans. On both sides of the Atlantic young people want not a paternalistic society with the old class distinctions but a true democracy with social justice, civilian control, and evolving political and economic institutions.

Yet too much youthful impatience either in or regarding Europe can only arouse expectations that are dangerous to disappoint and doomed to disappointment. For the reunification of Germany, to cite the number-one example and obstacle, will be a long process, not a surprise package. That process, with encouragement from the Four Powers, should at least begin now with exploratory talks, commercial relations, and contact on those human and logistical problems created by the artificial division of a people which has no ethnic, geographic, or other logic. Perhaps collaboration on common domestic concerns could then follow, then someday a confederation, then a loose federation. Perhaps the ultimate political framework will not fit any existing formulation. Perhaps some kind of international force could replace those of NATO and the Warsaw Pact in Central Europe. Perhaps an all-European federation will by that time have been built around Germany. All that is certain is that the final reunification of Germany is far off and cannot be pushed by outsiders. We should take no steps inconsistent with it, but we should not hold up all other progress toward European peace and reconciliation while awaiting its ultimate realization.

Nevertheless, until a final European settlement is reached, the problem of a divided Germany—particularly the isolated existence of West Berlin—will continue to present a potential source of conflict between East and West. We cannot abandon the brave West Berliners with whom the Kennedy brothers felt a special bond. But neither can the Soviets abandon their East German regime, which regards a free West Berlin as anathema, or abandon their anxieties over Germany's future, which they illustrated in the Czechoslovak crisis. The prospect of an autonomous, united, powerful Germany armed with nuclear weapons understandably terrifies any Soviet citizen old enough to remember his nation's suffering in the Second World War; and that prospect is also the Kremlin's most effective tool with which to bind the similarly fearful East Europeans. We must understand these fears; and both sides must understand the dangers of a new German war. A resurgence of neo-Nazi politics in West Germany, a revived East German attempt to squeeze West Berlin's lifeline, even a spontaneous incident at the grotesque Wall or on the Autobahn, could set off a chain reaction of frightening proportions. We must all keep cool in West Berlin if a hot war is to be avoided.

I have written at length elsewhere about the dangers to Soviets and Americans alike in resting a shaky Middle East truce upon an unstable East-West arms race and about the unavoidability of Arab and Israeli negotiators eventually signing a final, comprehensive settlement that recognizes the self-interests of both sides and the realities of geography and power. I will add here only that, in light of Robert Kennedy's call for "no more Vietnams," the American people do not equate South Vietnam with Israel —whether the comparison is one of governments, armed forces, or social and economic viability. Israel, Prime Minister Golda Meir told me, will never request American forces to fight Arabs. Nevertheless, U.S. security would suffer if the Arabs ever succeeded in crushing Israel.

Our hopes for any agreement with the Soviet Union are particularly complicated by its hostile relationship—and ours—with Communist China. No agreement on the control of nuclear weapons will be very meaningful for very long if the world's newest nuclear power is excluded. No grant of authority to the United Nations will be very meaningful for very long if nearly one-fourth of the human race is excluded. No peace settlement in Southeast Asia will be very meaningful for very long if the needs and views of the largest Asian power are excluded.

Americans understandably worry that the survivors of a post-Mao struggle for leadership may seek a rapprochement with the Soviet Union. The Chinese assail every Soviet hint of peace with the Americans as a sellout of Chinese interests. The Soviets have deep concerns—of which I received some flavor in Moscow—that the Americans may get together with the Chinese in a "new encirclement" of the Soviet Union.

Thus these three old maids stare suspiciously at one another, each convinced that the other two will conspire behind her back and each inwardly hoping that the other two will fight it out. When a similar triangular situation prevailed before the Second World War, the Soviets joined first with the Axis powers against the Allies and then with the Allies against the Axis powers; and the West would do well to make certain, if the game should ever again become two against one, that either the Soviets or the Chinese are on our side.

The situation is rapidly becoming more serious than any game. China's speed in developing a nuclear and then a thermonuclear capacity was remarkable. She is already believed to possess missiles of an intermediate range. She is expected to develop missiles of an intercontinental range, capable of reaching the United States, by the 1970s.

At the same time her people have developed a xenophobic suspicion and hatred of the United States, hardly surprising in view of repeated statements by their leaders to the effect that our military presence in Vietnam, the Straits of Formosa, Taiwan, Thailand, and Korea as well as our other Asian military and economic missions, our original anti-Chinese label on the ABM, and our refusal to recognize her, trade with her, or give her the Chinese seat in the United Nations are all in preparation for another white man's war against the Chinese mainland.

The Chinese—economically, militarily, or in any other way—will be no superpower for years to come, the size of China's population being more hindrance than help in her struggle toward that goal. Mao's revolutionary zeal has not in recent years been translated into military action (as distinct from subversion) far from his own borders. Nevertheless, to know that the most populous nation in the world is developing in isolation that particular combination of massive weapons of destruction and blind hatred of the United States is to see on the far horizon a danger we dare not ignore.

Possibly the disruptions of the cultural revolution or a post-Vietnam change in atmosphere will produce a surprising reversal in behavior or a disintegration too complete to pose any threat. But that seems doubtful today. The task of reducing that isolation and hatred is thus almost certain to be one of the most difficult this country has ever faced. It will require steps far bolder than any undertaken by JFK or proposed by RFK, yet consistent with their thinking on China and their actions toward the U.S.S.R. China's actions, in contrast with her words, have in fact offered no more danger or provocation to American interests than those of the Soviet Union. There is no foundation in fact or logic for our erecting higher, different, or added barriers between ourselves and Peking than we have between ourselves and Moscow. We need not—we dare not—await some major shift in China or China's posture before shifting our own.

Militarily, we can learn to consider China's security needs and fears as we have learned to consider Russia's. We can continue to reduce our naval, air, and other assistance and presence on Taiwan, Okinawa, and elsewhere in the area to a point where it clearly serves defensive purposes only, minimizes the risk of provocative action on our part, and symbolizes only our commitment to prevent a change by force. (The military convenience provided by our bases on Okinawa is far less valuable to our security than the good relations with Japan which our continued presence on Okinawa is undermining.) We can hasten the massive withdrawal of our troops from Vietnam (which will also help with Japan, our key Asian ally). We can stop foolishly calling our ABM an anti-China device inasmuch as that serves only to alarm our Asian allies that we could be indifferent to a Chinese nuclear attack—and, as mentioned, we can in fact halt the whole ABM program without loss to our security. While providing neighboring peoples with assurances against aggression, we can accept China's inevitable interest and influence in Asia and not attempt to install or maintain anti-Chinese governments around her borders. In short, without waiting for any reciprocal moves by China, we can start conforming less to Mao Tse-tung's view of how we behave militarily.

Diplomatically, we can do the same. We can at least change the atmosphere to one of hope instead of recrimination and can display some magnanimity on our part. Following up President Nixon's proposals in mid-1969, we can take more definitive unilateral steps to end restrictions on travel, cultural exchanges, and trips in both directions by business, news media, and political representatives. We can try to open more diplomatic channels like the one at Warsaw and make better use of that one. We can make certain China is included if other nations are brought into the Vietnam or post-Vietnam peace talks. We can seek her participation in disarmament and other international conferences. We can remove discriminatory barriers to non-strategic trade between the United States and China, offering neither paternalistic loans nor humiliating restrictions, beginning at least by untying the hands of American subsidiaries in Canada and other countries. Ending our wartime embargo does not require reciprocal action.

We can respond with interest to Peking's 1968 call for peaceful coexistence, her 1964 call for outlawing all nuclear weapons, and her repeated pledge not to be the first to use such weapons. We can offer cooperative research on medicine, agriculture, birth control, and other areas of mutual concern. We can put on the table a standing offer to send surplus food without strings attached. We can encourage our allies not to isolate China but to help bring her into the world community.

All these moves will be difficult for the American people after twenty years of emotional and political agitation about the Red Chinese, even though they would be beneficial to our interests as well as China's. Such actions on our part could in time help thaw the present atmosphere and at least open a door that someday one of the factions contending to succeed Mao and Lin Piao could see as an alternative to Russian aid and trade. The task of internal industrialization may preoccupy Chinese resources and attention for some years to come; and future leaders might well prefer economic collaboration with the United States to any military adventures. But there is little basis for such hope today, unless China's fear and hatred of the Soviet Union have so surpassed its fear and hatred of the United States that an accommodation with us is deemed necessary.

As a result, any move on our part that depends on reciprocal action, with the possible exception of two-way trade, is almost certain to be rejected by the Chinese in their present state of uncertainty.

This will be particularly true until the issues of UN credentials and U.S. diplomatic recognition are settled. Both of those issues turn in China's mind on the question of Taiwan. Our disapproval of Peking's conduct, language, and system cannot logically compel us to deny the fact that Mao Tse-tung is, despite internal challenges and convulsions, the ruler of China, entitled to be so recognized by the United States and the United Nations. (Neither Chiang nor Mao will ever agree that there are "two Chinas," and it is patently absurd to recognize Chiang as the ruler of 750 million Chinese on the mainland.) Surely we no longer claim that Mao is a Soviet puppet imposed on a captive nation by Moscow. The added exposure of Peking to the U.S. and vice versa might in time enable both to judge better each other's intentions and conduct, despite the almost certainly disruptive nature of any UN delegation representing the current Chinese government.

We have, however, no moral or legal right simply to deliver the thirteen million people on Taiwan, many of whom are already unhappy under the thumb of Nationalist Chinese exiles, over to Communist Chinese control without regard to the principle of self-determination. Nor can we—aside from preventing the use of force to change the *status quo*—make the decision here as to whether Taiwan should ultimately be a separate nation, an autonomous part of China, or something else. What we can do, in direct negotiations with Peking, is devise a compromise formula of deliberate ambiguity that recognizes Peking as the factual ruler of the Chinese mainland entitled to sit in the UN without immediately terminating or otherwise permanently settling our relations with Taiwan or its constructive role as one of the larger members of the UN.

Mao would presumably refuse to exchange ambassadors with the U.S. or to accept UN membership on these terms, thus deferring any change in the Security Council. But such an initiative on our part may at least encourage the eventual emergence of more moderate Chinese leaders willing to negotiate these issues and willing to participate in UN-related arms-control conferences. Meanwhile, we can still initiate the trade, demilitarization, and other measures mentioned, just as we improved trade and other relations with the Soviet Union long before we exchanged ambassadors. As Senator Edward Kennedy pointed out in a remarkable attack on our hostile China policy on March 20, 1969, we can seek to re-establish consular offices even before a formula for full diplomatic recognition is achieved. "It takes two sides to make a lasting peace," he said, "but it only takes one to make the first step."

It is the issue raised by the continuation of Chinese and other Communist-sponsored subversion, insurrections, and "wars of liberation" that will pose one of the most difficult choices facing American foreign-policy makers in the post-Vietnam period. Secretary Rusk's fears notwithstanding, no one of us who endorses Robert Kennedy's principle of "no more Vietnams" is advocating a return to isolationism, a withdrawal of all missions to a Fortress America. We have never suggested that our painful experience in Vietnam should cause us to turn our backs on, for example, our hopes for the United Nations and arms-control measures, ties with Western Europe and Latin America, and a variety of other obligations directly related to our national interests.

Most doves recognize that history more than choice has

made us a world leader with heavy responsibilities to use our size, strength, and wealth in a way that is beneficial to mankind. We recognize as well that this nation cannot afford to have any other continent in the world dominated by a power hostile to America's interests, that we cannot afford to be alone—politically, economically, or militarily alone—in a dangerous and explosive world. We want allies; we want friends; we are not isolationists.

On the contrary, the modern-day isolationists, in my view, are those in our midst who have only contempt for world opinion, who have cost us the respect of other peoples by persistently pursuing hard-line cold-war policies of militancy and military responses. They are willing to "go it alone" if our allies balk at any step on the ladder of escalation. They have cut back economic aid to nations unwilling to endorse all aspects of our foreign policy or to accept all aspects of our domestic system. They oppose the delays and dilutions inevitable in seeking multilateral solutions through such bodies as the UN or the OAS. It was their policies on Vietnam which distorted our budget, price levels, and balance of payments to a point where unprecedented restrictions had to be placed on American investments abroad, new restrictions were attempted on American tourism and trade, and severe blows were suffered in the wars against American poverty and discrimination which are essential to our standing overseas. It is this kind of thinking, not the concept of "no more Vietnams," that helps isolate us from other nations.

Instead, our experience in Vietnam has taught us—or should have taught us—other lessons that RFK, McCarthy, Fulbright, and others have helped to crystallize. We should have learned not to Americanize with a predominance of our own troops a war in which we are committed to propping up an unpopular, unrepresentative government rife with corruption, opposed to reform, and unable to mobilize its own repressed population or even with much success its own politicized army. Such a regime is unable to oppose with all-out vigor a small but determined enemy of the same nationality who is prepared to fight indefinitely and, despite heavy casualties, against all odds and all comers under the banner of nationalism.

We should have learned that American military might, particularly if engaged on the Asian mainland next door to Communist China, cannot win a war of attrition against an elusive and disciplined guerrilla force employing terror and ambush on its native terrain, generally unopposed by the peasantry, and constantly receiving supplies and reinforcements from its immense manpower reserves across unsealable borders from a territory too rural to be knocked out by bombing.

We should have learned that unilateral American military solutions advocated by eternally overconfident generals will not succeed in meeting primarily political problems requiring changes in the *status quo,* changes which this nation has difficulty in imposing without contradicting our belief in self-determination or risking our prestige and investment. Thus our initial error becomes self-serving and self-perpetuating, growing like a cancer until it weakens and deforms the body politic itself.

We should have learned, finally, that to make a testing place of our national will and word out of a small threatened alteration in the boundary between the Communist and non-Communist world can be more costly to our security—and cost the people we are supposedly saving far more of their own lives, property, and even national aspirations—than would the establishment of an independent coalition or even Communist government that little alters the real balance of power.

All that, at any rate, is what this follower of Robert Kennedy means in carrying on his admittedly ambiguous declaration of "no more Vietnams." Recognizing the realistic limits of our military capability does not mean America resigning from the world. It does not mean ignoring the dictates of our conscience, our national interest, or our obligation as the only counter to the nuclear blackmail potential and massive armies of the Soviets and Chinese. Abjuring open-ended military commitments in defense of reactionary regimes that repress the revolutionary aspirations of their people is not pacifism. It does not prevent the United States from relying on collective-security arrangements against genuine threats to world peace and American security. It does not prohibit multilateral economic assistance to needy peoples of every ideology and system. Nor does opposing the excessive militarization of American foreign policy mean abandoning those responsibilities of leadership we fulfill through imaginative diplomacy, constructive assistance, and an inspiring example of justice and opportunity here at home.

Without ignoring the past and present threats posed by other nations with less innocent motivations than our own, the Kennedy legacy urges the United States to cool down and move beyond the outworn slogans of the cold war, to seek creative world-wide peace-keeping arrangements, and to use its power with more care and selectivity as our national interests and abilities permit. We need to pause and think through our strategy, our commitments, and our goals before continuing past errors. We need to re-examine once successful but now outmoded policies that were appropriate two decades ago when our power was paramount, our commitments limited, our adversary monolithically strong, and our allies wholly weak—particularly those policies that serve today only to divide our people and alienate many of our brightest youth. We must tune in to a new generation of leaders in such key countries as West Germany and Japan who question their governments' ties to an America too enmeshed in anachronistic trade, defense, and cold-war policies to respond to their changing needs.

This kind of new foreign-policy posture will not be as simple as some of my fellow Vietnam critics have assumed. There is little value in pledging to prevent conventional military conquests in the less developed areas of the world if its would-be perpetrators simply substitute the indirect take-over of an unwilling majority through an armed internal minority. Yet there is no value in pledging "no more Vietnams" if we intervene on behalf of every shaky despot in every civil war that bears a made-in-China label. To list in advance those countries we will assist and those we will not assist invites the subversion of those we have omitted; yet to leave both sides in doubt about our intentions may bring on local wars requiring our intervention that a clear-cut stand would have deterred.

Even our special concern for this hemisphere does not justify our assertion of military hegemony over Latin America—despite its being graced by so revered a label as "the Monroe Doctrine." President Johnson, at the time of the Dominican Republic invasion, explained this country's direct military intervention in a sovereign state in words that have rightly been compared to the post-Czechoslovakia Brezhnev doctrine: "American nations cannot, must not, and will not permit the establishment of another Communist government in the Western Hemisphere," whatever force is required, whether or not force is requested, and regardless of the wishes of either the people of that nation or the other governments in the OAS. The Soviets denounced such an "arbitrary, unlawful" assertion of authority on our part, just as we denounced theirs in Czechoslovakia. To be sure, neither power is willing to do more than verbally challenge actions taken by the other power within the latter's "sphere of influence"; but that hardly makes it right for either power to initiate such actions.

In short, there is no list, geographic or otherwise, of countries in whose external or internal conflicts we will always intervene. The challenge to our policy-makers is not how to draw up such a list but where to draw the line, how to set forth hardheaded, coherent criteria for *ad hoc* application to each situation. The slogan taken up by Robert Kennedy and subsequently everyone else that we cannot be "policemen for the world" surely does not mean that we have been intervening in more than a small fraction of the world's armed disputes—for we have not—and it cannot mean that we should withdraw from involvement in all of them. To me it means an attitude paralleling in reverse RFK's (and JFK's) favorite quotation from Shaw. When previously faced with a decision on whether the United States should intervene in a local dispute in which one side is termed Communistic but our own security is not directly jeopardized, there has been since the days of Dulles a tendency in some quarters to say, "Why not?" Now it is hoped the tendency will be to say, "Why?" Thinking people will ask that question if the government does not, and any President unable to give a satisfactory answer had best not attempt such an intervention.

If a nation is about to choose a system that is contrary or even hostile to our own, then the principles of self-determination and diversity do not permit our intervention. If a government seeks our military assistance, without evidence that our arms are required to offset similar outside assistance being furnished to its adversary, then we should question whether that government is committed to social justice and reform among its own people and not merely to anti-Communism. If it threatens to ask Moscow or Peking for assistance if we fail to deliver it, then we should question that government's commitment to anti-Communism. If a nation's neighbors inform us that their own security will be undermined if it comes under Communist rule, then their forces should be joined and in the field before ours.

If the number of insurgents in a friendly country has grown, we should inquire whether this has mirrored an increase in American aid and whether more American aid will not produce more insurgents. If the rulers of a nation seek help against a Communist insurgency, we should ascertain whether that is actually the case or simply their label. (Of 164 internationally significant outbreaks of violence in the eight years preceding late 1966, according to Robert McNamara, only 15 were military conflicts between two states; and of the 149 serious internal insurgencies, Communists were involved in only 58 of them, including 7 in which Communist regimes were the target.)

In short, there are no automatic tests, as JFK discovered early in 1961. A leftist regime insisting on radical land reform may be more worth supporting than a regime that is cooperative with our CIA and military attachés. A "revolt of the colonels" may bring into power a government better organized to obtain revolutionary progress than its civilian predecessor. Whenever any national sparrow falls from its nest, our moral fervor usually urges our government to do something—but we cannot do everything. We can prevent American funds, arms, and trade from flowing to South Africa, Portuguese Africa, and Rhodesia; but, however moral it may seem to those who preach the immorality of violence elsewhere, we cannot use our military might to overthrow these entrenched governments.

We can airlift more food and medicine to the thousands of starving black children in Biafra and Nigeria with at least the same ingenuity and courage we displayed in airlifting white missionaries out of rebel-held areas of the Congo; but we cannot intervene militarily or otherwise to help Biafra achieve what most African nations fear would be a dangerous precedent for tribal secession. We have no right or obligation to fill every "power vacuum." The United States simply cannot play God, and some sparrows must unfortunately fall from their nests without our moving to help them. Indeed, in some cases nonaction on America's part may help world peace and even world freedom more than any unilateral action on our part. In more than one instance local nationalists have ejected Communists without our intervention more easily than they could have had their domestic standing been compromised by our presence.

All these decisions on military assistance and intervention in the developing world are difficult enough. But they will be unnecessarily complicated if we insist on maintaining an income as vendor of old armaments to small and impoverished nations; or on retaining obsolete overseas bases; or on choosing sides in a local dispute according to the wishes of American corporations in the area or hypocritical interest groups here at home; or on replacing the British forces now being withdrawn from Asia; or on extending our overextended commitments in the name of the now tarnished domino theory. To be sure, the close of the Vietnam war will leave us with an airlift, sealift, and combat-troop capacity to intervene quickly and conventionally anywhere in the world. But the Soviets are also acquiring such a capacity. Only the kind of caution exercised by both sides in the nuclear-missile crisis can prevent their nonnuclear forces from being drawn into a

dangerous confrontation. We would in fact do well to reduce our forces in recognition of the hard fact that their
mere existence may often hamper rather than facilitate
the establishment of a peaceful atmosphere and peaceful
solutions.

Confrontation will become less avoidable if large parts
of the so-called third world are allowed to sink into
chaos, political or economic, and are torn by poverty,
hunger, racial wars, civil insurrections, tribal struggles, or
anarchy. The result might then be Chinese or Soviet
domination or exploitation of the third world, or—even
more nightmarish to contemplate—an eventual confrontation between the world's impoverished peoples of every
color and ideology and the world's more comfortable
nations, including nonwhites such as the Japanese and non-
capitalists such as the Russians. This is not idle speculation.
As the economic gap between rich states and poor states
continues to widen, the scale and number of outbreaks of
violence in the poor countries of the world have already
risen ominously. The United States must work with the
other twenty-six developed states, including the Soviet
Union, who with us possess twenty-eight per cent of the
world's population but eighty-three per cent of its wealth,
to assist these nations struggling to emerge from primitive
agriculture directly into the space age.

Regional cooperation by the nations of each developing
area on political and military as well as economic problems
should be encouraged. Self-help internal reforms, including the political reform, land reform, tax reform, and
decentralization sought by JFK in the Alliance for Progress particularly, must accompany external assistance. It
is a tragic fact that the developing nations are spending
for armies and weapons twice as much as they are receiving

in foreign aid and at least as much as they are spending on health and education. But the more fortunate nations of the world will still have to dig deeper into their national pockets to help finance the economic and social development that is a necessary foundation for peace.

The United States, the richest nation in the history of mankind, must contribute its proportionate share. From Iran to Taiwan, from Pakistan to Tunisia, our aid programs have achieved more successes than usually noted. But such vast nations as India and Indonesia have only sunk deeper into economic difficulty. Perhaps the pessimists like Gunnar Myrdal will be proven right. Perhaps many of these nations will steadily decline until life becomes intolerable, and a series of revolutions and convulsions produce new dictatorships of one brand or another, ruthlessly allocating resources among decimated populations. But believers in the Kennedy legacy cannot stand by and let that happen.

We must not impose our economic or political system upon these nations nor tailor their institutions to the expensive standards of our society. The more we can use the World Bank, improve the other multilateral agencies, and induce other prospering nations to make available their share of capital, the more we can avoid an unequal portion of the burden, avoid suspicion of our motives, avoid duplication of our effort, and avoid the Vietnam type of political consequences. We cannot, however, shirk such unilateral programs as the Peace Corps, technical training, aid to cooperatives and trade unions, and incentives for private investment. Of more importance to many poor countries than the developed world's aid is its willingness to open its doors to their trade—and the United States has recently been closing as many trade doors as it has opened.

Among all the developing nations of the world, those in Latin America deserve our special attention. This must be given through the Alliance for Progress, not through continued military assistance. Both the appeal and the threat of Castroism have dwindled throughout the hemisphere. Castro's irritation with his generous Soviet benefactors over their comparative caution in promoting Latin American revolution has apparently lessened. Nevertheless, it indicates the possibility that Cuba may (even under his leadership) someday resume its peaceful place in the hemispheric system as a nonaligned, nonsubversive Socialist or Communist state, a development contemplated by JFK in his last months which we should be brave enough to encourage as a gain for all concerned. But democracy in Latin America is still threatened—less by Soviet or Chinese Communism than by the kind of impoverished internal disintegration that produces not only right-wing juntas but deep human despair and ultimately violent disruption. Whether the next outbreak of massive violence is in Haiti, the Dominican Republic, Chile, Peru, or elsewhere on the continent, the United States is certain to be condemned if it intervenes and assailed if it fails to intervene. To prevent that choice, we must help Latin America now—and that means more than throwing the proverbial fifteen-foot rope toward our Latin American neighbors drowning twenty feet away.

Robert Kennedy tried to alert this nation to the growing problems of Latin America. One to which he pointed, despite his religion, was the problem of overpopulation. In most of the developing world, the crucial race is not between Communism and capitalism, neither of which most of their populations have ever heard of, but between population and food supply, between the stork and the plow. Already three and a half million children die each year from hunger and malnutrition. Before the world population doubles again by the year 2000, we must learn to make better use of our surpluses and fertilizers, to develop low-cost high-protein food substitutes, to extract food and fresh water from the ocean depths, and to increase the use of modern farm machinery and productivity. But all this will be insufficient if there are 350 million more mouths to feed every year.

Nearly all the rapid rise in the world's population today is occuring in those countries already short of arable land, food, and resources. Most families in those countries cannot now feed the children they have, despite allocating more than twice the proportion of their meager incomes to food as the average American family does. A new agricultural revolution, with our help, may be coming in many of these areas; but even with better storage and distribution facilities, even with the necessary land, tax, and credit reforms, famine and collapse may face India, Brazil, China, and others before another generation has passed. By 1975 the number of dependent children in the developing world will equal the total population of the developed world. There are more hungry people on this planet now than there were fifteen years ago, when our food shipments began. National and international measures to encourage the systematic limitation of populations by artificial means will continue to meet religious, cultural, educational, financial, and practical obstacles. But adopting such measures by free choice now is surely strongly preferable to facing in the future a terrible choice between compulsory methods and chaos. It is not "demographic imperialism" to seek means now of preventing the misery and starvation that will engulf the poor nations, and the congestion and depletion that will damage the rich nations, if this Malthusian tide is not turned back.

There is something terribly, tragically askew in a world on the brink of a technological and scientific revolution that offers simultaneously the prospects of such enormous misery and such enormous opulence, such unprecedented opportunities and such unprecedented dangers. The same is true of our own country—that more of its citizens than ever before should be crying out in anger and despair at the very time that more of its citizens than ever before are enjoying its blessings and bounty. Some people blame the will of God; but John Kennedy reminded us that "here on earth God's work must truly be our own." Some people recognize the crises that will lead to catastrophe but do no more than look forward to watching it all happen on television. Some blame the world's poor for being poor, the hungry for being hungry, the slow learners for being slow learners; and then they settle back to the affluence they have hardly shared, to that permanent passport to opportunity known as white skin, and to their complaints about high taxes and foreign aid. They smugly refuse to admit that America could ever be wrong, refuse to change their ways when the pressure is not on, refuse to respond to peaceful protests or listen to reason—and then wonder why students and minorities and others finally lash out in violence. John and Robert Kennedy proved by their very lives that the individual could take on the established forces and folkways and effectuate change. But they are gone, and today's young and oppressed are understandably skeptical about whether the Kennedy legacy will take hold.

Yet the presence of George Wallace's name on every state ballot in 1968 demonstrated how thorough organization can change the usual system. The absence of Lyndon Johnson from any ballot demonstrated the power remaining with the people when aroused. Americans can be generous, as they showed in the Marshall Plan. They can invest large public sums to solve problems not directly affecting the majority, as they showed in TVA. They can vanquish seemingly ineradicable blights, as they showed in the depressed-areas program. And they can focus their energies, money, and brains with striking results, as they showed in the Manhattan Project that developed the atomic bomb and in placing a man on the moon.

All that was demanded of us in those efforts combined is now demanded of us again. We should not require a domestic Pearl Harbor to galvanize us into action. To live up to the Kennedy legacy, we must pre-empt the extraordinary before the extremists seize it for their own. We must enlighten our own behavior before new chemical agents, electronic implants, and genetic controls are used upon us. Even though we are now taxed more lightly at all levels than any major industrial nation in the Western world, we must reallocate from military to domestic use the resources that are equal to the task that faces us. We must firmly persist in these efforts without losing interest and turning to new crusades. We must genuinely fix high standards and high goals without overpromising quick results. Planning programs, passing laws, and providing appropriations will not be enough. To regain the respect of the young, to make violent change unnecessary, we must devise a new strategy for living instead of fighting, a new kind of leadership that can catch America up with history—not a Man on Horseback but abler men in the councils of man. The Talmud distinguished a city from a village not by its size or population but by its more responsible, less narrow, and less provincial outlook. The United States must become the leading city of the world, not one of its largest villages.

Perhaps I am an idealist in believing that these principles of the Kennedy legacy can be carried out. But, like John

Kennedy, I am "an idealist without illusions"; and I have no illusions about man's eagerness to make sacrifices for the common good, only faith in his ability to change our society radically, swiftly, and peacefully if only he would try. Try we must, for our own sake and for the sake of our brothers. For if ever a man loved his younger brothers, that man was John Kennedy. If ever a man loved his older brother, that man was Robert Kennedy. If ever two men taught us all to love each other like brothers, it was John and Robert Kennedy. That is the heart of the Kennedy legacy.

Index